WONDER WOMAN

PSYCHOLOGY

Lassoing the Truth

Edited by
Travis Langley and Mara Wood

#PsychGeeks #WWpsych

STERLING
New York

STERLING
New York

An Imprint of Sterling Publishing Co., Inc.
1166 Avenue of the Americas
New York, NY 10036

ISBN 978-1-4549-2343-5

Distributed in Canada by Sterling Publishing Co., Inc.
c/o Canadian Manda Group, 664 Annette Street
Toronto, Ontario, Canada M6S 2C8
Distributed in the United Kingdom by GMC Distribution Services
Castle Place, 166 High Street, Lewes, East Sussex, England BN7 1XU
Distributed in Australia by NewSouth Books
45 Beach Street, Coogee, NSW 2034, Australia

For information about custom editions, special sales, and premium and corporate purchases,
please contact Sterling Special Sales at 800-805-5489 or specialsales@sterlingpublishing.com.

Manufactured in Canada

2 4 6 8 10 9 7 5 3 1

www.sterlingpublishing.com

Dedication
To Rebecca Manning Langley
and Michelle Taff,
our Wonder Women

CONTENTS

Acknowledgments:
Our Sensations

I.

Travis Langley, PhD

series editor/volume co-editor

Be a sensation, not sensationalistic.

Myths and misconceptions abound regarding Wonder Woman's history both behind the scenes and in the fiction. Yes, her creator and the women who inspired her creation lived an unusual lifestyle, but the specific details may not neatly fit the claims and assumptions that people popularly repeat. Insinuation and inference presented with a veneer of heavy research can leave folklore mistaken for historical fact, filling in the gaps in our knowledge of these sensational people by sensationalizing their lives. We thank William and Elizabeth Marston's son Pete and Pete's daughter Christie for sharing their time and thoughts and for granting us access to the Wonder Woman Network Family Museum's archives in our efforts to get some things right. And yes, we acknowledge that characters got tied up a lot in those earliest stories, but make no mistake: The stories and characters are much richer than that. Read the originals and take it all in. The ropes and chains here and there in those first few years were not intended to promote sadistic delight in seeing someone suffer, according to Marston, but were instead about things he considered important: becoming free, learning to break out of restraints, submitting to those who mean us well while overcoming any who mean us harm, and escaping the symbols used by the women's suffrage movement to represent the limits they strove to overcome in his lifetime. As he put it, "The reader's wish is to save the girl, not to see her suffer."[1]

Thank you, Christie, for welcoming us into the Wonder Woman Network. It is a pleasure and an honor. Wonder Woman does have friends and fans all over the globe.[2] We thank David Chapman and Geoffrey Prince for being great conversationalists and our first readers. Other wonderful people we've been pleased to meet through Christie and company include David Berger, Alice and Art Cloos, Susan Torres Christensen, Barbara A. Moss, and Valerie Perez. Pete Marston "decided it was time to board his invisible jet and head to Paradise Island" as this book was going to press, and so we remember him with a salute and our deep thanks for sharing his time and recollections with us.[3]

When we began working on the first books in this Popular Culture Psychology series, *The Walking Dead Psychology: Psych of the Living Dead* and *Star Wars Psychology: Dark Side of the Mind*, Mara Whiteside Wood told me that if we ever covered Wonder Woman, she wanted to be heavily involved. In addition to writing chapters for books in the series, Mara has proven herself to be an insightful, conscientious, knowledgeable editorial assistant on several volumes, more than capable of co-editing *Wonder Woman Psychology: Lassoing the Truth*. Her contributions have been invaluable.

Sterling Publishing editor Connie Santisteban and I each separately decided on the same day that the time had come to examine Wonder Woman. At the very moment Connie was in a meeting saying that she hoped we would want to work on a Wonder Woman book, I happened to be writing my email to broach the subject with them. Imagine her surprise ten minutes later when she got to her computer. Kate Zimmermann took over the editorial reins on Sterling's side along the way. We congratulate Connie and her husband, Josh, on the birth of little J. J., and we look forward to seeing Connie again. This Popular Culture

Psychology book series grew out of a conversation Connie and I had in the hallway at New York Comic Con, and my gratitude to her will never end. When writers I know grumble about their editors, I can only praise Connie and Kate. Many other fine folks at Sterling also deserve praise for giving us the support necessary to bring these books to you: Ardi Alspach, Toula Ballas, Michael Cea, Marilyn Kretzer, Sari Lampert, Rodman Neumann, Blanca Oliviery, Lauren Tambini, Theresa Thompson. My literary agent, Evan Gregory of the Ethan Ellenberg Literary Agency, handles many details, sometimes suggesting great subtitles—although for this one, we must credit my own subconscious mind because *Lassoing the Truth* came to me on a book cover in a dream.

Without our chapter contributors, of course, this series could not exist. Janina Scarlet has written for every volume, and Jenna Busch, Lara Taylor Kester, Martin Lloyd, and Billy San Juan for all but one. Jenna also adds valuable touches as editorial assistant. I met them, Mara Wood, and many of our other contributors through conventions and conferences where they showed that they know their psychology, know their fandoms, and know how to bring them together in ways that are interesting and informative for audiences of all kinds. I thank Nicholas Langley and Matthew Smith, whose work led me to my first Comic-Con and therefore set this long chain of events in motion. I thank the organizers of the Comics Arts Conference (Peter Coogan, Randy Duncan, Kate McClancy), San Diego Comic-Con International (Eddie Ibrahim, Gary Sassaman, Cathy Dalton, Laura Jones, Sue Lord, Adam Neese, Amy Ramirez, Chris Sturhann), Atlantic City Boardwalk Con (Sean McHugh, Carl Horosz), Los Angeles Comic Con (Stan Lee, Regina Campinelli, Jade Cresko, Keith Tralins), New York Comic Con (Lance Fensterman), River City Expo (Brent Douglass), so many Wizard World cons (Christopher Jansen, Peter Katz, Ryan Ball, Donna Chin, Shelby Engquist,

Kate Gloss, Tony B. Kim, Jerry Milani, Mai Nguyen, Alex Rae, Katie Ruark), and more for the variety of opportunities that make this work possible. Speakers who joined us on convention panels where we've discussed Wonder Woman include Eric Bailey, Genese Davis, Rick Klaw, Elizabeth Ann Kus, Patrick O'Connor, Peter Sanderson, Janey Tracey, Jessica Tseang, and Nicky Wheeler-Nicholson. Comics and cartooning professionals such as Paul Benjamin, Danny Fingeroth, Phil Jimenez, Denny O'Neil, Trina Robbins, Greg Rucka, Peter Sanderson, J. J. Sedelmaier, Gail Simone, Marguerite Van Cook, and Len Wein helped us form our thoughts regarding the Amazon princess through panels, conversations, and other communications over time.

Henderson State University administrators President Glendell Jones, Provost Steve Adkison, and Dean John Hardee encourage creative ways of teaching. When I first mentioned to Dr. Jones that I was about to work on a Wonder Woman book, he then described why Wonder Woman is the greatest superhero, citing a specific Justice League story to make his point. Not just any school would have let a group of faculty members (David Stoddard and others named elsewhere herein) create a comics studies minor. Huie Library director Lea Ann Alexander and staff maintain a well-stocked graphic novel collection and reading room. David Bateman, Lecia Franklin, Carolyn Hatley, Ermatine Johnston, Salina Smith, Connie Testa, and Flora Weeks help me and my students go all the places we need to go. Millie Bowden, Denise Cordova, Renee Davis, Sandra D. Johnson, and many other staff members make sure other essentials get done. Our faculty writers group (Angela Boswell, Matthew Bowman, Davis Sesser, Suzanne Tartamella, Michael Taylor, Melanie Wilson Angell) reviewed portions of this manuscript. My fellow psychology faculty members put up with my crazy schedule. Through groups such as our Comics

Arts Club and the Legion of Nerds, our students prove that geeky passions belong in higher education.

Rebecca Manning Langley gets my greatest appreciation, adoration, respect, and love for being my superheroine—my wife, best friend, sounding board, colleague, and partner in all things in this life. Our sons, Nicholas and Alex, each played critical roles in paving the path that led to this series of books. Family not by blood Katrina Hill, Marko Head, and Renee Couey helped pave it, too. My mother Lynda read comic books to me when I was little, which motivated me to learn to read them myself. After our television died, my father Travis Sr. worked many extra hours while juggling his seminary studies to make sure his kids would have a TV, the one on which I first saw Wonder Woman in animation and live action. Importantly, my parents let me be me.

Comics scholars (David Beard, Carolyn Cocca, Elisa G. McCausland) helped us identify where specific comic book images came from. Facebook friends and a Twitter legion (Matt Beard, J. MacFEARlane, Chris Murrin) helped us brainstorm, find facts, and confirm quotes. While wikis are tricky, they often point us in the right direction to track down back issues and other resources, and so we must thank the many volunteers who, often anonymously, maintain sites such as the Grand Comics Database (comics.org), DC Comics Database (dc.wikia. com), and Wikipedia's WikiProject Comics. Comic Book Resources (comicbookresources.com), Comic Vine (comicvine. com), Mike's Amazing World of DC Comics (dcindexex.com), and many others aided our quest to get facts right.

We can't thank DC Comics Vice President Jay Kogan and Rights & Permissions Manager Mandy Noack-Barr enough for the images from DC Comics/Warner Bros. publications, along with Kitty Lindsay for the *Ms.* magazine cover. For reasons diverse and sometimes difficult to explain, we also thank Benjamin

Cruz, Dianne Currie, Athena Finger, Carmelina Frasca, Jeffrey Henderson, Gaye Hirz, Charlotte Bollinger Izzo, DC Librarian Benjamin LeClear, Jim and Kate Lloyd, Sharon and Audrey Manning, Chase Masterson, Dustin McGinnis, Marc Nadel, Trish Nelson, Jacque Nodell, Ed O'Neal, Bill Ostroff, Kaja Perina, Paul Simon, Ann Taylor, Carol Tilley, Michael Uslan, the United Nations, Melynda Williams, the Wonder Woman Creative Collective, Dan Yun's NerdSpan crew, and the makers of Underoos (thanks to which, editorial assistant/contributor Jenna Busch's first cosplay was as Wonder Woman).

A special note of appreciation goes to Chelle Mayer and Golden Age comic book artist Irwin Hasen for previously sharing their recollections of Chelle's grandfather Sheldon Mayer. He was the cartoonist who, as an editor for the companies that would become DC Comics, gave Marston his opportunity to create a superhero, worked with him and provided critical guidance along the way, and trimmed the character's name down from "Suprema the Wonder Woman" to the more elegant and powerful "Wonder Woman." Credited as Mayer's associate editor on *Wonder Woman*, tennis champion and WWII spy Alice Marble created the comic's "Wonder Woman of History" feature and completed a number of Marston's stories.

We owe a great debt to Lynda Carter for being Wonder Woman, embodying the character's spirit, values, and grace to this day. Voice actresses Shannon Farnon and Susan Eisenberg brought Wonder Woman to life in animation more often than did any other performers. We particularly thank Susan for speaking to us for a feature in this book and for helping in other ways. Hundreds of writers, artists, and other creators kept this great hero going, refining and shaping her over the decades. From among the many, we express special appreciation to my friend Denny O'Neil for talking with me about his controversial *Wonder Woman* revamp in the 1960s and to Trina Robbins for writing this book's fantastic foreword. We are honored beyond words to be able to present, for the first time in publication anywhere, the memoir of Elizabeth Holloway Marston.

Our utmost gratitude, naturally, goes to psychologist/attorney Dr. William Moulton Marston ("Bill") for creating Wonder Woman, attorney/psychologist Elizabeth Marston ("Sadie" in her younger days, "Betty" later on) for telling him to make his new superhero a woman, and journalist Olive Byrne ("Dotsie") for her important place in their lives and in Wonder Woman's. Both Betty and Dotsie worked with Bill in psychology and helped shape his iconic creation. They all were and forever remain sensations.

II.

Mara Wood, PhD
volume co-editor

None of this could have happened without Travis. From *Batman and Psychology: A Dark and Stormy Knight* to this volume, Travis has shown that we can learn from our heroes. Working with him and the other professionals on this series has taught me even more about psychology and about unapologetically loving comics. I thank the writers of this and previous volumes for keeping me sharp and challenging me to be a better psychologist and a better fan.

I would like to thank my husband, Matt Wood, for putting up with my deep dive into Wonder Woman comics. There were many nights of quietly reading comics and taking notes. Thanks to Matt and his talent at hunting for comic trades, my Wonder Woman collection is wonderful.

Thanks, Mom, for introducing me to comics and sharing your love for the hero and the antihero with me. I want to thank my co-workers in the Rogers Public School district for their support in working on *Lassoing the Truth*. Nobody tuned me out while I explained why a bound Wonder Woman was important or how Pérez brought the character back to her roots. I am a graduate of the University of Central Arkansas, and I am thankful for the support of the psychology department, particularly Ron Bramlett, when I expressed an interest in researching comics. Allen Thomas, you are my favorite research partner. Please continue using comics and popular culture to help others.

Thank you to the Talking Comics family for taking me on in 2012, putting me behind the microphone on the podcast, and giving me a place to express my love. Thank you, Bobby Shortle, Bob Reyer, Steve Seigh, Joey Braccino, Melissa Megan, Stephanie Cooke, Maria Norris, Carolyn Cocca, and Huw Parry for helping me grow as a comics fan and learn to be critical while still loving what I love. The Talking Comics podcast listeners hold a special place in my heart for the culture they represent and the insights they have regarding the industry.

References

Hull Funeral Home (2017, January 17). *Moulton "Pete" Marston*. Hull Funeral Home: http://www.hullfuneralservice.com/notices/Moulton-Marston.
Richard, O. (1940, October 25). Don't laugh at the comics. *The Family Circle*, pp. 10–11, 22.
Wonder Woman Network (n.d.). *Welcome!* http://wonderwomannetwork.com.

Notes

1. Byrne, writing as Richard (1940), p. 22.
2. Wonder Woman Network (n.d.).
3. Hull Funeral Home (2017).

Foreword:
The Lasso and the Pendulum

Trina Robbins

I must have been about ten years old when I discovered Wonder Woman. I didn't know at the time that "Charles Moulton" (Dr. William Moulton Marston, under his pen name) had died the year before but had left behind a pile of scripts that were still being published, still illustrated by Harry G. Peter, so the Wonder Woman I was reading was still the original Amazon princess that Marston had created.

I had never heard of Amazons before and I was instantly captivated by the idea of an island of beautiful, competent, and courageous women, with no men allowed. *Especially* with no men allowed! I lived in a time of "No Girls Allowed." Although we were taught in school that anyone born in America could become president of our country, it was universally accepted without question that only *men* born in America could be president. Even Marston, Wonder Woman's feminist creator, could only envision a woman as president a thousand years into the future.[1]

Men ruled and women served. A woman might be a nurse but never a doctor. She could be a stewardess but never a pilot. As a secretary, she could take dictation but not do the dictating. Even Wonder Woman, when she joined the all-superhero Justice Society, had to be the secretary.[2]

Years went by and at a certain point I stopped reading Wonder Woman. Her adventures had become boring to me. It seemed that all she cared about was whether or not she should marry Steve Trevor, and she was no longer drawn in the style I had enjoyed. I didn't know that Marston's scripts had been used up[3] and now she was being written by Robert Kanigher, or that Harry Peter, whose art had so perfectly complemented Marston's writing, had retired.[4] All I knew was that my favorite heroine wasn't any fun anymore.

Fast-forward forty years: 1988 found me suffering from some mystery fever that left me aching and weak, sometimes feeling too awful to even read, so that all I could do was lie on my recliner and watch television. Coincidentally, PBS was airing the immortal *Joseph Campbell and the Power of Myth*, a six-part series featuring Joseph Campbell being interviewed by Bill Moyers about psychology and mythology. And because of my mystery fever, I was watching it in an altered state. Lying there on the recliner with Joseph Campbell holding forth on the small screen in front of me, I suddenly understood the spell that Wonder Woman had cast over me back in 1948 and why decades of other comic book heroines had failed to cast the same spell. Wonder Woman was the classic mythic hero! Born of a virgin mother, given life by a deity (in Diana's feminist case, her divine parent is usually written as the goddess Aphrodite), she receives the call when Steve Trevor crashes his plane on her island, going off with him to heal the damaged land, "Man's World."

In the world of comics, arguably only four characters can claim the title of mythic, thus true, heroes (Superman, Batman, and the original Captain Marvel being the other three), and the Amazon Princess is the only woman among them. Sadly, Wonder Woman is only a fictional character owned by DC Comics. As such, since Marston's death she has been a slave to whoever writes and draws her. Many of those have not really liked her, have perhaps felt threatened by the strongest woman in comics. Thus they have diminished her through the years, by turning her into a family show composed of woman, girl, tot, and mom; by taking away her costume and powers and dressing her in Emma Peel jumpsuits; or by drawing her to look like a pole dancer.

I am happy to see that the many contributors to *Wonder Woman Psychology: Lassoing the Truth* have avoided the above versions, but instead have concentrated on analyzing Marston's original version or those of the few creators who got it right, like George Pérez, Gail Simone, and Greg Rucka.

Pendulums swing, as we learned from our 2016 presidential election. Wonder Woman's pendulum has swung from Marston writing about the kind of heroine he felt should become president, to writers who characterized her and her sister Amazons as violent and warlike, and artists who couldn't keep their hands off her costume and kept redesigning it, to creators who see her as more woman-friendly. I only hope that her pendulum will continue to swing in the direction she's been going recently, and we will continue to enjoy the Amazon princess we love: beautiful, strong, brave, compassionate—and feminist.

 Retired underground cartoonist and current comics historian **Trina Robbins** has been writing graphic novels, comics, and books for almost half a century. Her subjects have ranged from Wonder Woman and *The Powerpuff Girls* to her own teenage superheroine, *Go Girl!*, and from women cartoonists and superheroines to women who kill. She's won an Inkpot Award and was inducted in the Will Eisner Hall of Fame at the San Diego Comic-Con. She lives in a moldering, 100+-year-old house in San Francisco with her cats, shoes, and dust bunnies. She illustrated and co-authored the comic book series *The Legend of Wonder Woman*.

Comic Book References

All Star Comics #13 (1942). "Shanghaied into Space." Script: G. Fox. Art: J. Burnley.
Wonder Woman #7 (1943). "America's Wonder Women of Tomorrow!" Script: W. M. Marston. Art: H. G. Peter.
Wonder Woman #28 (1948). "Villainy Incorporated." Script: W. M. Marston. Art: H. G. Peter.

Wonder Woman #97 (1958). "The Runaway Time Express" Script: R. Kanigher. Art: H. G. Peter.

Notes

1. *Wonder Woman* #7 (1943).
2. *All-Star Comics* #13 (1942).
3. Marston's last story appeared in *Wonder Woman* #28 (1948).
4. Peter's last story appeared in *Wonder Woman* #97 (1958).

Introduction: Truth

TRAVIS LANGLEY

Princess Diana of the Amazons is a strong, healthy character. As Wonder Woman, she is one of the world's most famous superheroes, and she is the most famous female among them— some argue the most famous heroine of any kind.[1] Superheroes tend to embody the hope that individuals who step up to do the right thing can make the world better. Wonder Woman goes further by demonstrating hope that every individual can improve. She wants to help people discover the best in their own true natures. Diana's magic lasso, known for compelling people to speak honestly, represents her dedication to truth itself.

Why put together a book on the psychology of a superhero who's mentally healthy and whose enemies are not widely known? When I wrote *Batman and Psychology: A Dark and Stormy Knight*, people understood why: The Dark Knight has serious issues, his enemies fill an asylum, and no superhero has foes more famous than his. Using psychology to look at those characters and stories seemed the obvious thing to do, and mining that fiction for examples to explain psychology made sense. Personal trauma does not drive Diana to become a hero. Real-life heroes' backgrounds tend not to include a single driving tragedy.[2] As comic book writer Len Wein observed, "Some of them become heroes because it's simply the right thing to do."[3] There are many kinds of heroes, though, and many areas of psychology. Not all of them are dark.

Truth is incomplete when we seek it only in the darkness. Hunting for secrets in the dark of night, no matter how many great discoveries that might reveal, falls short and even misleads us if we overlook other truths that shine in the light of day. A look at mental illness makes little sense unless we contrast it with mental health. How can we evaluate a person's "impairment in social, occupational, or other important areas of functioning"[4] without considering what counts as *un*impaired functioning in the first place? How can we discuss "abnormal" without defining "normal"? Questions like these nagged at Wonder Woman's creator.

A psychologist created Diana the Amazon princess at the suggestion of his wife, Elizabeth Holloway Marston, who was also a psychologist by the standards of the time.[5] Dr. William Moulton Marston—therapist, professor, and entrepreneur—became an educational consultant for the companies that would eventually merge to become DC Comics.[6] When editor Sheldon Mayer gave him the opportunity to create a new superhero, Bill Marston went home full of excitement about the prospect. According to their son Pete, Elizabeth made the crucial recommendation: "Let's have a super woman! There's too many men out there."[7] Under the pen name Charles Moulton, until his death of cancer at age fifty-three, Bill dedicated the last six years of his life to writing stories about this character who combined his views about women's superiority to men,[8] his DISC theory about how people influence each other,[9] and his science of truth.[10]

Not just any psychologist, William Moulton Marston occupies an important place in the history of both forensic psychology and personnel psychology, in the history of seeking truth in courtrooms and careers. He is often called—incorrectly and yet with good reason—the "inventor of the lie detector"[11] for using systolic blood pressure to identify signs of deception. Even though he did *not* invent the *polygraph* (*poly-* for "multiple" and *-graph* for "measurement"),[12] Marston popularized the use of measuring a physiological reaction when attempting to evaluate honesty in criminal proceedings.[13] He appeared as the

STARRING...
WONDER WOMAN

CREATOR: Dr. William Moulton Marston, a.k.a. Charles Moulton.

ORIGINAL ARTIST: H. G. Peter.

DEBUT: *All-Star Comics* #8 (1941), concluded in *Sensation Comics* #1 (1942).

DEBUT OF HER OWN TITLE: *Wonder Woman* #1 (1942).

UNAIRED TELEVISION PILOT: *Who's Afraid of Diana Prince?* (1966 short). Played by Elle Wood Walker as Diana Prince and by Linda Harrison as her Wonder Woman alter ego.

FIRST TELEVISION APPEARANCE: *The Brady Kids* (animated series) episode 1–13, "It's All Greek to Me" (December 2, 1972). Voiced by Jane Webb.

FIRST TELEVISION SERIES: *Super Friends* (animated series), beginning with episode 1–1, "The Power Pirate" (September 8, 1973). Voiced by Shannon Farnon.

FIRST LIVE ACTION APPEARANCE: *Wonder Woman* (1974 television movie). Played by Cathy Lee Crosby.

FIRST LIVE ACTION SERIES: *Wonder Woman,* beginning with *The New Original Wonder Woman* (1975 pilot/television movie), followed by episode 1–1, "Wonder Woman Meets Baroness von Gunther" (April 21, 1976). Played by Lynda Carter.

FIRST THEATRICAL APPEARANCE: *The LEGO Movie* (2014 motion picture). Voiced by Cobie Smulders.

FIRST LIVE ACTION THEATRICAL APPEARANCE: *Batman v. Superman: Dawn of Justice* (2016 motion picture). Played by Gal Gadot.

FIRST THEATRICAL STARRING ROLE: *Wonder Woman* (2017 motion picture). Played by Gal Gadot.

Hippolyta reveals the lasso's divine power in *Sensation* Comics #6 (1942).
Art: H. G. Peter. ®DC Comics.

lie detection expert in a landmark court case[14]—admittedly, the
case that led an appellate court to rule and set the enduring legal
standard[15] that his lie detection method should *not* be admissible in court.[16] In Marston's Wonder Woman comics of the
1940s, the characters Wonder Woman and Steve Trevor each
use systolic blood pressure measurements at times to identify
liars and spies.[17] No matter which physiological sign an expert
records to assess veracity, each test for an abnormal deviation
that supposedly indicates a lie requires a *baseline* measurement
for comparison, an assessment of what the person looks like in
that individual's normal state—in this case, what the person
looks like when telling the truth.[18]

Wonder Woman would become well known for wielding
a magical Lasso of Truth[19]—which is itself a widely shared
mistruth, a misnomer because the lasso compels obedience,
not simply confessions.[20] Marston considered obedience and
loving submission to others to be good, healthy, and important for personal growth,[21] and this would become a recurring

THE PUBLISHER:
IT'S ALL DC

Wonder Woman originated in publications from All-American Comics, one of the companies that would merge to become what is now known as DC Comics:

- **All-American Publications:** founded in 1938. Merged with **National Allied Publications** (founded in 1934, a.k.a. **National Allied Newspaper Syndicate**) and **Detective Comics, Inc.** (founded in 1937) to form **National Comics Publications** in 1944 under the greater corporate entity of **National Periodical Publications**.
- **Superman-DC:** unofficial branding of many National publications starting in 1940; later simply **DC**.
- **DC Comics:** officially rebranding of the company in 1977.

PARENT COMPANY: **Warner Communications**, which merged with Time to form **Time Warner** in 1989. Time Warner made DC Comics a subsidiary of **DC Entertainment** in 2009.

LOCATION: New York, NY, until 2015. Burbank, CA, since 2015.

Because most comics cited in this book were published by All-American/National/DC Comics, references will identify a comic book's publisher only for the few instances in which an outside company such as Fawcett or Nedor Comics published the work.

theme throughout his stories. The lasso could even compel a person to lie,[22] but Wonder Woman's dedication to seeking truth as an integral part of her personality makes that aspect the lasso's most identifiable attribute, to the point that even comic book writers forgot for many years that it does more than elicit honest answers. "We looked at the golden Lasso of Truth," writer Greg Rucka said about revisiting the heroine's origin for the DC Rebirth event, "but it's not the lasso that does it; it's Diana who brings the truth."[23]

Together with Superman and Batman,[24] Wonder Woman is one of only three superheroes to stay in steady publication from their Golden Age debuts through the present day.[25] The respective children of science fiction, street crime, and myth, these three persist for diverse reasons. At one point in the 1950s, theirs were the only superhero titles left in publication.[26] Superman was our first comic book superhero—bright and impossible. Batman "expanded that meme by adding the coin's other side, the dark and improbably possible."[27] What, then, was Wonder Woman? She was neither the first superheroine[28] nor the first mythological superhero,[29] but maybe she was the first psychological superhero.[30]

"Frankly, Wonder Woman is psychological propaganda for the new type of woman who should, I believe, rule the world," said the character's creator in a letter to comics historian Coulton Waugh. "There isn't love enough in the male organism to run this planet peacefully." [31] During World War II, a time when the wars men waged threatened lives across the globe, he believed that female leaders who would emerge in the aftermath would take the future in a more enlightened direction. "There's great hope for this world. Women will win! When women rule, there won't be any more [war] because the girls won't want to waste time killing men—I regard that as the greatest—no, even more—as the only hope for permanent peace."[32] In the best-known versions of her origin, Diana leaves her island home and becomes Wonder Woman to fight against war itself, as is sometimes embodied in the form of war god Ares or Mars. "The first casualty of war," as Diana puts it, "is truth."[33]

> *"When you need to stop an asteroid, you get Superman.*
> *When you need to solve a mystery, you call Batman. But*
> *when you need to end a war, you get Wonder Woman."*
> —comic book writer Gail Simone[34]

Why has she endured? Is it the strength of the name itself, *Wonder Woman*? Marston originally wanted to call her Suprema the Wonder Woman in the vein of Robin the Boy Wonder and many other characters of the time, but editor Sheldon Mayer disliked that and said to cut it down to Wonder Woman.[35] She was not a direct spin-off of a male superhero (no more so than any other superhero ultimately derives from Superman, that is), not in the way that Hawkgirl, Supergirl, and Batgirl followed Hawkman, Superman, and Batman. Nor was she created to be a male superhero's love interest (Hawkgirl, Bulletgirl), relative (Mary Marvel, Supergirl, She-Hulk), inspired fan (Batwoman, Batgirl), team token (Invisible Girl, Marvel Girl), or femme fatale (Catwoman—sometimes a hero, sometimes not). Among superheroes, she was the independent woman—*woman*, not *girl*. She may have joined the Justice Society initially to help out as their secretary, but in her own stories she was the hero.

Depictions of her have varied, notably with regard to how violent she might be and how much fun she's having. In her early stories, she refuses to kill, she sports a good sense of humor, and she has fun throughout her adventures. Over the decades, she would undergo a number of revisions, partly because her roots in World War II no longer held up as the decades progressed but also because women's roles and rights changed over time.

We look at the strong, healthy character for some of the same reasons recent psychologists now charge psychology with a criticism her creator made long ago: Too much of psychology has focused on that which is abnormal without exploring that which is normal—hence Marston's classic book, *Emotions of Normal People*. Whereas other psychologists and other fictional characters might view humankind pessimistically, William Moulton Marston and Wonder Woman look for the best in us all and hope for our world. In the twenty-first century, a psychologist best known for studying the causes and consequences of learned helplessness[36] promotes *positive psychology* on the belief that psychology has overemphasized the worst parts of human nature to the neglect of trying to understand the best.[37] Perhaps more than any other superhero, Princess Diana of Themyscira embodies the virtues that positive psychologists look for in us all (wisdom, courage, justice, temperance, transcendence, and humanity[38]), which the Virtue Files at the end of each section in this book will explore.

She is a wonder. Behold.

Comic Book References

Action Comics #1 (1938). "Superman, Champion of the Oppressed." Script: J. Siegel. Art: J. Shuster.

Detective Comics #27 (1939). "The Case of the Chemical Syndicate." Script: B. Finger. Art: B. Kane.

Jungle Comics #2 (1940). [Untitled origin of Fantomah]. Script & Art: F. Hanks (as B. Flagg). Fiction House.

The Legend of Wonder Woman #1 (1986). "Legends Live Forever." Story: T. Robbins & K. Busiek. Art: T. Robbins.

The Legend of Wonder Woman #4 (1986). "Splitting the Atom." Story: T. Robbins & K. Busiek. Art: T. Robbins.

Sensation Comics #3 (1942). "A Spy in the Office." Script: W. M. Marston. Art: H. G. Peter.

Sensation Comics #6 (1942). "Summons to Paradise Island." Script: W. M. Marston. Art: H. G. Peter.

Thrilling Comics #2 (1940). [Untitled origin of the Woman in Red]. Script: Unknown. Art: G. Mandel. Nedor Comics.

Whiz Comics #2 (1940). [Untitled origin of Captain Marvel]. Script: B. Parker. Art: C. C. Beck. Fawcett Comics.

Wonder Woman #4 (1942). "The Rubber Barons." Script: W. M. Marston. Art: H. G. Peter.

Wonder Woman #329 (1986). "A Universe Besieged!" Script: G. Conway. Art: D. Heck.

Wonder Woman #1 (1987). "The Princess and the Power!" Story: G. Potter & G. Pérez. Art: G. Pérez & B. Patterson.

Wonder Woman: The Circle (2008). Script: G. Simone. Art: T. Dodson & R. Dodson.

Wonder Woman Rebirth #1 (2016). "Wonder Woman Rebirth." Script: G. Rucka. Art: M. Clark, L. Sharp, & S. Parsons.

Other References

Allison, S. T., & Goethals, G. R. (2011). *Heroes: What they do and why we need them*. New York, NY: Oxford University Press.

American Psychiatric Association. (2013). *Diagnostic and statistical manual of mental disorders* (DSM-5). Washington, DC: American Psychiatric Association.

Benussi, V. (1914). Die Atmungssymptome der Lüge [The respiratory symptoms of lying]. *Archiv fuer Die Gesamte Psychologie, 31*, 244–273.

Bio Staff (2014, July 17). *Fact or fiction: Inventor of the lie detector also created Wonder Woman?* Biography: http://www.biography.com/news/fact-or-fiction-inventor-of-the-lie-detector.

Bunn, G. C. (2012). *The truth machine: A social history of the lie detector*. Baltimore, MD: Johns Hopkins University Press.

Comic Vine (2015, June 3). *William Moulton Marston*. Comic Vine: http://comicvine.gamespot.com/william-moulton-marston/4040-43411/.

Committee to Review the Scientific Evidence on the Polygraph (2003). *The polygraph and lie detection*. Washington, DC: National Academic Press.

Daniels, L. (1995). *DC Comics: Sixty years of the world's favorite comic book heroes*. New York, NY: Bulfinch.

Daniels, L. (2004). *Wonder Woman: The complete history*. San Francisco, CA: Chronicle.

DC Comics (n.d.). *Wonder Woman*. DC Comics: http://www.dccomics.com/characters/wonder-woman.

DC Database (n.d.). *Lasso of Truth*. DC Database: http://dc.wikia.com/wiki/Lasso_of_Truth.

Diaz, E. (2016, July 29). *Celebrating 75 years of Wonder Woman*. Nerdist: http://nerdist.com/celebrating-75-years-of-wonder-woman/.

Duncan, R., & Smith, M. J. (2009). *The power of comics: History, form, & culture*. New York, NY: Continuum.

Fernandez, C. (n.d.). *The first ever superheroes*. Ranker: http://www.ranker.com/list/the-first-ever-superheroines/chinofernandez.

Fisher, J. (2008, January 7). *The polygraph and the Frye case*. Jim Fisher: http://jimfisher.edinboro.edu/forensics/frye.html.

Hanley, T. (2014). *Wonder Woman unbound: The curious history of the world's most famous heroine*. Chicago, IL: Chicago Review Press.

Johnston, R. (2016, April 11). *The continuity of Wonder Woman to be made sense of—DC Rebirth details*. Bleeding Cool: http://www.bleedingcool.com/2016/04/11/the-continuity-of-wonder-woman-to-be-made-sense-of-dc-rebirth-details/.

Joyce, N. (2008). Wonder Woman: A psychologist's creation. *American Psychologist, 39*(11), 20.

Karlin, S. (2016, Jun 17). *Psychology's first superhero: Celebrating Wonder Woman at 75*. Fast Company: https://www.fastcocreate.com/3060996/creation-stories/psychologys-first-superhero-celebrating-wonder-woman-at-75.

Keeler, L. (1933). Scientific methods for criminal detection with the polygraph. *Kansas Bar Association, 2,* 22–31.

Langley, T. (2012). *Batman and psychology: A dark and stormy knight.* New York, NY: Wiley.

Larson, J. A. (1932). *Lying and its detection.* Chicago, IL: University of Chicago Press.

Letamendi, A., Rosenberg, R., Langley, T., & Wein, L. (2011). *The superhero battlefield: Resiliency in the face of loss and destruction.* Panel presented at San Diego Comic-Con International, San Diego, CA.

Littlefield, M. M. (2011). *The lying brain: Lie detection in science and science fiction.* Ann Arbor, MI: University of Michigan Press.

Madrid, M. (2013). *Divas, dames, & daredevils: Lost heroines of the Golden Age of comics.* Minneapolis, MN: Exterminating Angel.

Marston, W. M. (1917). Systolic blood pressure symptoms of deception. *Journal of Experimental Psychology, 2*(2), 117–163.

Marston, W. M. (1928). *Emotions of normal people.* London, UK: Kegan Paul, Trench, Trubner.

Marston, W. M. (1929, October 29). Why men are organizing to fight female dominance. *Hamilton Evening Journal,* feature section, p. 1.

Marston, W. M. (1944). Women can out-think men! *Ladies Home Journal, 61* (May), 4–5.

Marston, W. M. (1947). Lie detection's bodily basis and test procedures. In P. L. Harriman (Ed.), *Encyclopedia of psychology* (pp. 354–363). New York, NY: Philosophical Library.

McMillan, J. J. (1973). Professional standards and the master's level psychologist. *Professional Psychology, 4*(3), 296–299.

Meyer, R. G., & Weaver, C. M. (2006). *Law and mental health: A case-based approach.* New York, NY: Guilford.

Morrison, G. (2011). *Supergods: What masked vigilantes, miraculous mutants, and a sun god from Smallville can teach us about being human.* New York, NY: Spiegel & Grau.

New York Times (1993, April 3). Elizabeth H. Marston, inspiration for Wonder Woman, 100 (obituary). *New York Times* (late edition), section 1, p. 11.

Peterson, C., & Seligman, M. E. P. (2004*). Character strengths and virtues.* Washington, D.C.: American Psychological Association.

Reynolds, R. (1994). *Superheroes: A modern mythology.* Jackson, MS: University Press of Mississippi.

Richard, O. (1940, October 25). Don't laugh at the comics. *The Family Circle,* pp. 10–11, 22.

Seligman, M. E. P. (1972). Learning helplessness. *Annual Review of Medicine, 23*(1), 407–312.

Seligman, M. E. P. (1998). Building human strength: Psychology's forgotten mission. *APA Monitor, 29*(1), 1.

Seligman, M. E. P., & Maier, S. F. (1967). Failure to escape traumatic shock. *Journal of Experimental Psychology, 74*(1), 1–9.

Seligman, M. E. P., Steen, T. A., Park, N., & Peterson, C. (2005). Positive psychology progress: Empirical validation of interventions. *American Psychologist, 60*(5), 410–421.

Notes

1. DC Comics (n.d.); Hanley (2014); Morrison (2011).
2. Allison & Goethals (2011).
3. Letamendi et al. (2011).
4. American Psychiatric Association (2013), p. 21.

5. McMillan (1973).
6. Daniels (1995).
7. *New York Times* (1993); Marston, P. (personal communication, 2016).
8. Marston (1929, 1944).
9. Marston (1928).
10. Marston (1917, 1947).
11. e.g., Bio Staff (2014).
12. Marston (1917) followed Benussi (1914). Larson in 1921 (described in 1932) and Keeler (1933) expanded the polygraph to multiple physiological channels.
13. Bunn (2012); Committee to Review the Scientific Evidence on the Polygraph (2003).
14. *Frye v. United States* (1923), cited in Fisher (2008).
15. Bunn (2012); Fisher (2008); Committee to Review the Scientific Evidence on the Polygraph (2003).
16. Meyer & Weaver (2006).
17. e.g., *Sensation Comics* #3 (1942); *Wonder Woman* #4 (1942).
18. Littlefield (2011).
19. DC Database (n.d.).
20. *Sensation Comics* #6 (1942).
21. Marston (1928).
22. e.g., *Sensation Comics* #6 (1942).
23. Johnston (2016).
24. Diaz (2016); Reynolds (1994).
25. Superman since *Action Comics* #1 (1938), Batman since *Detective Comics* #27 (1939), and Wonder Woman since 1941 except for a two-month hiatus between *Wonder Woman* #329 (1986) and *The Legend of Wonder Woman* #1 (1986), then five months between *The Legend of Wonder Woman* #4 (1986) and *Wonder Woman* #1 (1987).
26. Duncan & Smith (2009).
27. Langley (2012), p. 6.
28. Fantomah debuted in *Jungle Comics* #2 (1940), the Woman in Red debuted in *Thrilling Comics* #2, and others followed. See Fernandez (n.d.) and Madrid (2013) for more of Wonder Woman's predecessors.
29. e.g., the original Captain Marvel, whose comics would outsell Superman's: debuted in *Whiz Comics* #2 (1940).
30. Joyce (2008); Karlin (2016).
31. Quoted in Daniels (2004), pp. 22–23.
32. Richard (1940), p. 19.
33. *Wonder Woman Rebirth* #1 (2016).
34. *Wonder Woman: The Circle* (2008).
35. Mayer, C. (personal communication, 2016).
36. Seligman & Maier (1967); Seligman (1972).
37. Seligman (1998); Seligman et al. (2005).
38. Peterson & Seligman (2004).

WHILE THE WORLD WENT TO WAR, A PSYCHOLOGIST CREATED A CHARACTER, GUIDED BY HIS PSYCHOLOGIST WIFE. THROUGHOUT THIS NEW HERO'S STORIES, FUN AND ADVENTURE BLENDED TO PROMOTE THE CREATOR'S PSYCHOLOGY OF TRUTH, DOMINANCE, AND MENTAL HEALTH.

PART I

CREATOR'S WORLD

CHAPTER ONE

Psychology on Trial: The Other Legacy of William Moulton Marston

MARTIN LLOYD

"Whew! Lila's blood pressure jumped 50 millimeters! She's lying about that envelope!"
—Wonder Woman (using the Marston blood pressure test)[1]

"The behavior of the b.p. does not act as the least indicator of the objective validity of the story told by any witness, but it constitutes a practically infallible test of the consciousness of an attitude of deception."
— Psychologist William Moulton Marston[2]

Readers who are at least passingly familiar with the legal system or, indeed, even with courtroom dramas on television or in film are doubtless aware that mental health practitioners (e.g., psychologists and psychiatrists) sometimes testify in court. These expert witnesses may be called upon to offer opinions about whether a defendant has the mental capacity to stand trial or should be considered "sane," meaning that the accused is culpable for criminal conduct. Mental health experts may also be asked to explain psychological concepts[3] such as the validity of repressed memories or multiple personalities. Although mental health professionals are a common fixture in the courtroom today, this was not always the case. Through a large part of the twentieth century, mental health testimony was more limited in scope than it is now, typically allowed to focus only on diagnosis.[4] Psychologists, lacking the medical degrees of their psychiatric colleagues, were even more limited in their ability to testify, sometimes being ineligible to be considered expert witnesses.[5]

Change was slow over the first half of the twentieth century, but various legal decisions gradually increased psychologists' participation in the criminal justice system. One of the key early figures in that development was none other than Wonder Woman's creator, William Moulton Marston. Marston's work and his involvement in the legal system helped pave the way for psychologists to testify as expert witnesses and shaped the rules that allow experts in any scientific field to offer testimony. Marston's impact on the field of forensic psychology shaped the rules for expert testimony and paved the way for modern efforts at the detection of deception.

Under Pressure: Marston and the Detection of Deception

Although best known for the creation of Wonder Woman, William Moulton Marston began his professional life as a classically trained psychologist. He received both a law degree and, in 1921, a doctorate in psychology from Harvard University.[6] While at Harvard, he was apprenticed to Hugo Münsterberg, a German psychologist who developed an early psychological laboratory at Harvard to apply experimental methods to normal psychological phenomena.[7] In that laboratory, Münsterberg established what are now widely accepted findings about the fallibility of memory and the tendency of normal people to lie for self-serving reasons. Münsterberg hoped that some of his findings—and by extension psychological science—would ultimately be admissible in court. He never achieved that goal, but his student would eventually make significant strides in that direction.[8]

While completing his graduate studies, Marston made an unanticipated experimental finding. In 1915, he discovered a correlation between deception and rises in systolic blood pressure.[9] He found significant differences in the systolic blood pressures of individuals when they were known to be telling the truth and when they were verifiably lying.[10] His explanation was that the rise in blood pressure was an emotional reaction, specifically the result of fear and, less consistently, anger. Liars, according to Marston, would experience a rise in blood pressure because they were reacting to the dangerous state of being caught or detected while consciously trying to ignore that fear.[11]

Marston became a great promoter of his blood pressure test's ability to differentiate truth from lies. In his early writing on the matter, he described the test's ability to identify those who were consciously lying as "practically infallible."[12] He later claimed that his test made accurate determinations over 95 percent of the time.[13] His faith in his test would ultimately bring him to the attention of the legal system.

The Lie Detector on Trial

It would take a murder for Marston to be able to introduce his systolic blood pressure test to the general public—specifically, the murder of one Dr. R. W. Brown, shot in the head by an

A deceptive character shows a jump in blood pressure, demonstrating Wonder Woman creator Marston's lie detection method. *Sensation Comics* #3 (1942). Art: H. G. Peter. ®DC Comics.

unknown assailant. After approximately a year with no suspects, James A. Frye confessed to the crime while being questioned on an unrelated matter. Frye initially claimed he had killed Brown in self-defense, but he later denied any involvement in the murder to his lawyers, stating that he had confessed in order to share the reward money with one of the investigating detectives. No physical evidence linked Frye to the crime scene, but his alibi proved to be false. Thus, his defense attorneys were left with few means of avoiding the death penalty other than trying to prove that the confession had been false.[14]

The attorneys believed they had found the solution to their problem when they learned of Marston's work. The psychologist readily agreed to evaluate Frye for free. To Marston's apparent surprise, his test indicated that Frye was truthful in his claim of innocence. Frye's attorneys called Marston to testify, submitting his dissertation and scientific papers to the court so that he could be acknowledged as an expert witness. Upon reviewing the supporting documents, however, the trial judge ruled that Marston could not testify, as it was the jury's job to determine if witnesses were being truthful (and yet the discussion about the test's admissibility had nevertheless revealed to the jurors that Frye had passed a so-called lie detector test).[15]

The Legacy of *Frye*

Although he was unable to testify at trial, Marston's involvement in the Frye case would have lasting implications for the field of forensic psychology and for anyone looking to testify as an expert witness. Frye's case, specifically the decision to disallow Marston's testimony, was ultimately appealed.[16] The appellate case set a landmark precedent that would govern the admission of expert testimony in the United States for decades. The court of appeals ruled that for expert testimony to be admissible, the means of arriving at the expert's opinion must have achieved general acceptance within that expert's field.[17] Marston's technique was novel. That is, his findings were relatively new and the psychological field as a whole was not actively using, or necessarily even aware of, his test. Thus, the exclusion of Marston's testimony was upheld, and his deception test was never part of the official record in the *Frye* case.[18] Nonetheless, the *Frye* decision did not automatically exclude testimony by psychologists. In fact, by the rule *Frye* created, if the systolic blood pressure test had been recognized as a test for deception by the psychological community as a whole, Marston would have been able to testify about it.

Despite Marston's inability to have his testimony admitted in the *Frye* case, the rule that grew out of the case would govern the admissibility of expert testimony for some time. For many years, the test that would govern the admissibility of expert testimony was *general acceptance*, though this was not to last. In 1975, Congress passed the Federal Rules of Evidence, intended to govern the admissibility of evidence in the federal courts. Rule 702 specifically governs the admission of expert testimony, holding that such testimony should be useful to the trier of fact (e.g., the jury), based on sufficient data and arrived at by reliable means.[19] Although 702 was in place, the *Frye* rule generally held sway in the courts until a 1993 Supreme Court case led to the formal adoption of the Federal Rules of Evidence for the federal courts. The *Daubert* rule, in addition to formally adopting the Federal Rules of Evidence, held that judges should consider several additional factors in deciding whether to admit expert testimony: whether the science can be tested, whether there is a known error rate, whether it has been subject to peer review and then published, and whether it is generally accepted within the relevant field (the *Frye* criterion).[20] The *Daubert* ruling held that these rules would apply to the federal court system, and numerous states have replaced *Frye* with the *Daubert* standard, but several states continue to use the *Frye* rule (Washington, California, Utah, Kansas, Minnesota, Illinois, Alabama, and Pennsylvania, along with several states that use modified versions of the standard).[21] Although the *Frye* rule is no longer used as frequently, it seems to make little difference in terms of what testimony is actually admitted.[22]

Although the rule governing admissibility of expert testimony that Marston helped shape is used increasingly infrequently, his involvement in the *Frye* case nevertheless paved the way for expert testimony by psychologists. The *Frye* decision allowed for any scientific testimony that had achieved general acceptance within the relevant field, and this allowed psychology to be considered a field of scientific inquiry. Later decisions would grow the seed planted in this decision and further expand psychologists' ability to testify. The fact that the courts were beginning to recognize the need for such testimony was evident in *Brown v. Board of Education*,[23] the landmark Supreme Court case that outlawed school segregation. This was the first Supreme Court case to cite psychological research. The decision arguably leaned heavily on the research of psychologist Kenneth B. Clark, cited in a foot-

NO LASSO OF TRUTH

MARTIN LLOYD AND TRAVIS LANGLEY

Most readers are doubtless familiar with Wonder Woman's Lasso of Truth. The fact that this lasso, which compels absolute truthfulness, was created by the inventor of the lie detector (or at least an important component of it) makes for a fantastic bit of trivia. Unfortunately, it's not entirely true. When Marston was writing Wonder Woman, she did not have the Lasso of Truth. She had a magical lasso[24] with numerous powers, primarily the ability to make those it encircled obey her commands. This ability to compel obedience derived from the goddess Aphrodite's power to make others submit to her will.[25] Wonder Woman could use this ability to make others tell the truth,[26] but this was always in the context of their obeying her; there was no inherent compulsion for truthfulness. In the time before she had the lasso, Wonder Woman made do with Marston's systolic blood pressure test to detect deception.[27]

There appears to be some debate about when the lasso of Truth, with which modern readers are familiar, became a Lasso of Truth. It was never called by that name during Marston's tenure, and he never described it as being linked exclusively to truthfulness. The modern form of the lasso first appeared after the universe-reshaping events of *Crisis on Infinite Earths* in the 1980s.[28] Though they may have coined the name "Lasso of Truth," it seems that neither writer George Potter nor artist George Pérez ever actually invented a lie detector.

note, which concerned the effects of segregation on psychological development.[29] Other decisions would more directly address the admissibility psychological experts' testimony. Several court decisions in the 1960s held that psychologists could testify as experts.[30] The landmark decision, however, is generally thought to be *Jenkins v. U.S.*,[31] which established that psychologists can testify as an expert.

Marston's work opened the door for those in his profession to be more actively involved in the legal system. This perhaps begs the question: Is it a good thing for psychologists to be allowed to testify in court? There is certainly evidence to suggest that psychologists have something to offer the legal process above and beyond what their medically trained psychiatric colleagues might offer. Clinical psychologists typically have substantially more training in research than psychiatrists do and also spend several more years in formal study of human behavior.[32] Likely as a result of this extra training, judges, attorneys, and law professors performing blind reviews rated forensic reports by psychologists to be more thorough and of higher quality than those completed by psychiatrists.[33] Thus, William Moulton Marston, by tipping the first domino in a line that allowed psychologists to testify as recognized experts, directly contributed to better information and higher-quality work being used in the legal process. In this respect, much like his famous creation, he was a warrior for truth and justice.

The Lie Detector: The Fate of Marston's Other, Other Legacy

Aside from its impact on the admissibility of expert testimony, Marston's work on the systolic blood pressure test is notable for contributing to what is now known as the polygraph or, more colloquially, the lie detector. The modern polygraph is more than just the systolic blood pressure test; it consists of a number of indices, including heart rate, respiration, and galvanic skin response.[34] Thus, Marston's test remains a component of the lie detector, but it is not the only element of the modern test. This test is still used in a number of settings. In some jurisdictions, courts can offer to release defendants who pass the polygraph, and courts vary on whether polygraph evidence is admissible.[35] Though the polygraph remains in use, there are questions about its validity. Studies over the years have reported much higher error rates than Marston reported, ranging from 25 to 75 percent—meaning that the polygraph leads to incorrect conclusions at least a fourth of the time, if not substantially more.[36] A reason for the large error rate is that there does not appear to be a typical physiological reaction to deception. That is, people's bodies react differently when they lie, making it difficult to know what signs to look for.[37]

In general, many psychologists express doubt about the effectiveness of the polygraph. A majority of psychophysiological researchers surveyed said that the polygraph is not a theoretically sound technique and should not be admitted in court.[38] In the absence of general acceptance, this means that nearly a century after Marston tried to introduce evidence about his systolic blood pressure test, the polygraph is still not admissible under the *Frye* standard. Although Marston's legacy has far-reaching implications for the practice of forensic psychology, his goal of supporting a test of deception to the point where it can be admitted as evidence remains unrealized.

Comic Book References

Sensation Comics #3 (1942). "A Spy in the Office." Script: W. M. Marston. Art: H. G. Peter.

Sensation Comics #6 (1942). "Summons to Paradise." Script: W. M. Marston. Art: H. G. Peter.

Sensation Comics #7 (1942). "The Milk Swindle." Script: W. M. Marston. Art: H. G. Peter.

Wonder Woman #1 (1942). "The Origin of Wonder Woman." Script: W. M. Marston. Art: H. G. Peter.

Wonder Woman #2 (1987). "A Fire in the Sky!" Script: G. Potter. Art: G. Perez & B. D. Patterson.

Other References

Benjamin, L. T., Jr., & Crouse, E. M. (2002). The American Psychological Association's response to *Brown v. Board of Education*: The case of Kenneth B. Clark. *American Psychologist, 57*(1), 38–50.

Brown v. Board of Education of Topeka, et al., 347 U.S. 483 (1953).

Daubert v. Merrell Dow Pharmaceuticals, 509 U.S. 579, 113 S.Ct. 2786 (1993).

Federal Rules of Evidence, Pub. Law 93–595 (1975).

Fiedler, K., Schmid, J., & Stahl, T. (2002). What is the current truth about polygraph lie detection? *Basic & Applied Social Psychology, 24*(4), 313–324.

Frye v. United States, 293 F. 1013 (D.C. Cir. 1923).

Iacono, W. G., & Lykken, D. T. (1997). The validity of the lie detector: Two surveys of scientific opinion. *Journal of Applied Psychology, 82*(3), 426–433.

Jenkins v. United States, 307 F.2d 637 (D.C. Cir. 1962).

JuriLytics (2016, July 25). Daubert and Frye in the 50 states. Retrieved October 2, 2016 from https://jurilytics.com/50-state-overview.

Kiesler, C. A. (1977). The training of psychiatrists and psychologists. *American Psychologist, 32*(2), 107–108.

Marston, W. M. (1917). Systolic blood pressure symptoms of deception. *Journal of Experimental Psychology, 2*(2), 117–163.

Marston, W. M. (1923). Sex characteristics of systolic blood pressure behavior. *Journal of Experimental Psychology, 6*(6), 387–419.

Pacht, A. R., Kuehn, J. K., Bassett, H. T., & Nash, M. M. (1973). The current status of the psychologist as an expert witness. *Professional Psychology, 4*(4), 409–413.

Petrella, R. C., & Poythress, N. G., Jr. (1983). The quality of forensic evaluations: An interdisciplinary study. *Journal of Consulting & Clinical Psychology, 51*(1), 76–85.

Saxe, L. (1994). Detection of deception: Polygraph and integrity tests. *Current Directions in Psychological Science, 3*(3), 69–73.

Shapiro, D. L., Mixon, L., Jackson, M., & Shook, J. (2015). Psychological expert witness testimony and judicial decision making trends. *International Journal of Law & Psychiatry, 42*(1), 149–153.

Slobogin, C. (1999). The admissibility of behavioral science information in criminal trials: From primitivism to *Daubert* to voice. *Psychology, Public Policy, & Law, 5*(1), 100–119.

Weiss, K. J., Watson, C., & Xuan, Y. (2014). Frye's backstory: A tale of murder, a retracted confession, and scientific hubris. *Journal of the American Academy of Psychiatry & the Law, 42*(2), 226–233.

Notes

1. *Sensation Comics* #3 (1942).
2. Marston (1917).

3. Slobogin (1999).
4. Slobogin (1999).
5. Pacht et al. (1973).
6. Weiss et al. (2014).
7. Weiss et al. (2014).
8. Weiss et al. (2014).
9. Weiss et al. (2014).
10. Marston (1917).
11. Marston (1917).
12. Marston (1917).
13. Marston (1923).
14. Weiss et al. (2014).
15. Weiss et al. (2014).
16. Weiss et al. (2014).
17. *Frye v. U.S.* (1923).
18. Weiss et al. (2014).
19. Federal Rules of Evidence (1975).
20. *Daubert v. Merrell Dow Pharmaceuticals* (1993).
21. JuriLytics (2016).
22. Shapiro et al (2015).
23. *Brown v. Board of Education* (1953).
24. *Sensation Comics* #6 (1942).
25. *Wonder Woman* #1 (1942).
26. e.g., *Sensation Comics* #7 (1942).
27. *Sensation Comics* #3 (1942).
28. *Wonder Woman* #2 (1987).
29. Benjamin & Crouse (2002).
30. Pacht et al. (1973).
31. *Jenkins v. U.S.* (1962).
32. Kiesler (1977).
33. Petrella & Poythress (1983).
34. Fiedler et al. (2002).
35. Iacono & Lykken (1997).
36. Saxe (1994).
37. Saxe (1994).
38. Iacono & Lykken (1997).

CHAPTER TWO

Dominance, Inducement, Submission, Compliance: Throwing the DISC in Fact and Fiction

MARA WOOD

"The training is strenuous, the discipline strict—will you submit?"
—Wonder Woman[1]

"The normal and efficient attitude in all love responses consists of inducing another individual only for the purpose of submitting to him."
—psychologist William Moulton Marston[2]

William Moulton Marston's Wonder Woman reflects his theory of interactions between forces, namely, the relationships people form. His theory of emotions, published in the 1928 text *Emotions of Normal People*, is illustrated in the way characters exhibit dominance, compliance, submission, and inducement in a variety of situations to obtain what they want.

To understand human behavioral responses to relationships, Marston looked to nature. He studied how the earth responds to gravity, how rivers shape landscapes, and how animals react to one another. His theory is grounded in observation, and many of the examples he provides describe how these forces relate to and interact with one another. He concluded that emotions people considered abnormal—sex complexes, emotional distress, and hidden fears—were all part of a normal human response.[3] The concept of survival of the fittest further supported Marston's theory in that dominance, compliance, submission, and inducement (DISC) are adaptive in some way. These basic emotions, as well as their combinations, interactions, and overabundance, form the human response.

Rather than being widely accepted as a general personality theory in its original form, Marston's theory has morphed into the acronym DISC and has been utilized to determine how a person generally sees the world.[4] It is sometimes used in the workplace ever since organizational psychologist Walter V. Clarke created an assessment for employees that was based on Marston's theory in the late 1940s.[5]

Marston's theory was published over a decade before Wonder Woman debuted. Though his theory in its original conception is not widely used in therapeutic settings today, it is nonetheless part of the history of psychology. Additionally, it is an integral part of understanding actions in Wonder Woman comics written by Marston.

Dominance

"Since our civilization is man made, dominance is probably
the emotion most universally admired by both sexes."
—William Moulton Marston[6]

The *dominance* response is activated when there is an encounter with an antagonistic weaker force.[7] Thought to be the most primitive, fundamental emotional reaction in humans and animals—an unlearned behavior, an inherent emotional response.

Dominance is one of the first forces presented in the Wonder Woman mythos. Hippolyta recounts the origin of the Amazons' exclusion from the general population to her daughter Diana. A major—and consistent—aspect of the Amazon exclusion is the dominance Hercules exhibits. Though Hippolyta bests him in a one-on-one contest, he captures the Amazons and forces them into compliance.[8] The Amazons, with the help of their patron goddess Aphrodite, exhibit a dominating force over Hercules and his men and escape their bonds. Rather than subject the men to the same treatment, the women depart with a ship to Paradise Island. Dominance is also activated when a weaker force gives chase. The pursuer desires to catch the fleeing force, as is seen in instances when Steve Trevor follows Nazi spies in order to gain information.[9]

Marston observed gender differences in the dominance response. Dominance is described as a competitive behavior. Marston noted that young boys engage in competitive play more often than young girls do.[10] Girls respond more positively to allied approaches than to antagonistic, competitive approaches. The type of play boys engage in is also an indication of dominance per Marston's research. Boys often engage in destructive play, such as knocking down blocks or vandalism. Marston goes so far as to state that the male sex hormone produces increased dominance. The sex differences in dominance are more pronounced in children than in adults; however, men often show dominant behavior in their professions and in sports. Women are not free from exhibiting dominant behavior. Often, women's use of dominant behavior occurs more in social situations in which rivals compete for status. Lila, Steve's secretary, exhibits dominance over Diana Prince when Diana tries to take her position.[11] Women also may exhibit dominant behavior in raising young children.[12] Wonder Woman's demonstration of dominance often codes as masculine. When approaching an antagonistic force, she will use physical force in order to get what she wants.[13]

Marston theorized that dominance is reinforced in a person because successful domination is pleasant. When people successfully dominate others, they get what they want and their needs are thus reinforced. A person who often uses dominance to resolve conflict may feel a surge of energy or emotion that enables him or her to remove opposition. Dominance, like other forces, can be viewed as passive or active. The passive form can be simple resistance to an antagonistic force. Active dominance, on the other hand, is the process of reestablishing control after an instance of compliance.[14]

People who tend to be dominating often seek out people who tend to be compliant.

When taken to the extreme, dominance becomes rage. Marston warned against rage each time he showed Wonder Woman without her bracelets. The bracelets, a symbol meant to remind the wearer never to submit to a man again, hold back Wonder Woman's destructive nature. Without them, she becomes free to destroy like a man.[15]

Compliance

"Positive pleasantness of compliance response seems only to occur when the compliance is a reaction to a motor stimulus of superior volume and moderate intensity . . ."
—William Moulton Marston[16]

Compliance is the response of a weaker force to a dominant one. Marston explains compliance in the natural world by examining the water cycle: The sun, a dominant force, causes water to comply by evaporating. Water changes its physical form to accommodate the stronger, antagonistic force.[17]

Marston suggested that children with an abundance of dominant behavior need to learn to comply. The compliant person becomes indifferent to the relationship, then experiences pleasantness as he or she adjusts to a new role.[18]

Diana creates compliance in Hippolyta after successfully winning the contest to take Steve Trevor back to America. Hippolyta does not want Diana to travel to America (losing her right to eternal life), but she complies with Diana's stronger, contrary force.[19] The early Diana Prince alter ego can be interpreted as an act of compliance to the more dominant Wonder Woman. While acting as Diana Prince, Wonder Woman feels jealous of the attention she gets while out in her true form.[20]

Compliance can also arise right after a dominance response.[21] Nazi spy Gross initially responds to Wonder Woman with a show of dominance by brandishing his gun. Even as Wonder Woman displays her dominance to him, he continues to resist her force by puffing out his chest and lacing his words with insults. Wonder Woman exerts more antagonistic force, and Gross complies by giving her the information she needs about the plot to kill Steve.[22] Marston saw this type of reaction as a normal one when a person first encounters a stronger force. When it becomes apparent that the stronger force will win out in the end, the weaker force readjusts and becomes compliant.[23] In excess, compliance can manifest as fear. Overcompliance to a dominant force is maladaptive to the compliant force. Baroness Paula von Gunther's slave girls are extremely loyal to her, but their loyalty is a result of fear. Carla, a slave of the baroness, becomes extremely distressed when Wonder Woman breaks her chains and urges her to leave.[24] Carla's fear results from the baroness beating her, and she is unable to act.

Submission

"Submission response, according to unanimous introspective agreement, is pleasant from beginning to end."
—William Moulton Marston[25]

Submission, like compliance, is a weaker force in an individual that changes in accordance with a stronger force. According to Marston, the submissive force wants to be controlled and led by a force that is similar to it yet stronger.[26] Marston believed that the process of submission is always pleasant. Because it involves the weaker force submitting to an allied stronger force, there is not a conflict of interests in the partnership.

Submission is a state that is supposedly learned much more readily than is compliance, which requires a stronger force commanding a weaker, antagonistic force. Submission's weaker force does not need as strong a force to induce it, and the stronger force does not go against the will of the submissive force. Submission, Marston notes, is more frequently associated with love than with any of the other emotions.[27] Submitting to another is an act of love, and Wonder Woman calls for loving submission from others, especially the women who are undergoing reformation.[28]

Marston noted gender differences in submission: Submission seems to exist more easily between women, especially mothers and daughters.[29] Except when Diana enters the contest to go to America, early *Wonder Woman* stories feature a Diana who regards her mother as a superior figure whose commands must be carried out.[30] The Holliday Girls are another example of a female force that submits to another female force. Wonder

Woman often calls upon them to carry out a mission. The Holliday Girls readily submit to the instruction, and they are portrayed as smiling and eagerly carrying out the command.[31]

True submission can never be unpleasant, according to Marston. The distinction Marston made between compliance and submission lies in the feeling it creates in the weaker force. The Holliday Girls of Beeta Lambda put new members through an initiation process that often is depicted as humiliating or degrading.[32] The girls who go through the initiation are an allied force to the stronger force because they want to submit to the members so that they can become members themselves.

Submission can evolve into jealousy. Diana Prince and Wonder Woman vie for Steve Trevor's attention. Wonder Woman often laughs at the idea of being her own rival.[33] As comical as the situation is, it evokes jealousy, especially in the civilian persona.[34] Diana Prince laments being less desirable than her true self and wants Steve to notice her in her plainness. She desires to submit to him, but Steve would rather submit to Wonder Woman—although Steve exhibits extreme jealousy during the Robert Kanigher era over Wonder Woman's relationship with Mer-Man.[35]

Inducement

"Inducement seeks rather to draw the stimulus person into such close alliance that the subject can submit to the other without further striving, or effort."
—William Moulton Marston[36]

In the submission–inducement relationship, *inducement* is the stronger of the two. Marston refined this view by explaining that the inducing force is distinct from the submissive force in that it initiates rather than responds.[37] Inducement is more like

THE GOLDEN LASSO: FORCE OF DOMINANCE OR INDUCEMENT?

When Diana receives the golden lasso from her mother in *Sensation Comics* #7, she gains the power to compel others to carry out her commands. Early instances of the lasso in use include commanding Mala to promise not to follow her, commanding enemies to surrender, and physically restraining dangerous people.[38] The lasso cannot be overcome by anyone, not even Wonder Woman,[39] making it the ultimate stronger force in Marston's comics. The lasso presents initially as a dominating force, especially since it is used so often against weaker, antagonistic forces. However, there are two components that complicate the relationship between the lasso and the bound individual: the woman controlling the lasso and the role of the truth as the person sees it. Wonder Woman is unlike many of the dominating forces in her comics. Often, brute force is used to create compliance, and Wonder Woman herself engages in some of that behavior. She is not a man or an evil mistress; rather, she is the perfect mistress to whom to submit. Additionally, lying can interfere with a person's genuineness and authentic life.[40] By admitting the truth, the bound individual moves a step closer to being authentic and genuine in his or her own life, even if it is "evil." Christianity and many other religions recognize the power of the truth in releasing people from their burdens.[41] In some stories, people, including Diana, willingly submit to the lasso to convey a point, thus making the lasso a clear force of inducement.[42]

The lasso allows for commands to be carried out regardless of an allied or antagonistic weaker force. Even with a beneficial mistress and emotional benefits from telling the truth, the lasso represents a dominant force more often than an allied force since it is often used against another person's will.

leading and fulfilling a leadership role among those who are similar. The alliance between inducement and submission can therefore be rewarding to both roles.

Inducement looks different in men and women. Female friendships are described as allied rather than competitive, and women are supposedly more likely to alternate in submissive and inducement roles in those friendships. Helen and Molly, two department store girls, are in an allied relationship in which the actions of each one are for the benefit of the other.[43] Wonder Woman often uses inducement when encountering other women, such as fearful Carla in the baroness's dungeon[44] or the real Diana Prince.[45] Women are supposedly taught to induce men so that they can receive the essentials they need in life, such as security, family, and money (think back to the status of men and women in the late 1920s). Women present themselves to men as an allied force and initiate in order to get men to submit to what they desire. Men may engage others through inducement, but their natural state of being a stronger force defaults toward dominance.[46] Boys may start out as allied forces, but competition can create antagonistic relationships. Men may use inducement on women in their romantic relationships, but there is a certain amount of appetite involved to facilitate that relationship.[47]

Inducement is essential in media. Advertising relies on inducing the audience to purchase an item.[48] Eroticism in films is a form of inducement of the audience and of controlling the power in scenes. In Marston's study of film, he found that women were drawn to scenes of inducement in the characters whereas men found scenes of dominance and submission exciting (a conclusion Marston reached by using his systolic blood pressure device and carefully chosen film scenes).[49] This finding supported his idea that men trend toward dominance and women toward inducement (although not necessarily his ideas regarding the reasons why).

The order of these forces is important in understanding the way Marston viewed the progression of relationships. Compliance is antagonistic, but it occurs because the dominant force is stronger. Submission is a pleasant experience that occurs in the presence of inducement, a skill in which Marston believes men to be deficit. Inducement is better suited to women and the relationships they develop with one another. Placing dominance and inducement on opposite sides in the theory and describing them as closely interacting with different genders indicates the stance Marston has outlined time and time again: Women are better suited for leadership positions than are men as a result of their innate nature.[50]

Lasting Impact

Marston set the foundation for what to expect from Wonder Woman comics in the early 1940s. Stories that take place after Marston's death carry the same elements, although not as overtly. Wonder Woman relies on inducement to lead others and fought against the practice of domination, sometimes in the form of corrupt regimes or abusive men. Compliance, including fear, is a cause of concern for Wonder Woman as she protects others.[51] She approaches her enemies with inducement rather than domination, extending her hand when she can.[52] Diana submits when appropriate, especially to her gods and her mother.[53] Without Marston's theory of emotions laying the foundation for his superheroine, Wonder Woman would not embody the spirit of loving submission readers have seen over the decades.

Comic Book References

All-Star Comics #8 (1941). "Introducing Wonder Woman." Script: W. M. Marston. Art: H. G. Peter.

Sensation Comics #1 (1942). "Wonder Woman Comes to America." Script: W. M. Marston. Art: H. G. Peter.

Sensation Comics #2 (1942). "Dr. Poison." Script: W. M. Marston. Art: H. G. Peter.

Sensation Comics #3 (1942). "A Spy in the Office." Script: W. M. Marston. Art: H. G. Peter.

Sensation Comics #4 (1942). "School for Spies." Script: W. M. Marston. Art: H. G. Peter.

Sensation Comics #5 (1942). "Wonder Woman versus the Saboteurs." Script: W. M. Marston. Art: H. G. Peter.

Sensation Comics #6 (1942). "Summons to Paradise." Script: W. M. Marston. Art: H. G. Peter.

Sensation Comics #8 (1942). "Department Store Perfidy." Script: W. M. Marston. Art: H. G. Peter.

Sensation Comics #13 (1943). "Wonder Woman is Dead!" Script: W. M. Marston. Art: H. G. Peter.

Sensation Comics #19 (1943). "The Unbound Amazon." Script: W. M. Marston. Art: F. Godwin.

Wonder Woman #1 (1942). "Wonder Woman versus the Prison Spy Ring!" Script: W. M. Marston. Art: H. G. Peter.

Wonder Woman #2 (1942). "Mars, the God of War." Script: W. M. Marston. Art: H. G. Peter.

Wonder Woman #3 (1943). "A Spy on Paradise Island." Script: W. M. Marston. Art: H. G. Peter.

Wonder Woman #4 (1943). "Mole Men of the Underworld." Script: W. M. Marston. Art: H. G. Peter.

Wonder Woman #125 (1961). "Battle Prize." Script: R. Kanigher. Art: R. Andru & M. Esposito.

Wonder Woman #10 (1987). "Paradise Lost." Script: G. Perez & L. Wein. Art: G. Pérez & B. Patterson.

Wonder Woman #25 (2008). "A Star in the Heavens Scene 3: Personal Effects." Script: G. Simone. Art: B. Chang.

Wonder Woman #28 (2009). "The Blood of the Stag." Script: G. Simone. Art: A. Lopresti & M. Ryan.

Wonder Woman Rebirth #1 (2016). Script: G. Rucka. Art: M. Clark, L. Sharp, & S. Parsons.

Other References

Marston, W. M. (1928). *Emotions of normal people.* New York, NY: Harcourt, Brace.

Olenina, A. (2015). The doubly wired spectator: Marston's theory of emotions and psychological research on cinematic pleasure in the 1920s. *Film History, 27*(1), 29–57.

Rogers, C. R. (1961). *On becoming a person: A therapist's view of psychotherapy.* Boston, MA: Houghton Mifflin.

Rohm, R. (1993). *Positive personality profiles.* Atlanta, GA: Personality Insights.

Scullard, M., & Baum, D. (2015). *Everything DISC manual* (pp. 185–187). Hoboken, NJ: Wiley.

Notes

1. *Wonder Woman* #4 (1943).
2. Marston (1928), p. 604.
3. Marston (1928).
4. Rohm (1993).
5. Scullard & Baum (2015).
6. Marston (1928), p. 228.
7. Marston (1928).
8. *All-Star Comics* #8 (1941).
9. *Sensation Comics* #4 (1942).
10. Marston (1928).
11. *Sensation Comics* #5 (1942).
12. Marston (1928).
13. *Sensation Comics* #1 (1942).
14. Marston (1928).
15. *Sensation Comics* #19 (1943).
16. Marston (1928), p. 299.
17. Marston (1928).
18. Marston (1928).
19. *All-Star Comics* #8 (1941).
20. *Sensation Comics* #5 (1942).
21. Marston (1928).
22. *Sensation Comics* #3 (1942).
23. Marston (1928).
24. *Sensation Comics* #4 (1942).
25. Marston (1928), p. 395.
26. Marston (1928).
27. Marston (1928).
28. *Wonder Woman* #3 (1943).
29. Marston (1928).
30. *Sensation Comics* #6 (1942).
31. *Sensation Comics* #2 (1942).
32. *Sensation Comics* #3 (1942).
33. *Sensation Comics* #1 (1942).
34. *Sensation Comics* #13 (1943).
35. *Wonder Woman* #125 (1961).
36. Marston (1928), p. 445.
37. Marston (1928).
38. *Sensation Comics* #6 (1942); *Wonder Woman* #2 (1942), #3 (1943).
39. *Wonder Woman* #1 (1942).
40. Rogers (1961).
41. John 8:32.
42. *Wonder Woman* #3 (1943); *Wonder Woman Rebirth* #1 (2016).
43. *Sensation Comics* #8 (1942).
44. *Sensation Comics* #4 (1942).
45. *Sensation Comics* #1 (1942).
46. Marston (1928).
47. Marston (1928).
48. Marston (1928).

49. Olenina (2015).
50. Daniels (2000); Marston (1928).
51. *Wonder Woman* #28 (2009).
52. *Wonder Woman* #25 (2008).
53. *Wonder Woman* #10 (1987).

CHAPTER THREE

Marston, Wertham, and the Psychological Potential of Comic Books

TIM HANLEY AND TRAVIS LANGLEY

"The comics have their foibles, but I believe that picture-story education holds vast possibilities."
—psychologist William Moulton Marston[1]

". . . I think Hitler was a beginner compared to the comic-book industry."
—psychiatrist Fredric Wertham[2]

If Dr. William Moulton Marston and Dr. Fredric Wertham had ever met, it's unlikely that they'd have been friends, but they certainly would have had a lot to talk about. These two men are the best-known psychological professionals involved with the early years of the comic book industry,[3] and both have spent decades getting dismissed by some as crackpots. Marston, the creator of Wonder Woman, sometimes was viewed as a

charlatan with a bondage fetish.[4] Wertham, the author of
Seduction of the Innocent, was regularly decried as a writer of a
screed against comic books who sought to discredit and destroy
the entire industry.[5] Recent historians of the superhero genre,
though, have painted a fuller picture of the two doctors, cred-
iting Marston for the unique pro-woman values he imbued
in Wonder Woman[6] and recognizing Wertham's progressive
psychiatric work.[7]

Opposite Paths over Common Ground

The two men shared much in common, even in their
approach to the comic book phenomenon that swept America in the 1940s. Their backgrounds—Marston's in psychology,
Wertham's in psychiatry—led them to see potential in the new
medium; with millions of comic books being sold each month
and shared in playgrounds across the nation, comics were an
ideal means to reach and influence young minds. Marston and
Wertham recognized the power of comic books to steer an
entire generation, but they diverged in their reactions. Whereas
Marston wanted to harness that potential for good, Wertham
wanted to constrain it. Two sides of the same coin, their differing responses exerted massive influence on the world of comic
books both in their own time and in ways that have reverber-
ated ever since.

Origin Stories

Marston and Wertham were born just two years apart but
half a world away—Marston in Saugus, Massachusetts, in
1893 and Wertham in Munich, Germany, in 1895. Both were
well educated on their respective continents. Marston earned

several degrees at Harvard, culminating in a PhD in psychology in 1921, while Wertham studied in a variety of institutions, including King's College London and the University of Munich, before earning an MD from the University of Würzburg, also in 1921.

At Harvard, Marston was mentored by Hugo Münsterberg, known as the founder of both applied psychology and forensic psychology.[8] In Europe, one of Wertham's mentors, Emil Kraepelin, developed scientific psychiatry, and when Wertham moved to the United States in 1922, another mentor, Adolf Meyer, came to focus on psychobiology.[9] Despite Marston and Wertham's different specialities, their mentors were united in their lack of interest in Freudian psychoanalysis. They appreciated aspects of Freud's work but ultimately found his focus on individualistic interpretive analysis lacking in comparison to more rigorous, empirical methods.[10] Their rejection of Freudian methods had a strong influence on their pupils, who carved their own paths throughout the early twentieth century even as Freud's theories rose in prominence in American psychology and became the dominant school of thought by midcentury. Wertham corresponded and met with Freud, who advised him against writing about psychiatry for the popular press.[11]

Inspired by their work with patients, both Marston and Wertham developed their own theories. Marston's primary text was his 1928 *Emotions of Normal People*, in which he proposed his DISC theory.[12] It placed all human interactions—friendly, instructive, parental, romantic, sexual, or otherwise—on axes with points corresponding with dominance, inducement, submission, and compliance. Marston crafted a variety of permutations of those four points, but the core of his theory boiled down to two pairs of factors: active versus passive and antagonistic versus favorable.[13]

For Wertham, treating a patient involved delving into mental, physical, and societal conditions in order to compile a thorough, unified assessment of that individual's current state.[14] The roots of violence and aggression became a major focus for Wertham that would continue in his later work on comics, and he developed several new theories that expanded the psychiatric lexicon. Those ideas included the *catathymic crisis*—the process by which violent fantasies turn into violent acts[15]—and the *Orestes complex*, a counter to Freud's Oedipus complex that focused on hostility toward a mother figure.[16]

Even though Marston and Wertham had very different ideas and approaches, their work led them to a similar conclusion: Mental health wasn't rooted solely in personal issues; it was rooted in societal issues as well. For Marston, DISC theory applied to interpersonal relationships between two people, but the tenets of the theory had wider implications in that groups and institutions could embody dominant or submissive behavior as well. For Wertham, factoring in the wider environmental issues that affected his patients made him increasingly aware of the role societal influences play not just individually but corporately. Both men realized that addressing these societal issues could have a widespread effect on mental health, and they pursued this notion in ways that corresponded with their own progressive causes.

Marston focused on gender and women's rights. As a college student, he was a supporter of the women's suffrage movement, and he later lived in an unconventional relationship with two well-educated women: Elizabeth Holloway and Olive Byrne. Byrne was the niece of Margaret Sanger, a champion of women's reproductive rights.[17] Marston surrounded himself with smart, forward-thinking women, and they clearly influenced his view of the world.

In his psychological writing, Marston applied his theories to American patriarchal culture. He argued that men were more likely to be dominant, as evidenced by their penchant for greed and aggression. Through maternal affection and sexual allure, women were more loving and thus better at inducing submission. As such, Marston ultimately contended that "women, as a sex, are many times better equipped to assume emotional leadership than are males" because "there isn't love enough in the male organism to run this planet peacefully."[18] Patriarchy was psychologically damaging for the nation, and so it was time to try something different.

Wertham's focus was race. The *mental hygiene movement* sought to make psychiatric care more accessible, but Wertham noticed that minority communities were underserved. He opened his own clinic in a basement office in Harlem in 1946, charging only a quarter for counseling.[19] Engaging with the community opened Wertham's eyes to the harmful structural issues that people of color faced in America.

He began to use his work to address this racial imbalance. He often testified as a psychiatric expert on his patients' behalf if they got into legal trouble, and his book *Circle of Guilt* examined an unjust murder conviction that highlighted the rampant racism and prejudice toward Puerto Ricans in the American legal system.[20]

Both men played important roles in landmark legal cases. Marston was the lie detector expert in *Frye v. U.S.*[21], the case that led the courts to determine that lie detectors should *not* be admissible in criminal proceedings.[22] Wertham testified in the *Brown v. Board of Education* case[23] that led to the desegregation of American schools, presenting an account of the harmful psychological effects of segregation on black children, and was heralded as one of the most captivating experts who spoke on behalf of the plaintiffs.[24]

Having realized the ways in which societal issues could influence people psychologically on a large scale, both Marston and Wertham recognized that popular culture could have a similar effect. As comic books exploded in popularity in the 1940s, they took note of the new medium's capability for influencing young minds, but the two men diverged in their response to the funny books.

Comic Book Potential

Marston and Wertham's approaches to comics highlighted the stark differences in what each man saw as the end goal of his work: Marston wanted to progress, and Wertham wanted to protect. This was made clear in their chosen causes. Marston saw patriarchy and wanted to flip the system entirely by putting women in charge and creating a new paradigm, while Wertham saw racism and sought to stop harmful inequality by leveling the playing field, raising minorities up to the status enjoyed by white citizens. Marston sought to shape comics in a way that would, in his view, help kids, whereas Wertham sought to spare children from comics that could harm them.

In 1940, as comics starring Superman and Batman took the nation by storm, Marston praised the new medium and its educational potential in a *Family Circle* article titled, "Don't Laugh at the Comics."[25] His tone was one of enthusiastic optimism. He saw the best in the emerging comic book industry and was so effusive that the head of All American Publications, Max Gaines, quickly hired him to be part of his new content advisory board.[26]

When All American editor Sheldon Mayer soon offered him a shot at creating his own superhero, Marston seized the opportunity. By then, his feminist beliefs had evolved past the point

THE QUEER QUESTION

The fact that Diana grows up on an island occupied only by women has led a number of people, not just Wertham, to feel that same-gender sexual activity logically must be common among the Amazons, including Wonder Woman.[27] The few stories that address Diana's sexual history indicate that she remains a virgin[28] prior to DC Comics' 2011 "New 52" reboot.[29]

Comic book scribe Greg Rucka, writing *Wonder Woman* during DC's "Rebirth" storylines, states outright that gender does not determine with whom Diana will or will not have sexual relations and that canonically "Themyscira is a queer culture." He explains: "It's supposed to be paradise. You're supposed to be able to live happily. You're supposed to be able . . . to have a fulfilling, romantic, and sexual relationship. And the only options are women."[30]

Rucka takes the position that "an Amazon doesn't look at another Amazon and say, 'You're gay.' They don't. The concept doesn't exist."[31] Because theirs is not a *heteronormative* culture—one treating heterosexuality as the preferred standard[32]—sexual orientation is not something they consider, and therefore it is not a key part of Diana's *self-concept* (how she sees herself) or *self-schema* (the pattern or scheme of all concepts she associates with herself). Sexual orientation is not equally important to all people in terms of how they think of themselves,[33] and culture can play an important role in determining its perceived importance to a person's identity.[34]

If a person's sexual orientation is not critical to the way she thinks about herself, what does worrying about it say about the worriers?

where he thought that female rule would be preferable; now he considered it inevitable.[35] He teamed with artist H. G. Peter to create Wonder Woman, Marston's exemplar for the kind of woman he believed should rule the world.[36] She was a counter to the "blood-curdling masculinity" of the violent male super-heroes who dominated the newsstands as well as a means to get young readers used to the idea of powerful women in order to ease the transition when the impending matriarchal revolution arrived.[37]

Wonder Woman is the princess of Paradise Island, a hidden utopian society of Amazons, and is drawn into World War II when American pilot Steve Trevor crash lands into their home.[38] She battles in the war abroad and fights for local justice and women's rights in America, embodying strength and love throughout her adventures. Wonder Woman isn't the only powerful female presence in the stories either; she surrounds herself with a panoply of daring women. She fights along-side her Amazon sisters, befriends a sorority of plucky young women known as the Holliday Girls, and even works with reformed villains such as the scientist Paula von Gunther.

Wonder Woman's early stories encapsulate Marston's psycho-logical theories in many ways, most controversially through the metaphor of bondage imagery. On Paradise Island, binding is a fun game that demonstrates the joy of willing submission to others and the benefits of female rule. Out in the world of men, bondage is harsh and unpleasant, mirroring the antago-nism of male dominance pervading patriarchal society.[39] The metaphor held nonetheless. Even though Gaines was uncom-fortable with the elements of bondage, the comics sold so well that Marston was largely allowed to do as he liked.[40] Soon after Wonder Woman's first appearance in 1941, she was starring in several series.

Attacking a Ghost

Marston died of cancer in 1947, a week short of his fifty-fourth birthday and too soon to challenge the psychiatrist whose campaign would damage the industry Marston had helped build. At the time, Wertham was conducting a two-year study of juvenile delinquents. Trying to make sense of the post–World War II jump in juvenile delinquency, researchers in Europe developed *attachment theory*, attributing the change to wartime disruption of family bonds, while Wertham in New York blamed comic books. Regarding comics, he said, "So far we have determined that the effect is definitely and completely harmful."[41]

Ten months after Marston died, Wertham launched his public crusade with a symposium titled, "The Psychopathology of Comic Books."[42] The psychiatrist's remarks from the symposium appeared in a *Saturday Review of Literature* article titled "The Comics—Very Funny!"[43] as if in delayed response to the *Family Circle* interview that first brought Marston to Gaines's attention, "Don't Laugh at the Comics."

By the early 1950s, the superhero boom had imploded. Series featuring Wonder Woman dwindled to just one, and she soon became one of only three featured superheroes to remain consistently in print. New genres took over the newsstands, including crime, horror, and Westerns, that often featured dark, grisly content. The medium had been criticized by parental and educational groups since its inception, and a rise in juvenile delinquency in the United States fanned the flames even higher. With Wertham's involvement, the alleged link between comics and juvenile delinquency quickly became a national issue.

Whereas Marston saw hope in the ability of comics to influence young readers, Wertham saw horror. Wertham's interest in

INTERVIEW: THE VOICE OF WONDER WOMAN

JENNA BUSCH

Actress Susan Eisenberg has played the role of Wonder Woman longer than anyone else. She has voiced Wonder Woman in the animated series *Justice League* and *Justice League Unlimited* as well as video games, such as *Injustice: Gods among Us*. Eisenberg spoke with us about the defining qualities of Wonder Woman as well as her ongoing popularity.

Busch: What would you consider the defining qualities of Diana Prince/Wonder Woman?

Eisenberg: You mentioned compassion and I would say her goodness *and* compassion. I wouldn't say there is one defining quality. I think that's what makes her so spectacular. She's not one-dimensional. One of my favorite things about the series was the relationships with the other characters. For instance, with J'onn, Martian Manhunter, she related to him because they were both outsiders. They both came from distant places and then came to the League, and were both trying to acclimate and figure it out, and you saw that effort. Then you've got the kickass "I'm going to fight for justice" side, which most of the superheroes will have. But, like Superman, I think that she is a genuine good girl. A really good girl. I love that about her.

Busch: What do you think has contributed to the character's ongoing popularity? When you say "female superhero," hers is always the first name that comes up.

Eisenberg: Well, I don't think that she has much competition! It's not like when we were growing up in the '70s, we had many heroes that we could look up to as women. Because of the goodness, because of the compassion, because of that outsider quality she has, I think she resonated with so many fans. And she still does. The fact is there wasn't that much of her and people wanted more and more—it's not like we were inundated with Wonder Woman. In fact, people have been yearning for a Wonder Woman feature movie for so long, live-action, and they're finally getting it. Men responded to her, women responded to her, kids responded to her. There is that vacuum that she fills, especially when she first came onto the scene. Throughout time, she has just spoken to different generations with all those qualities. The qualities still exist in her. I think they will always exist. They are universal qualities. People respond to that goodness. People respond to that compassion. People respond to that sense of fighting the good fight and fighting for what's right. And also having your friends' backs.

juvenile delinquency stemmed from his stance against segregation, and he viewed both as societal ills that adversely affected
the psychological health of America's youth.[44] He also saw comic
books as a contributing factor in both phenomena; in his *Brown
v. Board of Education* work he often decried racist storylines and
stereotyped depictions of people of color in comics, and with
juvenile delinquency he was appalled by the comics' high levels
of crime and violence, which he feared would influence young
readers. Wertham knew that comic books weren't the only
cause of juvenile delinquency, but he argued that "there can be
no doubt that they are the most unnecessary and least excusable
one."[45]

Wertham's opposition to comics was rooted in one of the
major components of the mental hygiene movement: *preventive
psychology*. As Wertham explained about a different case, "The
real problem is prevention. That requires . . . modification not
only of individual impulses but of social institutions."[46] He
focused on societal influences to prevent them from harming
people, not to shape them into something that would help.
Thus, Wertham's approach to comic books was critical rather
than idealistic.

And *critical* was the word. Starting in the late 1940s, Wertham
tore into the medium, penning pieces with inflammatory
titles such as "The Betrayal of Childhood,"[47] and his research
culminated in the ominously named book *Seduction of the Innocent* in 1954.[48] After his work caught the attention of a Senate
subcommittee that was investigating juvenile delinquency,
Wertham told the lawmakers that "Hitler was a beginner
compared to the comic-book industry. They get the children
much younger."[49]

Wertham contended that young readers lacked the ability
to discern the moral lessons of comic books; for example,

if a story featured twelve pages of violent crimes or hateful actions followed by one page of resolution in which the evildoers were punished, as was the case in many comics, children were more likely to internalize the negative behavior that made up the majority of the story rather than the brief punishment that followed. Wertham believed that crime, horror, and other offensive comic books shouldn't be sold to young readers.

Seduction of the Innocent and Wertham's Senate subcommittee testimony prompted publishers to band together and self-regulate content with the Comics Code Authority.[50] Several publishers went out of business for failing to meet the code's strict guidelines, and Wertham has been blamed for the code ever since.

The "Morbid Ideal"

Seduction of the Innocent's treatment of Wonder Woman shows the fundamental difference between Marston's and Wertham's worldviews. For all his progressive work, Wertham was a traditionalist at his core. He didn't seek to change the status quo of American society and values but rather tried to bring those who were excluded from them up to that level. Ultimately, Wertham embodied the dominant beliefs of the time, especially when it came to women.

Wertham's first mention of Wonder Woman condemned her for being "physically very powerful" and he declared, "While she is a frightening figure for boys, she is an undesirable ideal for girls, being the exact opposite of what girls are supposed to want to be."[51] He complained about female superheroes generally: "They do not work. They are not homemakers. They do not bring up a family. Mother-love is entirely absent."[52] For Wertham, a woman's place was in the home, raising children.

Anything outside of that role presented "a morbid ideal" for young readers.[53]

Furthermore, Wertham perceived something homoerotic about heroes who weren't part of a standard family unit. In the book's most famous passage, he argued that "a subtle atmosphere of homoerotism . . . pervades the adventures of the mature 'Batman' and his young friend 'Robin.'"[54] This accusation was significant; in the mid-1950s, homosexuality was considered sexually deviant and there were antisodomy laws on the books in every state. Even though Wertham did not call Batman and Robin homosexual characters, he described their lifestyle as "a wish dream of two homosexuals living together."[55] He included accounts from several of his male patients who saw gay undertones in Batman and Robin's adventures. Those accounts have been partly discredited as fraudulent because Wertham cut and combined their words as he saw fit, often neglecting to mention other characters in which those gay youths saw similar undertones.[56] Still, several young readers supposedly noticed the homosexual subtext that Wertham was so concerned about, and he made a point of including their thoughts.

He did no such thing with Wonder Woman. Instead, her adventures were "plainly lesbian" because she is not a home-maker and she often hangs out with other women.[57] Wertham even extrapolated the Holliday Girls as "the holiday girls, the gay party girls, the gay girls."[58] That was the bulk of his evidence. There were no personal accounts of young women who perceived lesbian subtext in *Wonder Woman*. Instead, Wertham saw a strong female superhero without a husband or children and viewed that as gay. He even decried a sweet, very maternal story in which Wonder Woman briefly takes care of a young girl when her parents go missing as having "lesbian overtones."[59] Somehow he saw something sexual in the mere act of rescuing one's friends from danger, a staple of many stories from a wide range of genres. Never mind that her primary romantic interest since her first appearance is the soldier Steve Trevor[60] and that that remains the case until Steve's 1969 death,[61] after which Wonder Woman rarely has any main love interest in her stories for many years.

Marston had a positive viewpoint on alternative approaches to sexuality, particularly among women. In *Emotions of Normal People*, he advocated for "female love relationships," which were sexual relationships between women practiced in addition to their insufficient heterosexual relationships.[62] Marston worked alternative practices into his Wonder Woman comics, albeit very much between the lines. *Emotions of Normal People* featured an examination of the effects of binding in sorority "baby parties," in which new members were blindfolded, bound, and initiated.[63] Marston said that these activities invoked sexual pleasure in many of the participants. Scenes with the same kinds of female activities appeared in his comics, particularly with the Holliday Girls, who regularly initiate new members, and the Amazons with their binding games.

Morbid Horror versus Utopian Hope

Wertham's "morbid ideal" was Marston's utopian ideal, and history appears to favor Marston's vision. Comic books continue to exist. And while the matriarchal revolution has yet to materialize, Marston's Wonder Woman has remained an iconic character. Today she's a major player in comic books and superhero television shows, movies, and video games. By trying to envision a better future instead of simply working to preserve the present, Marston's optimism may ultimately have more of a lasting effect on Wonder Woman, comic books, and popular culture than has Wertham's criticism.

Comic Book References

All-Star Comics #8 (1941). "Introducing Wonder Woman." Script: W. M. Marston. Art: H. G. Peter.

Wonder Woman #180 (1969). "A Death for Diana!" Script: D. O'Neil. Art: M. Sekowsky & D. Giordano.

Wonder Woman #10 (1987). "Challenge of the Gods, Part 1: Paradise Lost!" Story: G. Pérez & L. Wein. Art: G. Pérez & B. Patterson.

Other References

Aumer, K. (2014). The influence of culture and gender on sexual self-schemas and satisfaction in romantic relationships. *Sexual & Relationship Therapy, 29*(3), 280–292.

Baker, J. H. (2011). *Margaret Sanger: A life of passion.* New York, NY: Hill & Wang.

Beaty, B. (2005). *Fredric Wertham and the critique of mass culture.* Jackson, MS: University Press of Mississippi.

Berlatsky, N. (2015). *Wonder Woman: Bondage and feminism in the Marston/Peter Comics, 1941–1948.* New Brunswick, NJ: Rutgers University Press.

Brigham, J. C., & Grisso, J. T. (2003). Forensic psychology. In D. K. Freedheim (Ed.), *Handbook of psychology, volume 1: History of psychology* (pp. 291–412). Hoboken, NJ: Wiley.

Bunn, G. C. (1997). The lie detector, Wonder Woman and liberty: The life and work of William Moulton Marston. *History of the Human Sciences, 10*(1), 91–119.

Crist, J. (1948, March 27). Horror in the nursery. *Collier's Weekly,* pp. 22–23, 95.

Daniels, L. (2004). *Wonder Woman: The complete history.* San Francisco, CA: Chronicle.

Deutsch, A. R., Hoffman, L., & Wilcox, B. L. (2014). Sexual self-concept: Testing a hypothetical model for men and women. *Journal of Sex Research, 51*(8), 932–945.

Franks, A. (2005). *Margaret Sanger's eugenic legacy: The control of female fertility.* Jefferson, NC: McFarland.

Garcia, L. T. (1999). The certainty of the self-concept. *Canadian Journal of Human Sexuality, 8*(4), 263–270.

Greenberg, J. (1994). *Crusaders in the courts: How a dedicated band of lawyers fought for the civil rights revolution.* New York, NY: Basic.

Hajdu, D. (2008). *The ten-cent plague: The great comic-book scare and how it changed America.* New York, NY: Farrar, Straus, & Giroux.

Hanley, Tim. 2014. *Wonder Woman unbound: The curious history of the world's most famous heroine.* Chicago, IL: Chicago Review Press.

Huss, M. T. (2009). *Forensic psychology: Research, clinical practice, and applications.* Malden, MA: Wiley-Blackwell.

Hutchison, M. (2000). *15 years without a man: Is Wonder Woman gay? Paradise Island? Or Isle of Lesbos?* Fanzine: http://www.fanzing.com/mag/fanzing27/feature3.shtml.

Joyce, N. (2008). Wonder Woman: A psychologist's creation. *APA Monitor, 39*(11), 20.

Kluger, R. (1975). *Simple justice: The history of Brown v. Board of Education and Black America's struggle for equality.* New York, NY: Knopf.

Langley, T., Kus, E. A., O'Connor, Scarlet, J., & Kistler, A. (2016, March). *Comics psychology from Wonder Woman and Wertham to the World Wide Web.* Comics Arts Conference, WonderCon, Los Angeles, CA.

Marston, W. M. (1928). *Emotions of normal people.* New York, NY: Harcourt, Brace.

Marston, W. M. (1944). Why 100,000,000 Americans read comics. *The American Scholar, 13*, 35–44.

New York Times (1937, November 11). Marston advises 3 L's for success: "Live, love and laugh" offered by psychologist as recipe for required happiness. *New York Times,* p. 27 C7. http://query.nytimes.com/gst/abstract.html?res=9D06E0D8133DE23AB-C4952DFB767838C629EDE.

Nielsen, J. M., Walden, G., & Kunkel, C. A. (2000). Gendered heteronormativity: Empirical illustrations in everyday life. *Sociological Quarterly, 41*(2), 283–296.

Nyberg, A. K. 1998. *Seal of approval: The history of the Comics Code.* Jackson: MS: University Press of Mississippi.

Rashidian, M. Hussain, R., & Minichiello, V. (2013). "My culture haunts me no matter where I go": Iranian-American women discussing sexual and acculturation experiences. *Culture, Health, & Sexuality, 15*(7), 866–877.

Richard, O. (1940, October). Don't laugh at the comics. *The Family Circle,* pp. 10–11, 22.

Santori-Griffith, M. (2016, September 28). *Greg Rucka on queer narrative and Wonder Woman.* Comicosity: http://www.comicosity.com/exclusive-interview-greg-rucka-on-queer-narrative-and-wonder-woman/.

Surdam, D. G. (2015, March 24). *Comic books and censorship in the 1940s.* Oxford University Press: http://blog.oup.com/2015/03/comic-books-censorship-history/.

Tilley, C. (2012). Seducing the innocent: Fredric Wertham and the falsifications that helped condemn comics. *Information & Culture, 47*(4), 383–413.

U. S. Senate (1954). *Hearings before the Subcommittee to Investigate Juvenile Delinquency of the Committee on the Judiciary, United States Senate.* https://archive.org/stream/juvenilede-linque54unit/juveniledelinque54unit_djvu.txt.

Warner, M. (1991). Introduction: Fear of a queer planet. *Social Text, 9*(4), 3–17.

Weiss, K. J., Watson, C., & Xuan, Y. (2014). Frye's backstory: A tale of murder, a retracted confession, and scientific hubris. *Journal of the American Academy of Psychiatry & the Law, 42*(2), 226–233.

Wertham, F. (1937). The catathymic crisis: A clinical entity. *Archives of Neurology & Psychiatry, 37*(4), 974–978.

Wertham, F. (1941). *Dark legend.* New York, NY: Book Find Club.

Wertham, F. (1948a). The betrayal of childhood: Comic books. *Proceedings of the Seventy-Eighth Annual Congress of Correction,* American Prison Association, 57–59.

Wertham, F. (1948b, May 29). The comics—very funny! *Saturday Review of Literature,* p. 6.

Wertham, F. (1954). *Seduction of the innocent.* New York, NY: Rinehart.

Wertham, F., Legman, G., Mosse, H. L, Elkisch, P., & Blumberg, M. L. (1948, March). *The psychopathology of comic books.* Symposium presented at the meeting of the Association for the Advancement of Psychotherapy.

Wertham, F. (1956). *The circle of guilt.* New York, NY: Rinehart.

Wertham, F. (n.d.), *Episodes: From the life of a psychiatrist* [unpublished manuscript].

Notes

1. Quoted by Byrne, writing as Richard (1940), p. 22.
2. U.S. Senate (1954).
3. Langley et al. (2016).

4. Berlatsky (2015).
5. Hajdu (2008); Nyberg (1998).
6. Joyce (2008).
7. Beaty (2005); Surdam (2015).
8. Bunn (1997); Huss (2009).
9. Beaty (2005).
10. Beaty (2005); Brigham & Grisso (2003).
11. Wertham (n.d.).
12. Marston (1928).
13. Marston (1928)
14. Beaty (2005).
15. Wertham (1937).
16. Wertham (1941).
17. Baker (2011); Franks (2005).
18. Marston (1928), 258; second quote is from a letter from Marston to Coulton Waugh, March 5, 1945.
19. Beaty (2005), p. 89.
20. Wertham (1956).
21. *Frye v. U.S.* (1923).
22. Weiss et al. (2014).
23. *Brown v. Board of Education of Topeka* (1954).
24. Greenberg (1994); Kluger (1975).
25. Richard (1940).
26. All American Publications and National Comics later officially combined to become DC Comics.
27. Hutchison (2000).
28. e.g., *Wonder Woman* #10 (1987).
29. Sue (2013).
30. Santori-Griffith (2016).
31. Santori-Griffith (2016).
32. Nielsen et al. (2000); Warner (1991).
33. Deutsch et al. (2014); Garcia (1999).
34. Aumer (2014); Rashidian et al. (2013).
35. *New York Times* (1937).
36. Daniels (2004).
37. Marston (1944), p. 42.
38. *All-Star Comics* #8 (1941); *Wonder Woman* #32 (2016).
39. Hanley (2014), p. 46.
40. Daniels (2004).
41. Crist (1948), p. 22.
42. Wertham et al. (1948).
43. Wertham (1948b).
44. Beaty (2005), p. 135.
45. Wertham (1954), p. 166.
46. Wertham (1941), p. 34.
47. Wertham (1948a).
48. Wertham (1954).
49. U.S. Senate (1954).
50. Nyberg (1998).
51. Wertham (1954), p. 34.

52. Wertham (1954), p. 234.
53. Wertham (1954), p. 193.
54. Wertham (1954), pp. 189–190.
55. Wertham (1954), p. 190.
56. Tilley (2012).
57. Wertham (1954), p. 193.
58. Wertham (1954), p. 193.
59. Wertham (1954), p. 234.
60. Starting with *All-Star Comics* #8 (1941).
61. *Wonder Woman* #180 (1969).
62. Marston (1928), p. 338.
63. Marston (1928), pp. 299–313.

CHAPTER FOUR

The Tale of a Manx Cat (A Memoir from the Woman Who Gave Us Wonder)

ELIZABETH HOLLOWAY MARSTON

Editor's Note: Elizabeth Holloway Marston (1893–1993), known as "Sadie" in her youth and "Betty" later in life, received her bachelor's degree in psychology and held advanced degrees in both psychology and law. She conducted research on the psychophysiology of deception at Harvard University, collaborating with her fiancé/future husband, William Moulton Marston, on the development of a lie detector test. Although this memoir, which she began writing late in life, remained unfinished when she died at age 100, it nevertheless provides an intriguing look at the Marstons' early life as people and as both students and professionals in the field of psychology. We thank the Marston family for allowing us to share this abridged and previously unpublished memoir here in Wonder Woman Psychology.

Of course you know a feline Manx Cat has no tail, but a human Manx Cat is entitled, at least, to a tale. This human was born February 20, 1993, in a house on Finch Road, Douglas, The Isle of Man.

I don't remember the exact date of our sailing for the United States. Our first living quarters were a boarding house on Beacon Hill until my mother got her bearings. Evidently I was old enough for kindergarten. Very soon we left to live with distant relatives in Beachmont. From there my mother checked out various suburbs. Our first try was a tiny six-room cottage in Revere, Mass. The house was right on the edge of the marsh but many yards higher up. Standing there I could look over to the white gate of the Saugus Racetrack, located in a part of Saugus called Cliftondale, where my future husband was growing up.

Finally my mother found a house she really liked: 42 Morton Avenue, Cliftondale, MA. The house was pleasantly located right across the street from a large florist's establishment growing all sorts of flowers, vines, and trees. Living up the street, a few houses beyond ours, was an Irish family whose mother killed herself by attempting to abort a fetus with a wire clothes hanger. That memory affected me so much that I have always been in favor of legal abortions. Once, the two boys in the family got my brother down and were pummeling him. I jumped on their backs and banged their heads on the pavement.

Beyond our home was the home of a printer who operated his press with his feet. Then beside his house was another Irish family. The man of the house often got drunk. He sometimes knocked on our back door asking to borrow something. When he did, I'd run and get our weapon—an [ebony?][1] stick, our only defense weapon—and stand behind my mother, ready to defend her in case he got offensive.

It was in the eighth grade that I first met Bill, who was also in the eighth grade. He very soon maneuvered into a seat across the aisle from mine. In the ninth grade he was President of the class and I was Secretary.

Bill prepped for Harvard at Malden High. Before my family left for Dorchester while we were still in Cliftondale, I had a real tiff with Bill. I was on one side of Cliftondale Square when I met face to face with Bill and his friend Lionel Hopkins. Around the square I spotted a friend of mine, Alice Suaridge. I called over to her, "Alice, come over and help me get rid of this rubbish." The boys were insulted and rightfully so. (Incidentally, I was supposed to marry Hoppy and Bill was supposed to marry Hoppy's sister. Hoppy later did marry and wrote me a letter: "It was a black night, Sadie. . . ." His sister never married.) Enraged, they left me to my own devices. I didn't care. Later, in an attempt to make up, Bill sent me notes, brought to me by his childhood friend Lester Hatch. I did not read them but tore them up right then and there. Lester and Bill were friends from early childhood, which brings up another story. In those days, baby boys graduated from dresses to kilts and then to pants. When Bill's family tried to induce him to wear pants by saying Lester wore them, Bill said, "Baby Hatch may wear trousers if he wishes to, but I shall wear kilts." And he did. We have a picture.

Bill solved the problem of again being in touch with me by organizing a class reunion. Of course as President he had to work with the Secretary. We had our reunion and from then on Bill had to travel all the way from Cliftondale to Dorchester to see me.

My first Greek courses were given by a teacher in Dorchester High School. The prose I really didn't give a hoot about. What did I care if "from here they marched twenty stades five parasangs into the country" but the poetry was something else again. "Devious minded immortal Aphrodite, weaver of wiles." "The moon has set and the Pleiades; 'tis the middle of the night, the hours pass by but I sleep alone." "Would that my lot might lead me." I still have a Wharton's *Sappho* and still read it.

In college I majored in psychology but minored in Ancient Greek. Mount Holyoke College required a course in either chemistry or physics. I knew if I chose chemistry I'd blow the place up, so I chose physics—which my roommate said I passed in spite of the laws of learning and because I liked the professor's dog. I was asked to come back to the Psychology Department, and I would have if Bill could have been there with me.

Bill had cousins, the Whittemores, living in South Hadley Falls about five miles from South Hadley. In those days, the rule was that students couldn't ride the streetcar with a man without a chaperone. I talked to the Dean about this, who agreed with me that it was a stupid rule. So what happened? Bill came up and stayed with the Whittemores. I suppose I traveled to South Hadley Falls alone by streetcar, but when I was ready to return, Bill and I walked the five miles, threw a pebble at my room window, and my roommate came down and opened the front door, which was locked.

I graduated from Mount Holyoke College in June, 1915, with an A.B. degree. My mother by this time had bought a small farm in Abington, thinking she could make it produce some income. For me it was home all the years I was in college.

Bill and I were married September 16, 1915, in the living room of my mother's house with Pearl as Maid of Honor[2] and Hoppy as Best Man. When the ceremony was over, the Minister said, "The last time I was in this house, this is where the coffin stood." That same day Bill and I traveled by train to Liberty, Maine, where we had a two-week honeymoon.

Our first home was a small apartment on a very short street running between Brattle and Mount Auburn in Cambridge. Bill, as a professional psychologist, was given custody of a Back

Bay boy whose problem was masturbation. During the day there was always someone there to watch him. At night we gave a friend, rent free, a front room converted to a bedroom, which the boy shared with him to be sure the boy was under supervision 24 hours a day.

While living in this apartment, Bill went to Harvard Law, which didn't take women. I went to Boston University Law. There were three women in the class. Before the examination for admission to the Massachusetts Bar, B.U. offered a course on practice and pleading. I finished the exam in nothing flat and had to go out and sit on the stairs, waiting for Bill Marston and another Harvard man, a graduate of a Canadian college, to finish. With students coming from all over the U.S.A., Harvard had to stress fundamental principles rather than local practice.

We were still living at [Remington Gables?][3] when World War I was declared. Bill was first lieutenant at Camp Upton, deception-testing suspected spies. When he needed supplies, he would send a colleague to do the buying and head for home, not telling his father and mother. His parents wintered at a Boston Back Bay hotel and had a chauffeur and Packard Twin Six to drive them anywhere they wanted to go.

On one of Bill's visits, his father's secretary saw us in the subway en route to South Station. I got a phone call from Bill reporting this to me. I immediately phoned Govie, Bill's father, and gave him hell for causing trouble between us. It ended by his saying, "Well, you can't deny you were on the subway with some man."

Another time when they suspected Bill might be home—and he was—they drove to the apartment and had the chauffeur bang on the front door. When he got no answer, he climbed onto the piazza and banged on a door that led to the dining room. Bill was hiding in our bedroom.

During the war, women left at home were bored stiff. The Boston Opera House closed, so their Ballet Mistress started classes on her own. A friend of mine and I joined the class. It was marvelous, a real French ballet. Lucille and I would part at the subway station, Lucille saying, "Good night, Sadie. Take yourself home, kiss yourself Good Night, and put yourself to bed." I would do just that.

In those days people looked over the fence and said, "Very worthy people." When you got to Lowell Street and our house, our neighbor was an Elementary School. Across the street from us lived three old maids. Next to them was a bootlegger. Nonetheless they looked over their fence and said, "Very worthy people." We lived there while Bill was working on his Ph.D. I was working with him but refused to take the Ph.D. exam because Harvard required proficiency in German. I refused to accept the idea that it was necessary to read the German scientists if you were to keep up in your field, regardless of having completed the other requirements. I went to Radcliffe, signed some forms, criticized them from the legal point of view, wrote a thesis on Studies in Testimony, and was granted an M.A. Later a friend of ours, who was traveling in Europe with the Radcliffe Dean, reported that the Dean almost had a heart attack when he read my suggested changes.

In those days, suing the Boston Elevated was called shaking the plumtree and tort attorneys had to be ham actors (maybe they still are). One day I was sitting inside the bar taking notes for my Radcliffe thesis. The attorney, who knew my background, made an elaborate bow in my direction, saying, "There may be a Master Mind at work in this case." I didn't spit in his eye, but I would have liked to.

Soon after he got his degree, Bill, who had already been teaching at Radcliffe, went to Washington, D.C. to teach at one of the local colleges. I was alone in Cambridge, stone broke, and decided to do something about it. So I phoned Hoppy, then working at Lever Brothers,[4] and announced that I would like a job right away. He said, "You wouldn't demonstrate Lifebuoy soap, would you?" "Sure I would. I'll start tomorrow." "Okay, tomorrow morning be at the store next to the movie theater in Central Square." I did just that. It was Lent, so the movie business was slow. Hoppy induced the theater manager to authorize me to give a movie ticket to anyone who purchased fourteen dollars' worth of soap. One man did. He turned out to be the manager of the local Lever Brothers office. He went back carrying his basket of soap to face the hooting and laughter of the other employees.

I went from Cambridge to a Cleveland, Ohio food fair and started demonstrating Lifebuoy Soap. "Would you like to try some Lifebuoy soap, Madame?" "No, I wouldn't, it smells like a hospital." "You mean a hospital smells like Lifebuoy."

In the same unit with me was a woman we called "Blackie" because she dyed her hair with liquid shoe blacking. Her contribution to the joy of living was "God, Missus, there ain't a man on earth worth a foot in Hell."

Way back then, there were many traveling saleswomen who stuck together admirably. They would let each other know the names and addresses of people in towns you were headed to who would rent you decent quarters—room and board at a reasonable price. Only once did I have to go to a hotel, and that was the last town on my itinerary. As soon as I had saved enough cash to take care of my Cambridge needs for a while, I returned home and sold 17 Lowell Street at a decent profit.

By then Bill was in Washington, D.C., Professor of Psychology at a local university. Anxious to join him as soon as possible, I did not stay for the closing, which was handled by Bill's law partner and my father: $1,000 to be given to the partner to pay overdue rent. He kept the money for himself. Incidentally the rent was paid by Bill when I found it had not been paid. The balance was to be given to my father to pay for a second mortgage that my mother had advanced the money for, leaving a small amount to be sent to Bill. We never saw a cent. My father had kept it to cover a loss my parents had sustained from buying some stocks that Bill had recommended.

I will never forget the look on Bill's face when I showed up in Washington without staying for the closing.

My first job in Washington was with the Haskin Information Service in charge of inquiries on Agriculture, Home Economics, Domestic Relations, and Commercial Law. In the course of the morning I could dictate forty letters by using a speedup technique. Instead of dictating address and "Dear So and So," I numbered the letters, wrote #1 on the first letter and the stenographer wrote #1 on her first letter and took my dictation. "The Such and Such government office says, etc." It was easy to get through forty letters in the morning. The only exception to this procedure came when the letter was from a child, then I'd dictate, "What a pretty name . . ." Dictation finished, we would have the boss's chauffeur take us to the government departments specializing in our topics (the specialists in my topics were in the Smithsonian), go to lunch, then pick up the letters which had the answer written on them, return to the office, and then—finished for the day—go home. Sometimes Bill would join me and we would have a picnic.

The work at American University followed standard practice except when some offbeat chore came up. One time Bill was too lazy or didn't want to lecture to an offbeat group. He wished it on me. There was a group of four men up front who obviously were brainier than I was and who talked to each other while I was lecturing. So one day I called one of them up and said to him, "You know, So and So, nobody is going to give a good G.D. when you flunk this course." The next day they were scattered in seats far away from each other.

While indexing the documents of the first fourteen Congresses, I had to work in a locked cage lest someone try to steal them.

In 1927 we decided that if we were going to have children we'd better get started. During the pregnancy I was editor on the staff of the 14th *Encyclopaedia Britanica*—in charge of choosing the author, ordering and editing American copy in Psychology, Law, Home Economics, Medicine, Biology, Anthropology, Personnel Relations, and other miscellaneous subjects, about six hundred articles in all. Finally Bill said to me, "If you don't quit that job, that child will never be born." I quit on Tuesday. The baby was born on Friday at the Lenox Hill Hospital in Manhattan. I was thirty-five years old at the time.

At the time we were living in Darien, CT. When Pete was six months old, Bill accepted a job to come out to Hollywood and advise a movie producing company on how to strengthen the potential viewer appeal of new productions.

In those days traveling by train from New York to California, there was a stopover in Chicago. Bill's aunt Claribel Waterman lived there, so we went to her house to stay during the stopover. She was so intent on having her friends meet the "GRREAT Doctor Marston"[5] that the baby, my companion, and I were completely neglected. When the friends finally left, she turned to us. The baby got even. When she held him in her arms, his head bobbing over her shoulder, he burped all over her blouse. We should have gone to a hotel.

Editor's Note: The memoir ends here with a description of their house in Hollywood, before more family members, comic books, and Wonder Woman entered their lives.

Notes

1. That's how she typed it, question mark and all. She was apparently unsure of that detail.
2. Wharton Pearl Goddard, Elizabeth's closest friend during adolescence.
3. Again, that is how she typed it.
4. A cleaning products company.
5. She typed GRREAT in the manuscript with the double R. We will assume that's for emphasis and will not presume to change what she typed.

Justice

T R A V I S   L A N G L E Y

O f the virtues outlined in positive psychologists' *Character Strengths and Virtues* handbook,[1] one more than any other goes to the heart of what it means to be a superhero: *justice*, the pursuit of what is right, fair, and equitable for all. Law enforcement and the courts are not collectively referred to as the courage system, the wisdom system, or the temperance system. They belong to the justice system, in which William and Elizabeth Marston worked as both psychologists and lawyers.[2] The superhero teams that their Wonder Woman joins name themselves for this concept: the Justice Society of America in Golden Age comics[3] and then the Justice League in numerous iterations from the Silver Age onward.[4]

Justice as a core part of someone's personality is one of six *virtues*: favorable individual traits that psychologists Chris Peterson and Martin Seligman described when they developed the positive psychology manual *Character Strengths and Virtues: A Handbook and Classification* (CSV).[5] Like Wonder Woman's creator,[6] they saw a need to look at normal, healthy behavior and cautioned other psychologists against overemphasizing the abnormal and unhealthy.[7] A sort of "anti-DSM,"[8] the CSV identifies favorable characteristics that appear in mentally healthy people throughout the world, akin to the way the American Psychiatric Association's *Diagnostic and Statistical Manual of Mental Disorders* (DSM) categorizes and describes mental illnesses.[9]

Virtuous intent is insufficient without the strengths that enable a person to take action. According to Seligman, Peterson, and their colleagues, the virtue of justice depends on strengths in areas of citizenship, fairness, and leadership.[10]

Citizenship entails feeling both connected and obligated to the common good—at the simplest level, for the good of one's own group; at the broadest, for everyone everywhere. Although Diana's loyalty to her mother and her sister Amazons is great, a critical quality in her life, she leaves them to help all the world's people, believing at the time that she can never return.[11] Writer Greg Rucka calls this sacrifice for the greatest good "her defining heroic characteristic."[12] Though they make heroic choices, Superman does not choose to leave his dying planet[13] nor does Batman choose to lose his parents,[14] whereas Wonder Woman volunteers to give up everything she has ever known so that she can help (and see) the world.[15]

Trying to describe *fairness*—treating others in equitable ways—can produce endless debate: Should people be treated identically or should they be treated according to distinct abilities and needs? As children grow, fairness becomes an increasingly important aspect of their sense of morality.[16] Diane Nelson, president of DC Entertainment, sees Wonder Woman as an agent of "equality and fairness for people of all genders and likes."[17] The character's strength in treating people fairly and inspiring fairness in others makes her an enduring "symbol of hope, fairness, and heroism."[18]

Leadership, the power or ability to direct groups, can be official or unofficial, dictatorial or democratic, combative or cooperative, rigid or relaxed. Those who serve justice serve it best when they can get others to do the right thing, too. Though the Golden Age Wonder Woman initially joins the Justice Society (the greatest heroes of Earth-2) as their secretary during World War II,[19] she proves herself to be a strong, levelheaded leader in a number of their adventures.[20] From 1960 until the early 1980s, the Justice League (the greatest heroes of Earth-1) has a system of rotating chairmanship: Instead of having a single leader, every member takes a turn chairing the monthly meeting and assigning tasks during that month's adventures. Wonder Woman, the only woman on the team in the earliest published stories, from the outset takes turns equally with the other members.[21]

Comic Book References

Action Comics #1 (1938). "Superman, Champion of the Oppressed." Script: J. Siegel. Art: J. Shuster.

All-Star Comics #8 (1941). "Introducing Wonder Woman." Script: W. M. Marston. Art: H. G. Peter.

All-Star Comics #11 (1942). "The Justice Society Joins the War on Japan." Script: G. Fox. Art: J. Burnley, S. Moldoff, H. G. Peter, C. Young, B. Flinton, H. Sherman, & S. Aschmeier.

All-Star Comics #19 (1943). "The Crimes Set to Music." Script: G. Fox. Art: J. Gallagher, S. Aschmeier, J. Simon, J. Kirby, B. Baily, & S. Moldoff.

The Brave and the Bold #28 (1960). "Justice League of America." Script: G. Fox. Art: M. Sekowsky, B. Sachs, J. Giella, & M. Anderson.

Detective Comics #33 (1939). "The Legend of the Batman—Who He Is and How He Came to Be!" Script: B. Finger. Art: B. Kane.

Justice League of America #4 (1961). "The Doom of the Star Diamond!" Script: G. Fox. Art: M. Sekowsky & B. Sachs.

Wonder Woman #4 (2016). "Year One, Part Two." Script: G. Rucka. Art: N. Scott.

Wonder Woman #12 (2017). "Year One, Part Five." Script: G. Rucka. Art: N. Scott.

Other References

American Psychiatric Association. (2013). *Diagnostic and statistical manual of mental disorders* (DSM-5). Washington, DC: American Psychiatric Association.

Arakawa, D. (2008, May 14). *Thoughts on patience*. Positive Psychology News: http://positivepsychologynews.com/news/dana-arakawa/20080514748.

Cline, R. (2016, April 3). *"Sensation Comics": Wonder Woman collection proves heroine stands for hope, fairness*. The Gazette: http://www.thegazette.com/subject/life/books/sensation -comics-wonder-woman-collection-proves-heroine-stands-for-hope-fairness -20160403.

Georges, C. (2015, March 6). *The whys & how tos of strengths, passion, & purpose: Wisdom from the research & the people living the impact*. Seeing All the Good: http://www.seeingallthegood.com/seeing-all-the-good-blog/the-whys-how-tos-of-strengths -passion-purpose.

Hanley, T. (2014). *Wonder Woman unbound: The curious history of the world's most famous heroine*. Chicago, IL: Chicago Review Press.

Kohlberg, L. (1976). Moral stages and moralization: The cognitive-developmental approach. In T. Lickona (Ed.), *Moral development and behavior: Theory, research, and social issues*. New York, NY: Holt, Rinehart & Winston.

Lang, B. (2016, October 11). *Wonder Woman at 75: How the superhero icon inspired a generation of feminists*. Variety: http://variety.com/2016/biz/news/wonder-woman -75th-anniversary-dc-comics-1201884289/.

Marston, W. M. (1928). *Emotions of normal people*. London, UK: Kegan Paul, Trench, Trubner.

Narcisse, E. (2016, October 7). *Wonder Woman writer says haters need to "get over it" about Diana's new canon bisexuality*. io9: http://io9.gizmodo.com/greg-rucka-says-haters -need-to-get-over-it-about-wond-1787537688.

Park, N., Peterson, C., & Seligman, M. (2004). Strengths of character and well-being. *Journal of Social and Clinical Psychology, 23*(5), 603-619.

Peterson, C., & Seligman, M. E. P. (2004). *Character strengths and virtues: A handbook and classification*. Washington, DC: American Psychological Association.

Piaget, J. (1932). *The moral judgment of the child*. New York, NY: Harcourt Brace Jovanovich.

Seligman, M. E. P. (1998). Building human strength: Psychology's forgotten mission. *APA Monitor, 29*(1), 1.

Notes

1. Park et al. (2004); Peterson & Seligman (2004).
2. Hanley (2014).
3. *All-Star Comics* #11 (1942).
4. She was one of the original members in *The Brave and the Bold* #28 (1960).
5. Peterson & Seligman (2004), p. 5.
6. Marston (1928).
7. Seligman (1998).
8. As the CSV has been nicknamed by Arakawa (2008), Georges (2015), and others.
9. American Psychiatric Association (2013).
10. Peterson & Seligman (2004).
11. *All-Star Comics* #8 (1941); *Wonder Woman* #4 (2016); *Wonder Woman* #12 (2017).
12. Narcisse (2016).

13. *Action Comics* #1 (1938).

14. *Detective Comics* #33 (1939).

15. *All-Star Comics* #8 (1941).

16. Kohlberg (1976); Piaget (1932).

17. Lang (2016).

18. Cline (2016).

19. *All-Star Comics* #11 (1942).

20. *All-Star Comics* #19 (1943).

21. With Wonder Woman taking her first recorded turn in *Justice League of America* #4 (1961).

ANCIENT MYTHOLOGY LAY THE FOUNDATION FOR HEROIC TALES AND IDEALS ACROSS THE GLOBE AND THROUGHOUT TIME.

PART II

OLD WORLD

CHAPTER FIVE

A Perfect Place: Paradise Island and Utopian Communities

MARA WOOD

"Here is no want, no illness, no hatreds, no wars."
—Hippolyta[1]

*"What could we conclude from a successful
community of a thousand people?"*
—behavioral psychologist B. F. Skinner[2]

Sir Thomas More's term *utopia*, which he derived from Greek origins for his book *Utopia*, refers to a perfect place, a paradise for its inhabitants.[3] Originally called Paradise Island, the fictional Themyscira is home to a society of women of Greek origin who display a peaceful, advanced lifestyle there.[4] The location is unknown to the rest of the world, thus protecting their paradise. Paradise Island evokes feelings of comfort, relaxation, and seclusion. The Amazons' home is not without its flaws, but the unique, matriarchal society displays elements

of community psychology that highlight its ability to benefit
individual members.

Elements of a Utopia

In a hypothetical utopia, a group of people live together to
enhance shared values for some mutually agreed-upon purpose.[5]
The focus of this group of people is their shared vision of the
future, indicating some degree of homogeneity between the
members. With an agreed-upon end goal, the members can
find a reason to work together toward that goal. The Amazons'
shared values are reflected in Paradise Island, as established by
Aphrodite. The island is equipped with halls of justice, art, and
history, as well as icons that glorify the gods.[6] Paradise Island is
supplemented by Reform Island[7] and Science Island,[8] evidence
of the Amazons' interest in advancing scientifically as well as
reforming those who have lost their way. The Amazons unite
in establishing a culture based on these elements. Their shared
vision excludes men. Aphrodite forbids any man to set foot on
Paradise Island; if a man does, the Amazons will lose everything
they have accomplished.[9] The women of Paradise Island are to
set themselves apart from men and their way of thinking.[10]

Utopias have a goal of creating a society that is decentralized
and federated, made up of smaller autonomous communities.[11]
The most common way to reach this shared vision is expected
to be to separate from the larger society and create a smaller
community.[12] Separation from society is not a one-way ticket
to a utopia; a utopia has to be able to balance the autonomy
of the individuals and the sense of community of the whole.[14]
Members of the utopian community have to feel like individuals while also partaking in communion, interdependence,
cooperation, affiliation, intimacy, and belongingness with

their community.[13] The Amazons of Paradise Island may share a common goal, but each one fulfills a different role in the community to reach that goal. Mala is director of the island's reformation program for villains,[15] Phillipus the head guard,[16] and Io the blacksmith.[17] Many of the Amazons of Paradise Island have names, duties, and perspectives that may differ from the other members of their community, demonstrating the role of autonomy for the women. Despite any differences they may have with each other, the women continually work toward the benefit of the Amazons as a whole with few exceptions.[18]

Civil rights, unification, the addressing of global concerns, moral practices, and scientific advancement are widely considered the most important elements of a utopia."[19] The common thread in expectations for a future utopian society is adherence to the Golden Rule: Do unto others what you would have done unto you.[20] The Amazon culture is one that embodies most of these elements of a potential utopia. The rights of the individual women are protected within their community.[21] They follow their common religion, and they engage in the sciences to help create a technologically advanced society.[22] Significant worldwide events rarely come into the Amazons' field of vision, so more localized events make a significant impact on the community, such as Steve Trevor's arrival and Diana's subsequent sacrifice.[23]

Religion, science, and civil rights are the foundations of Amazon culture.[24] For centuries, religion has played a part in the concept of utopias. In many religions, an eternal paradise is the reward for adhering to moral precepts dictated by the religion. Utopian thought arises when an individual considers the possibility of establishing a similar paradise on Earth. The afterlife's paradise then becomes less important than the hope of using science and progress to live in paradise now.[25] The Amazons are able to establish a paradise on Earth because of their gods' goodwill, an earthly reward for their worship. With the favor and gifts from their gods, like the magic sphere,[26] the Amazons cultivate their culture to reflect their religious beliefs and the women they want to become.

Benefits of Utopian Membership

In both Marston's[27] and George Pérez's[28] accounts of Wonder Woman's background, the Amazons are mistreated and harmed by men. They feel like playthings to the gods, subjected to the whims of the higher beings and the mortal men around them. In one account, the Amazons receive the opportunity to escape their male captors if they do so without resorting to the level of destruction and violence the men display.[29] They gain their freedom and are rewarded with a place of seclusion. The societal problem, the subjugation and poor treatment of women, is addressed by removing the Amazons from men. Societal problems can be combated by a change in human behavior.[30] The Amazons' change in behavior starts with learning to live as a society of women, where their approach to life accounts for the loss of men and the traditional gender roles that come with a binary gendered society. Widespread social reform that eliminates sources of stress, such as an alteration in the social structures of the members, can prevent mental and emotional distress in the community members.[31]

Community members' ability to satisfy their psychological needs, honor their values, and achieve their goals is impacted by global events. A utopian society is separate from the general population in a way that many global concerns are minimized, especially those that are social in nature. In the case of the Amazons, their seclusion allows them to be wholly undisturbed by the goings-on of men. Wars, technological advancements, and religions pass them by. The women grow in their seclusion and develop their own history, separate from the one of humankind. Over the years, the global concerns that can impact the women psychologically are mostly related to the worship of their gods, advancement of their society, and ongoing perfection of their bodies and minds.[32]

It can be argued that the Amazons have a utopian mind-set. They work diligently throughout the years to create a society that lasts and prospers, and they have insights into social structures that prove over time to be effective. Individuals who have a utopian mind-set are likely to be prepared for extensive changes in society.[33] The Amazons therefore are open to the idea of widespread societal changes in their own community as well as the possibility of societal changes in man's world, when given the opportunity to integrate into the greater global society. Diana's work as Wonder Woman is not limited to heroic actions. For a time, she feels that her duty is best served as a teacher to global citizens and the sharing of cultures.[34] Diana acts as a diplomat for Paradise Island and offers her unique insight as a member of a utopian community.

In Wonder Woman's early stories, the Amazons demonstrate a utopian mind-set through the establishment of Reform Island (later called Transformation Island).[35] The purpose of the island is to teach women who have been corrupted by man's world the benefits of living like an Amazon. The residents of Reform Island, under Mala's tutelage, learn the Amazon lifestyle so that they may take that new perspective into their old lives.[36] After centuries of living and perfecting their society, the Amazons know what villainous women need in order to turn from their life of crime. The focus of Reform Island is on teaching love and *loving submission*, the concept of willingly submitting to a loving person.[37] The success of Reform Island is replicated in man's world for female prisoners, emphasizing that prisoners have a part in society and need to work as a team with others.[38]

Psychologist B. F. Skinner is best known for his contributions to behavioral psychology. He approached most problems with the idea that they could be solved using the basic principles of behaviorism, including community living. After World War II, Skinner felt that young men and women should experiment with different lifestyles instead of subscribing to the commonly held model of the time—traditional marriage and child rearing. He especially saw dissatisfaction in his wife's postwar life, when women were leaving the workforce. The dissatisfaction came from identifying herself a housewife, a life many women, especially those who had been productive and happy as part of the workforce, did not desire to live. Skinner's work on utopian living includes his 1948 novel, *Walden Two*. The utopian content of his novel includes streamlining activities to provide leisure for citizens and avoiding *aversive control*, that is, punishing people for their actions.[39] In post–World War II society, Skinner believed that many of the world's problems could be solved through behavior modification, and he hypothesized how a community based on ideals met through behavior modification would function.[40] Though *Walden Two* often curtailed personal freedom among its fictional citizens, the underlying utopian content can apply to the Amazons. The women of Paradise Island have jobs and responsibilities, but there is a focus on leisure activities and festivals.[41] They often engage in different sports, contests, and religious events. These activities are communal in nature, bringing together many of the women in a social context. There is also a lack of aversive control among the Amazons. Women are not often punished for their misdeeds, except in the context of loving submission, a commonly held belief among the Amazons.[42] Even the villains whom Wonder Woman stops from doing harm have the opportunity to reform with loving submission as the core feature of their rehabilitation. Skinner felt that the use of aversive control in a community context would induce poor emotional responses and damage the overall social relationships in the community. The Amazons rarely punish their own and are quick to forgive.[43] The result is the Skinnerian ideal for behavioral control in a community: humanization.[44]

Seclusion or Integration

Are the Amazons right in engaging in seclusion from the world for several thousands of years? They are able to create and maintain a utopian society, but some feel that something had been missing for all those centuries. After Diana journeys to man's world and has some success as a representative of Paradise Island, Hippolyta decides to consider allowing outsiders onto the island.[45] When offered the opportunity to engage with the outside world, the Amazons become divided.[46] Some feel that they have a divine duty to share with the rest of the world what they learned over all those years to improve the lives of everyone; others believe the integration of Amazon life and man's world will only doom the Amazon culture. The shared vision of the Amazons splits, and thus the utopian lifestyle of the Amazons changes.

There are some outsiders who, upon learning of the society created by the Amazons, resent them. Jeannette, a member of the Secret Six, despises the Amazons because of their decision to withdraw from the world and, she believes, abandon other women.[47] The Amazons, as a proud, fierce, independent nation of women, likely would not have developed as such without that isolation. Isolation from a society that does not support their views and values allows the women to concentrate on

A VISIT TO THEMYSCIRA

Themyscira becomes part of the greater world when Diana arranges for a delegation of outsiders to visit.[48] The purpose of the visit is to exchange ideas and explain how the Amazons have functioned as a society for thousands of years. The individuals whom Diana selects to visit Themyscira represent the world as a whole: Visitors range from religious leaders to political activists, scientists to historians, elders in society to youth.[49] They are, in her reasoning, the people who can show her sisters what man's world has to offer while also learning from the Amazon culture. Though the exchange of ideas has some rocky moments and interference by deities, all individuals leave the interaction having learned something about themselves and their culture. Notably, the people from man's world see Themyscira as the culture they could have had without centuries of wars and poor stewardship.[50]

creating a life that works best for them without the pressure of societal expectations or threats from outsiders.

An interesting aspect of the Amazons' seclusion is the homogeneity of the culture. The women may come from racially different backgrounds, but their culture is decidedly Greek.[51] A shared cultural heritage, plus thousands of years of seclusion, creates a very like-minded culture with limitations in diverse perspectives. The Amazons are well-read, with materials to study provided by the gods, but they lack interactions with people who have little in common with them.[52] Diana works to address the homogeneity of her community by bringing a diverse group of delegates to Paradise Island. The visitors may have one or two dimensions of similarity with the Amazons, such as being a woman or being devoutly religious, but the differences between the Amazons and the rest of the world are stark.[53] For the Amazons, joining the world stage includes learning to interact with radically different kinds of people.[54]

The Amazons are a race created by the gods to be an example to other people, and seclusion from the general population defeats the purpose of being a role model. Additionally, being a small community, their translation to a much larger society or culture may be impossible.[55] However, the impact of the Amazons thousands of years later, after they have perfected their community, shows the world the time and effort that go into creating a utopian community. The Amazons' entrance into the global community signifies their role as a savior society, one that has something to teach us.[56]

Comic Book References

All-Star Comics #8 (1941). "Introducing Wonder Woman." Script: W. M. Marston. Art: H. G. Peter.

Legend of Wonder Woman #4 (2016). Script: R. De Liz. Art: R. De Liz & R. Dillon.

Legend of Wonder Woman #9 (2016). Script: R. De Liz. Art: R. De Liz & R. Dillon.

Secret Six #14 (2009). "Depths, Part 5: Early Release." Script: G. Simone. Art: N. Scott.

Sensation Comics #1 (1942). "Wonder Woman Comes to America." Script: W. M. Marston. Art: H. G. Peter.

Wonder Woman #1 (1942). "The History of the Amazons: The Origin of Wonder Woman." Script: W. M. Marston. Art: H. G. Peter.

Wonder Woman #3 (1943). "A Spy on Paradise Island." Script: W. M. Marston. Art: H. G. Peter.

Wonder Woman #4 (1943). "Man-Hating Madness!" Script: W. M. Marston. Art: H. G. Peter.

Wonder Woman #30 (1948). "A Human Bomb." Script: R. Kanigher. Art: H. G. Peter.

Wonder Woman #169 (1967). "Wonder Woman Battles the Crimson Centipede." Script: R. Kanigher. Art: R. Andru & M. Esposito.

Wonder Woman #1 (1987). "The Princess and the Power." Script: G. Potter & G. Pérez. Art: G. Pérez.

Wonder Woman #8 (1987). "Time Passages." Script: G. Pérez & L. Wein. Art: G. Pérez & B. Patterson.

Wonder Woman #12 (1988). "Echoes of the Past." Script: G. Pérez & L. Wein. Art: G. Pérez & B. Patterson.

Wonder Woman #21 (1988). "The Cosmic Migration." Script: G. Pérez. Art: G. Pérez & B. McLeod.

*Wonder Woma*n #22 (1988). "Through Destiny's Door." Script: G. Pérez. Art: G. Pérez & B. McLeod.

Wonder Woman #37 (1989). "Strangers in Paradise." Script: G. Pérez & M. Newell. Art: C. Marrinan & S. Montano.

Wonder Woman #50 (1991). "Embrace the Coming Dawn." Script: G. Pérez. Art: J. Thompson & R. Tanghal.

Wonder Woman #196 (2003). "Down to Earth, Part One." Script: G. Rucka. Art: D. Johnson & R. Snyder.

Wonder Woman #17 (2008). "The Circle Conclusion: A Time of Reckoning." Script: G. Simone. Art: R. Randall.

Wonder Woman #39 (2010). "Warkiller, Part 4: Dawn before Darkness." Script: G. Simone. Art: A. Lopresti & M. Ryan.

Other References

Altus, D. E., & Morris, E. K. (2009). B. F. Skinner's utopian vision: Behind and beyond *Walden Two. The Behavior Analyst, 32*(2), 319–335.

Fox, D. R. (1985). Psychology, ideology, utopia, and the commons. *American Psychologist, 40*(1), 48–58.

Kinnier, R. T., Wilkins, K. G., Hauser, D. L., Hassert, S. M., & Petrolle, L. C. (2011). The main contributors to a future utopia. *Current Psychology, 30*(4), 383–394.

Marder, M., & Vieira, P. (2012). Utopia: A political ontology. In M. Marder & P. Vieira (Eds.). *Existential utopia: New perspectives on utopian thought.* New York, NY: Continuum.

Marston, W. M. (1928). *Emotions of normal people.* New York, NY: Harcourt, Brace.

Sargent, L. T. (2010). *Utopianism: A very short introduction.* New York, NY: Oxford University Press.

Skinner, B. F. (1948). *Walden two.* New York, NY: Macmillan.

Notes

1. *All-Star Comics* #8 (1941).
2. Skinner (1948), p. viii.
3. Sargent (2010).
4. *Wonder Woman* #1 (1942); *Wonder Woman* #1 (1987).
5. Sargent (2010).
6. *Wonder Woman* #1 (1987).
7. *Wonder Woman* #3 (1943).
8. *Wonder Woman* #169 (1967).
9. *All-Star Comics* #8 (1941).
10. *Wonder Woman* #1 (1987).
11. Fox (1985).
12. Sargent (2010).
13. Fox (1985).
14. Fox (1985).
15. *Wonder Woman* #3 (1943).
16. *Wonder Woman* #1 (1987).

17. *Wonder Woman* #196 (2003).
18. *Wonder Woman* #17 (2008).
19. Kinnier et al. (2011).
20. *Luke* 6:31
21. *Wonder Woman* #1 (1987).
22. *All-Star Comics* #8 (1941); *Wonder Woman* #1 (1942), *Wonder Woman* #1 (1987).
23. *Wonder Woman* #12 (1988).
24. *Wonder Woman* #4 (1943); *Wonder Woman* #1 (1987).
25. Marder & Vieira (2012).
26. *Sensation Comics* #1 (1942).
27. *All-Star Comics* #8 (1941); *Wonder Woman* #1 (1942).
28. *Wonder Woman* #1 (1987).
29. *Wonder Woman* #1 (1987).
30. Fox (1985).
31. Fox (1985).
32. *All-Star Comics* #8 (1941); *Wonder Woman* #1 (1987).
33. Fox (1985).
34. *Wonder Woman* #8 (1987).
35. *Wonder Woman* #4 (1943).
36. *Wonder Woman* #3 (1943).
37. Marston (1928).
38. *Wonder Woman* #30 (1948).
39. Altus & Morris (2009).
40. Skinner (1948).
41. *Wonder Woman* #3 (1943).
42. *Wonder Woman* #7 (1943).
43. *Wonder Woman* #39 (2010).
44. Altus & Morris (2009).
45. *Wonder Woman* #21 (1988).
46. *Wonder Woman* #22 (1988).
47. Secret Six #14 (2009).
48. *Wonder Woman* #37 (1989).
49. *Wonder Woman* #7 (1989).
50. *Wonder Woman* #37 (1989).
51. *Wonder Woman* #1 (1987).
52. *Wonder Woman* #1 (1987).
53. *Wonder Woman* #37 (1989).
54. *Wonder Woman* #50 (1991).
55. Skinner (1948).
56. *Sensation Comics* #1 (1942); *Legend of Wonder Woman* #4 and #9 (2016).

CHAPTER SIX

Individuation and the Psychology of Rebirth

CHRIS YOGERST AND CAITLIN YOGERST

"Amazons! Hear your Queen! Even as Apollo's sun gives birth to this glorious day, I have gathered you here to witness a birth of another kind! The champion has been chosen. The gods have been satisfied!"
—Hippolyta[1]

"But human kind is masculine and feminine, not just man or woman. You can hardly say of your soul what sex it is."
—psychiatrist Carl Jung[2]

Our experiences largely determine who we are as individuals. Psychiatrist Carl Jung referred to this process of individuation as a rebirth. Diana goes through a similar process to become Wonder Woman, with her mission, power, and identity all deeply rooted in her psychological makeup, as developed through a detailed rebirth. Wonder Woman's adventures showcase the character's solid foundation/origin, which developed into a clear mission, unique powers, and an inspirational identity that set her apart from other superheroes.[3]

Superheroes are generally strong, committed, resilient, skilled, and physically superior in mind and body,[4] all of which combine with feminism and mythology in Wonder Woman.[5] She can be seen as part love, inspiration, and vengeance in addition to mother figure, daughter, student, and leader. While Wonder Woman embodies these characteristics, her mythological foundation is created through the process of rebirth that helps each feature develop.[6]

The Archetype of Rebirth

*"The cave is the place of rebirth, that secret cavity in which
one is shut up in order to be incubated and renewed."*
—psychiatrist Carl Jung[7]

Carl Jung, an associate of Sigmund Freud, is widely known for his psychoanalytic approach to studying the *collective unconscious* and its *archetypes*. According to Jung, the collective unconscious consists of universal, innate instincts that do not develop consciously. Jung described the contents of this inherited collective unconscious as *archetypes*, instinctive patterns of natural behavior and transformations.[8] He interpreted these archetypes through numerous lenses, such as history and popular fiction. Such interpretation allows readers to look at Wonder Woman's mythology and see similar applications. For example, the Cavern of Souls, depicted in the 1987 series as a place where the Amazon women are reborn,[9] is exactly as Jung described the transformative process: a hidden location where a person is reborn and renewed.[10]

Each Amazon's soul is that of a woman previously murdered by a man, but Diana's soul comes from an unborn child who died with her murdered mother.[11] Wonder Woman is therefore born on Paradise Island as the only child in most versions of her history, immediately setting her apart from the others as special, and in the 1980s this becomes a story of rebirth. Before becoming Wonder Woman, Diana goes through a series of transformations. Jung outlined the phenomenology of rebirth with a series of transformative experiences that are life-changing and alter one's future personality and being. For Jung, to be reborn means to face primeval confirmations about life. Such transformations directly connect to Diana's birth and transformation into Wonder Woman.

Experiences Induced by Ritual

Jung's first stage of the *rebirth* archetype deals with supreme transformations, called *experiences induced by ritual*, which are "represented by the fateful transformations—death and rebirth—of a god or a godlike hero."[12] Ritualistic experiences can be religious in nature, such as praying in its various forms. Rituals can also be more simplistic, as seen in the common cultural practice of blowing out birthday candles and making a wish. In the Wonder Woman mythos, the rituals of a previously patriarchal life lead to the death of patriarchal cultural practices and the rebirth of new cultural practices.[13]

Immediate Experiences

Jung's second transformational stage is *immediate experiences*, which "represent an action in which the spectator becomes involved though his nature is not necessarily changed."[14] Representative actions that do not alter one's nature could be community involvement of many forms, such as participating in a club or volunteer group.

Diana is active on Paradise Island, but her nature is not altered to be more like that of her sisters. It is clear early on that Diana is her own person, with ideas that differ from those of her peers (particularly her mother). A good example of such independence is when Diana enters the competition, without her mother's approval, to win the job of taking Steve Trevor back to the United States.[15]

Diminution of Personality

Jung's third stage, the *diminution of personality*, occurs when "one no longer has any wish or courage to face the tasks of the day."[16] For example, when children begin to transition from following their parents' ideals to following their own. This process often includes questioning of established ideals and norms. As an adult, Diana does not share the same appreciation of Paradise Island that her sisters have (which is not to say she no longer feels loyal to them). Diana has not lived under the oppression her sisters have, which allows her to develop a different worldview.[17] As a child, she may feel just like everyone else around her, but it becomes clear that she has her own journey to take, which requires a transformation of personality, according to Jung.[18]

Enlargement of Personality

Next comes an *enlargement of personality*, which Jung argued happens in the first half of life "by new vital contents finding their way into the personality from outside."[19] Our personalities change (enlarge), as we encounter new things. Experiences such as meeting new people, hearing a song, or going somewhere new can have a lasting impact.

The obvious physical representation of such enlargement of personality is found with the landing (or crashing) of Steve

Trevor. While Hippolyta sees just another man fighting a war, Diana sees hope and possibilities for something new by creating a relationship with man, falling in love with him and his country.[20] Diana sacrifices immortality for the love of one man, his country, and the people of the world.

Change in Internal Structure

After the personality is transformed, according to Jung, the person undergoes *change in internal structure*, inwardly changing in order to act on newfound beliefs or ideals. This transformation is based on possession, such as when "some content, an idea, or part of the personality, obtains mastery of the individual."[21] A person may develop new convictions (which can be based on philosophy, theology, psychology, politics, etc.) that consume his or her thoughts and alter his or her future actions.

Diana's internal being changes when she meets Steve Trevor. Diana comes to possess the idea that both man and women can live together in harmony. Matriarchy may not be necessary to survive, which is why Diana believes she can return Steve to the United States and have a positive influence on the culture there.[22] Diana mirrors this step in Jung's *rebirth* archetype as her internal structure changes and she becomes Wonder Woman. Diana's transformation into Wonder Woman has been immortalized in images of Lynda Carter spinning into a costume,[23] but that iconic visual transformation is just a representation of the psychological change.

Identification with a Group

This internal change sparks additional identifiers for Diana, which leads us to Jung's next stage: *identification with a group*. Jung called this "the identification of an individual with a number of people who, as a group, have a collective experience of transformation."[24] Finding like-minded people through a political, religious, or volunteer group is a great way for someone to build on his or her passions and grow in new ways.

Diana identifies with Paradise Island as an active group member, but after meeting Steve she becomes able and willing to connect with the human race and the male gender as well. She quickly learns how humans differ from Amazons in situations ranging from stopping bank robbers to dealing with corrupt show managers.

Identification with a Cult-Hero

Idolizing a hero is an essential ingredient for Jung's rebirth. Jung described *identification with a cult-hero*: "Identification underlying the transformation experience is that with the god or hero who is transformed in the sacred ritual. Many cult ceremonies are expressly intended to bring this identity about."[25]

On one level, Wonder Woman is the hero others identify with.[26] In addition, the average citizen may see the armed forces as their hero, but the armed forces can see Wonder Woman as their hero.[27] Diana is also a hero to other women and other superheroes, and she is a role model whose many virtues many can appreciate. She is portrayed as an important figure and was even recognized by President Ronald Reagan.

Magical Procedures

When transformational rebirth moves beyond identification, according to Jung, *magical procedures* will take place—unnatural things that happen to the individual and play a major role in the transformation. This is part of the rebirth, as Jung stated that one "undergoes an ablution or baptismal bath and miraculously changes into a semi-divine being with a new character and an altered metaphysical destiny."[28] A person can be seen as reborn through *rite-of-passage* religious rituals, such as baptism, first communion, and bar and bat mitzvah.

Such magical transformation can be seen in Diana's birth from a clay creation with gods beside her. Her armor, bracelets, and lasso of truth are magical. Wonder Woman's entire origin involves magical procedures, from her soul being kept in Gaea to her body getting created out of clay and her special abilities coming from the goddesses (and, in some versions of the story, a god or two).[29]

Technical Transformations

For Jung, *technical transformations* are "elaborations of the originally natural processes of transformation." In other words, they are "techniques designed to induce the transformation by imitating this same sequence of events."[30] This can be seen as oral histories, stories passed from generation to generation, that influence current actions. Tangible examples of this would be heirlooms, pictures, and other artifacts that tell a story and hold special meaning.

Wonder Woman is initially transformed by those around her; the stories told of the Old World clearly drive the lifestyle on Paradise Island.[31] As Diana follows the lead of her elders, she begins to develop her own responses to life, based on her lived experience. Through meeting Steve Trevor and learning about the United States and the impact she could have there, Diana gets much closer to becoming Wonder Woman.

Natural Transformations

The rebirth is complete during the *natural transformation*, which is a creation of something entirely new to complete the process. Jung saw this as the completion of *individuation*, development as a whole individual. Jung asserted that this natural transformation is a rebirth into another being: "This 'other being' is the other person in ourselves—that larger and greater personality maturing within us, whom we have already met as the inner friend of the soul."[32] In his theory, this is a universal transformation, such as puberty when girls become women and boys become men. It might also represent the beginning of a new career, becoming a parent, or any other life change that forces us to become something new.

Diana becomes Wonder Woman and begins to influence those around her. She becomes her own person, standing out from the other Amazons. Jung saw the transformation after rebirth "as a prolongation of the natural span of life or as an earnest of immortality."[33] When Aphrodite recognizes that the last soul in the Cavern of Souls is different, Athena says to the other goddesses, "Aye, Aphrodite. That one has a special destiny. But her time is not yet come!"[34] Diana's time begins when she becomes Wonder Woman and embarks on her mission to bring mankind and womankind into harmony with one another. This is the completed natural transformation, where Princess becomes Wonder Woman and sets herself apart from the other Amazons.

It is the *natural* stage of Jung's transformative rebirth that shows us why Diana is important: She is destined to become this superheroine. Diana was the only child on Paradise Island and, in Jungian terms, "One of the essential features of the child motif is its futurity. The child is potential future."[35] In other words, Diana represents a future that only she can fulfill. The rest of Paradise Island is comfortable in their ways, while Wonder Woman wants to move forward. Jung has argued that the child can sometimes appear as a god or a hero, which was the case with Diana, as everyone around recognized her as special.

Her Journey

The rebirth is a process of individuation, which sets Diana apart from the other Amazons. While Diana's transformation into Wonder Woman is fantastical, it is also relatable because

CHILD AND MOTHER ARCHETYPES

Archetypes are elements of the collective unconscious, the inherited portion of the mind that Carl Jung believed developed over the history of our species. These elements are supposedly reflected in experiences, such as behavior, religion, myths, and dreams. Jung also saw archetypal patterns and transitions, such as rebirth, which apply to Wonder Woman directly.

According to Jung, the *Child* archetype represents possible future, just as Diana represents the future of Paradise Island by being the only child there. The prominent *mother* archetype is symbolized on Paradise Island by Hippolyta, who mothers the Amazons as well as her daughter Diana. Mythological Greek gods and goddesses, who give Diana powers that she will use to ultimately become Wonder Woman, invoke the *Spirit* and other archetypes related to their specific qualities. Becoming Wonder Woman showcases Diana as the Hero as well as the importance of individuation, which for Jung meant that a person's transformation is not complete until the individual becomes something truly unique.

people go through stages of rebirth. As we grow from children into adults, students into professionals, atheists into believers (or vice versa), or a married couple into parents, we live through a series of events that change us into new individuals who can take on new challenges. Like Diana, others go through changes in their life that may alter their philosophical, political, or theological views, but that process begins as a psychological rebirth.

Myth in the hero's journey is supposedly a "secret opening" where any possibility can become reality.[36] Wonder Woman personifies such a social and psychological creation. Jung's rebirth archetype and mythologist Joseph Campbell's hero's journey may each be just as applicable in real life as in fiction and mythology. Diana is born again as Wonder Woman, a new entity destined for new adventures, ultimately preparing her for the adventures ahead. Our lives work as a similar individuation process as we take on new roles, identities, and responsibilities that make us who we are.

Comic Book References

All-Star Comics #8 (1941). "Introducing Wonder Woman." Script: W. M. Marston. Art: H. G. Peter.
Sensation Comics #4 (1942). "School for Spies." Script: W. M. Marston. Art: H. G. Peter.
Wonder Woman #178 (1968). "Wonder Woman's Rival." Script: D. O'Neil. Art: M. Sekowsky & D. Giordano.
Wonder Woman #1 (1987). "The Princess and the Power." Script: G. Pérez & G. Potter. Art: G. Pérez & B. Patterson.
Wonder Woman #2 (1987). "A Fire in the Sky!" Script: G. Potter. Art: G. Pérez & B. Patterson.
Wonder Woman #4 (1987). "A Long Day's Journey into the Fright." Script: G. Pérez & L. Wein. Art: G. Pérez & B. Patterson.
Wonder Woman #8 (1987). "Time Passages." Script: G. Pérez. Art: G. Pérez & B. Patterson.
Wonder Woman: Earth One (2016). Script: G. Morrison. Art: Y. Paquette.

Other References

Campbell, J. (1949/2008). *The hero with a thousand faces.* Novato, CA: New World Library.
Coogan, P. (2013). The hero defines the genre, the genre defines the hero. In R. S. Rosenberg & P. Coogan (Eds.), *What is a superhero?* (pp. 3–10). New York, NY: Oxford University Press.
Jung, C. G. (1959/1990). *The archetypes and the collective unconscious.* Princeton, NJ: Princeton University Press.
Jung, C. G. (2012). *The red book: A reader's edition.* New York, NY: Norton.
Robbins, T. (1996). The great women superheroes. In C. Hatfield, J. Heer, & K. Worcester (Eds.), *The superhero reader* (pp. 53–60). Jackson, MS: University Press of Mississippi.
Stuller, J. K. (2010). *Ink-stained amazons and cinematic warriors: Superwomen in modern mythology.* New York, NY: Tauris.

Stuller, J. K. (2013). What is a female superhero? In R. S. Rosenberg & P. Coogan (Eds.), *What is a superhero?* (pp. 19–23). New York, NY: Oxford University Press.

Woogler, J., Woogler, B., & Woogler, R. J. (1989). *The goddess within: A guide to the eternal myths that shape women's lives.* New York, NY: Fawcett Columbine.

Notes

1. *Wonder Woman* #1 (1987).
2. Jung (2012), p. 227.
3. Coogan (2013).
4. Stuller (2013).
5. Robbins (1996).
6. *All-Star Comics* #8 (1941).
7. Jung (1959/1990), p. 135.
8. Jung (1959/1990).
10. *Wonder Woman* #1 (1987).
11. *Wonder Woman* #1 (1987).
12. Jung (1959/1990), p. 117.
13. *Wonder Woman* #1 (1987).
14. Jung (1959/1990), p. 118.
15. *All-Star Comics* #8 (1941); *Wonder Woman* #1 (1987).
16. Jung (1959/1990), p. 119.
17. *The New Original Wonder Woman* (1975 pilot/television movie).
18. Jung (1959/1990).
19. Jung (1959/1990), p. 120.
20. *All-Star Comics* #8 (1941).
21. Jung (1959/1990), p. 122.
22. *Wonder Woman* #2 (1987).
23. Beginning with *The New Original Wonder Woman* (1975 pilot/television movie), then the better-known magical transformation in *Wonder Woman* episode 1–1, "Wonder Woman Meets Baroness von Gunther" (April 21, 1976).
24. Jung (1959/1990), p. 125.
25. Jung (1959/1990), p. 128.
26. *Wonder Woman* #4 (1987).
27. *Wonder Woman* #8 (1987).
28. Jung (1959/1990), p. 129.
29. *Wonder Woman* #1 (1987).
30. Jung (1959/1990).
31. *Wonder Woman* #1 (1987); *Wonder Woman: Earth One* (2016).
32. Jung (1959/1990), p. 131.
33. Jung (1959/1990), p. 136.
34. *Wonder Woman* #1 (1987).
35. Jung (1959/1990), p. 164.
36. Campbell (1949/2008).

CHAPTER SEVEN

The Heroine and the Hero's Journey

LAURA VECCHIOLLA

*"Now is the plan of the Goddesses clear, Diana! You
were born into this world to be the most honored among all
Amazons!"*
—Menalippe, chief priestess of the Amazons[1]

*"We have not even to risk the adventure alone;
for the heroes of all time have gone before us;
the labyrinth is thoroughly known; we have
only to follow the thread of the hero's path."*
—mythologist Joseph Campbell[2]

Ancient cultures revered their heroes, passing on tales of
legendary figures and their conquests for generations.
Great hero myths of Sargon and Gilgamesh were spread in
ancient Babylonia as early as 2300 BCE.[3] Modern culture still
adores the hero story, as evidenced by blockbuster book and
movie ticket sales. The staying power of these heroes begs the

question: What about heroes and their stories has enchanted humankind for thousands of years?

The Hero Archetype

Myths that remain enthralling throughout generations often feature a great hero. But what makes a hero *a hero*? To understand Wonder Woman as a mythological hero, her origin is of great importance. With a character as long beloved as Wonder Woman, this story has been retold and reimagined, producing numerous renderings of the Wonder Woman character.[4] This is common practice with great myths. Wonder Woman remains, at her core, a true hero in every incarnation.

In 1941, psychologist William Moulton Marston and artist Harry G. Peter first introduced the world to Wonder Woman, a heroine whose story still captures people's imaginations.[5] In the midst of World War II, Wonder Woman embodied the same captivating attributes as the many heroes before her—a sense of duty, justice, and the herculean ability to overcome boundless obstacles. In examining the mythos of Wonder Woman, we can see that she shares a great deal in common with the heroes who have come before her. This becomes clear by examining her Hero's Journey.

Austrian psychoanalyst Otto Rank was one of the first to study the psychological themes in hero myths in order to find their commonalities and prevalent motifs. Rank described the uniformity in the hero myth sagas by using the metaphor of a skeleton, stating that all human skeletons, although each has its minor idiosyncrasies, is generally the same. Yet it is capable of housing figures that outwardly look vastly different from one another.[6]

Rank also summarized patterns of the hero's origin that comprise a "skeletal structure" of the hero's birth and upbringing. It is not uncommon for the time preceding the hero's birth to be riddled with strife, such as prolonged barrenness of the mother, rape or secret intercourse, or foreboding surrounding the pregnancy.[7] The time before the birth of Princess Diana, as depicted in George Pérez's tenure as writer of the *Wonder Woman* series, was indeed a time of violence and discord. The world had been ravaged by violence against women and Diana's own mother was herself a victim of man's brutality. Queen Hippolyta endured imprisonment and rape by the immoral demigod Heracles before eventually defeating his army and escaping to Paradise Island.[8] Rank also wrote that the relationships between the young hero and his parents are impaired, or even hostile. The hero's plight often requires him to sever ties with the parental figures or to leave his home. The hero moves out into the world to have adventures and then returns home to claim his fortune.[9] While Wonder Woman's relationship with her mother is generally depicted as loving and supportive, tension and doubt arise in their relationship when Princess Diana expresses her desire to leave Paradise Island. In a heated argument, Hippolyta forbids Diana to enter the tournament that will decide which Amazon will journey to America, forcing Diana to deceive her mother by disguising herself in order to enter and eventually win the tournament.[10] Rank dedicated himself primarily to exploring the origin of a hero and focused little on the conflict and conquest the hero endured. Developing a deeper understanding of Wonder Woman's story and its ongoing allure may require us to explore Joseph Campbell's notion of the monomyth.

First described in 1949 by Joseph Campbell, the Hero's Journey, or *monomyth*, is the universal structure of the hero and his quest story that is found in myths from various time periods and regions.[11] All heroes, despite the particulars of their stories, follow the same path—a path paved with anguish and adversity that inevitably leads to conquest and victory. Humanity feels connected to these stories on a much deeper level than simple entertainment. We crave stories that re-create our own experience of triumph over tragedy. The longevity of Wonder Woman's story offers substantiation of the deep connection we feel to her and to the ways in which her adventures mirror the experience of being human.

The Hero's Journey

Joseph Campbell chronicled the hero myth across the span of ancient and classic mythologies in order to understand the stages that lead to the hero's transformation from ordinary man to time-honored hero. In his 1949 book *The Hero with a Thousand Faces*, Campbell identified and described the universal narrative of the Hero's Journey that he termed the *monomyth*. He, like Rank, maintained that the hero and his journey are more than mere storytelling and entertainment—they form an archetypal narrative, psychologically embedded in the whole of humanity.[12]

The Hero's Journey is one of development and passage. The hero returns from his quest reborn, with new insight and knowledge. As such, the story unfolds as a primal rite-of-passage narrative: departure, initiation, and return.[13]

Departure

Departure first begins with the *call to adventure*—a cosmic request for the hero to depart from the ordinary world and venture into the unknown. According to Campbell, the hero can be summoned to embark on the journey in several ways. He can stumble upon the call seemingly by chance, leave of his own volition, or be beckoned by a herald.[14] The "stumbling into adventure" scenario depicts the hero's introduction to a strange and unfamiliar world by what appears to be an accident or blunder. In the story of Wonder Woman, Steve Trevor's crash landing on Themyscira represents the mishap that initiates Diana's journey.[15] What seems like a mistake to the hero is, in fact, fated to happen. Inspired by psychoanalytic theory, Campbell argued that the blunder symbolizes the suppression of desire and conflict; one's calling cannot be avoided and eventually one must confront destiny.[16] The hero's departure for his (or her, in this case) journey can also be motivated by personal volition or by a stirring within the hero and deep dissatisfaction with the world, which causes the hero to venture out into the unknown. Wonder Woman feels moved to fight injustice from the very beginning. Bestowed with great powers by the gods of Olympus, Diana openly accepts her fate.[17] For some heroes, it may take a while to become aware of or accept their destiny. Not so for Diana. Pérez depicted her as a character who, even as a young child, is eager to wield the sword and fight for those she loves. She once describes the stirring inside her to Steve Trevor, admitting, "As long as I can remember I've had dreams of being the one who reunites Themyscira with the outside world."[18] This inner desire, which moves Diana to action, is another form of the call. Campbell also wrote that a Hero's Journey can be initiated by the appearance of a herald.[19] The herald appears and asks the hero to leave the familiarity of the known world immediately and venture out into the unfamiliar. The statue of the goddess Athena comes to life to confirm Diana's calling, as she declares, "Aye, Diana! And purpose you shall have! The time has come!"[20]

The hero then responds to the call with a *refusal of the call*. In this next step in Campbell's monomyth, the hero denies the call to adventure.[21] At this point in the journey, the hero may feel unprepared for his destiny or may be convinced of his unsuitability for such a strenuous excursion. However, a refusal does not ensure failure or stagnation. This step in the journey is followed by the occasion of a divinely bestowed "revelation" that serves to ready the hero.[22] Although Diana herself does not show any indication of hesitation, she is thwarted temporarily by her mother, who prohibits her from leaving Paradise Island.[23] In this myth it seems as if her mother needs the experience of a revelation before the heroic journey can begin. Upon seeing her daughter's unparalleled tournament skills, Hippolyta finally fully accepts her daughter's destiny.[24]

Upon accepting the call, the hero then receives *supernatural aid*, the part of the journey when the hero has a transformative encounter with a protective figure.[25] This character provides supernatural aid that will assist the hero in defeating evil. Aid can come in the form of amulets or talismans that the hero will carry or wise words of counsel. In Wonder Woman's case, aid is bestowed in the form of her iconic bracelets and magical lasso.[26]

Having been prepared with the aid and the guidance of a protective figure, the hero moves on to the next step of the journey—*crossing the threshold* into the epic adventure.[27] The hero ventures forth into a destined journey until he or she reaches the threshold of the unknown world. For the first time, Wonder Woman pilots her invisible jet, through the veil between Themyscira and the outside world, to enter into a new and strange world.[28] Despite the danger and mystery that lie ahead, the hero crosses into the unknown and begins the final step of the departure stage—confronting the *belly of the whale*, the utter abyss of the unknown.[29] When Wonder Woman enters our world, she is immediately confronted with the dark and chaotic nature of an unknown world—America. She witnesses gender inequality when she encounters a young girl who is not allowed to play with her male counterparts.[30] In other renditions of her story, she becomes quickly exploited by the media—both scenarios truly highlight how very different she is in her new home.[31] In this stage, the hero must confront her despair and fear in order to be reborn into a hero; this is her metamorphosis.[32]

Initiation

The move into the *initiation* phase begins with the road of trials.[33] Emerging from the darkness of the belly of the whale, the hero is faced with a succession of tests. At this point, the amulets or aid given by the supernatural protective figure come into service and significantly benefit the hero in his encounters. There are countless stories that depict Wonder Woman's road of trials and the many enemies she must defeat, villains such as fierce and sadistic Ares, cunning Circe, and deadly Cheetah.[34] Campbell identified this as the phase of the journey that is most beloved by the audience.[35] This tends to be the most action-packed stage in the story, but more than this, the road of trials represents an intensifying symbolic representation of defeating one's own inner conflict to be reborn anew. When we see Diana defeating a villain, on some level we are watching ourselves overcome our own inner conflicts.

When all barriers are overcome, the hero encounters the next two steps of the journey—*meeting with the goddess* and *woman as the temptress*. These two steps in Campbell's monomyth are the most obviously male-centered, as they focus exclusively on male heroes. This creates some difficulty in modern-day applications of his theory. First, in meeting with the goddess, the hero is rewarded with a blessing of love and unity, joining with a pure and gentle lover who represents the divine feminine qualities our hero presumably lacks—creating a perfect union that serves to strengthen the hero. The temptress then enters the plot to spoil this perfect love by diverting the hero from

THE HEROINE'S JOURNEY

Therapist Maureen Murdock expressed frustration that Campbell's *monomyth* (one heroic myth) excluded female heroes.[36] The monomyth was man's journey, and Murdock wanted to know about woman's journey. She saw the journey of the heroine as one in which women endeavor to "fully embrace their feminine nature, learning how to value themselves as women and to heal the deep wound of the feminine."[37] Wonder Woman's saga corresponds with Campbell's monomyth, but in many ways the Heroine's Journey can provide insight into Diana's uniqueness as a *woman* warrior—highlighting the aspects of her experience that differ from those of her male counterparts. Though partially derived from the structure of the Hero's Journey, the language of the heroine's journey is specific to the experience of women. Murdock outlined the journey as occurring in a series of stages.[38]

- The heroine separates from the feminine. This is the onset of her adventure, and to begin she must reject her traditional feminine roles.
- The heroine identifies and adopts traditional masculine qualities as a means of preparing herself for the imminent quest.

his path.[39] If we examine these stages with gender neutralized, we can see that, in many variations, Diana does find her "other half." Traditionally, the union is with Steve Trevor, a gruff soldier who helps Diana navigate the strange ways of human beings. In some atypical depictions, she falls in love with Superman, who mirrors the godlike qualities of Diana.[40] In

- Similar to Campbell's steps, the heroine must complete her road of trials before receiving her ultimate boon.
- She receives the boon. However, in Murdock's journey, the rejection of the feminine renders it an illusory and unfulfilling reward.
- The heroine undergoes a spiritual crisis and figurative death.
- She begins her initiation stage and develops a deep understanding that to split the feminine and masculine is toxic and limiting.
- She yearns to reconnect to her once-rejected feminine side.
- Mother and daughter reunite.
- Healing begins and allows the masculine and feminine to reconcile and coexist.
- At the end of her journey, she returns wholly integrated and at peace.

Murdock offered her construct not as an alternative to Campbell's monomyth, but rather as a companion to it, to depict the experiences of women more accurately.

both cases, Diana's love interest is generally depicted as complementary to her own qualities. However, this love can never last, and the two must be separated for the hero to continue the journey. Many conflicts interrupt the tranquility of Wonder Woman's relationships—usually it's yet another bad guy getting in the way.

Fueled by the experience of love and loss, the hero reaches the next stage, *atonement with the father*. Campbell identified this as the process by which the hero learns to become one with all he is—good and bad, strong and weak.[41] This is often illustrated as yet another "trial," but this battle takes place internally within the hero's psyche. There are times in Wonder Woman's saga when she doubts herself, especially when reflecting on her ability to embody both an Amazon and a hero for humankind. In Pérez's version of the Wonder Woman origin story, Diana questions herself and confides in a friend, asking, "Will I leave man's world having taught people nothing more than my name?"[42] She pities the weakness in humans while at the same time valuing their humanity; it is a crisis of paradox. Yet, it is only through resolving this crisis that the hero reaches the next stage—*apotheosis*. This is the stage in which the hero truly becomes a hero.[43] With divine understanding and a transcendent self-awareness, the hero fully integrates all aspects of himself, even seemingly opposing characteristics.[44] For Diana, to reconcile her love and disdain for humankind is the ultimate atonement. When she is able to do so, she proclaims to the formidable god Hermes, "I love everyone . . . [but] you cannot make anyone love you until you love yourself."[45] These wise and apotheotic words reflect Wonder Woman's truly heroic nature.

The final stage of the initiation culminates in the hero receiving the *ultimate boon*. The quest officially ends with the hero overcoming all obstacles and experiencing a personal transformation.[46] The reward for the completion of such an endeavor may be a physical treasure or an exalted title that reflects the hero's worth. After falling in battle, Diana is welcomed by Athena to Olympus. There, as recompense for her "bold deeds and wise teachings," Diana is given her boon in the form of the title *goddess of truth*.[47]

Return

The third phase of the Hero's Journey entails the hero's return, beginning with a *refusal to return*, where the hero again resists change.[48] For Wonder Woman, this means a return to Themyscira.[49] After the experience of victory and transformation, it can be difficult to return to the ordinary world from whence the hero came. (To Diana, Themyscira is the ordinary world, no matter how extraordinary outsiders might consider it to be.) In the DC Animated Universe, Wonder Woman declines to leave man's world after her first conquest, choosing instead to remain with the Justice League. It is not until she watches a mother and daughter embrace that she accepts her need to return home.[50]

The hero is then aided in his return through the next two steps of the monomyth: the *magic flight* and the *rescue from without*. The magic flight phase of the journey is generally depicted as the hero's need to flee back to his home, while the rescue from without may involve the hero requiring help to find his way home and to reenter the ordinary world.[51] Unbeknownst to her, Diana's return is heavily aided. She approaches Themyscira's shores mortally wounded after defeating Ares. She is brought to these waters by her fellow Amazons, and Zeus and Poseidon infuse the water with healing powers that give Diana the strength to return home.[52]

In the next stage, the *crossing of the return threshold*, the hero again faces a threshold into a new phase of existence.[53] Unlike the unknown world that the hero previously faced, he now faces a new and different challenge: The hero must find a way to return back as a new and transformed person. In Diana's case, she can no longer return to Themyscira as the same woman she was when she departed. She is now intrinsically tied to the human world, forever changed by it. She does not return simply as a princess, but as an ambassador.[54]

Returned, the hero now possesses knowledge and experience that sets him apart from the everyday world. He is knowledgeable of his world and the adventure world, making him a *master of two worlds*.[55] This phase demonstrates that the hero did not need to choose between a life in two worlds, as he can now move freely between the two. Equipped with this mastery, the hero has reached the final stage of the journey: the *freedom to live*.[56] Accomplishing these final stages is what permits Wonder Woman to be the enduring hero audiences have adored for over seventy-five years. Diana, princess of the Amazons, flies from Themyscira to America, where she is our Wonder Woman. She moves between the two worlds with ease and strength and she is an inseparable part of both.

The Eternal Hero

The story of Diana, the princess and the warrior—the Wonder Woman—has permeated modern culture since 1941.[57] It is through the great stories of heroes like Wonder Woman that we learn to ready ourselves for our own perilous life journeys. She, like all heroes before her, has carved a path ahead of us, a path that allows us to venture more bravely into the unknown, defeat our enemies within and without, and return to our communities improved and impassioned.

Comic Book References

All Star Comics #8 (1941). "Introducing Wonder Woman." Script: W. M. Marston. Art: H. G. Peter.

Justice League #12 (2012). "Rescue from Within." Script: G. Johns. Art: J. Lee.

Sensation Comics #2 (1942). "Wonder Woman Comes to America." Script: W. M. Marston. Art: H. G. Peter.

Sensation Comics #6 (1942). "Summons to Paradise Island." Script: W. M. Marston. Art: H. G. Peter.

Wonder Woman #1 (1987). "The Princess and the Power." Script: G. Pérez & G. Potter. Art: G. Pérez.

Wonder Woman #2 (1987). "A Fire in the Sky." Script: G. Pérez & G. Potter. Art: G. Pérez.

Wonder Woman #7 (1987). "Rebirth." Script: L. Wein. Art: G. Pérez.
Wonder Woman #9 (1987). "Blood of the Cheetah." Script: L. Wein. Art: G. Pérez.
Wonder Woman #19 (1988). "The Witch on the Island." Script/Art: G. Pérez.
Wonder Woman #128 (1997). "Shell Game." Script/Art: J. Byrne.
Wonder Woman #10 (2012). "Vows." Script: B. Azzarello. Art: Kano & T. Akins.

Other References

Campbell, J. (1949/1968). *The hero with a thousand faces.* Princeton, NJ: Bollingen.
Campbell, J., with Bill Moyers (1991). *The power of myth.* New York, NY: Anchor.
Murdock, M. (1990). *The heroine's journey: Woman's quest for wholeness.* Boston, MA: Shambala.
Preister, B. J. (2012, April 30). *The heroine's journey: How Campbell's model doesn't fit.* Fangirl Blog: http://fangirlblog.com/2012/04/the-heroines-journey-how-campbells-model-doesnt-fit/.
Rank, O. (1959). *The myth and the birth of the hero, and other writings.* New York, NY: Vintage.

Notes

1. *Wonder Woman* #2 (1987).
2. Campbell (1949/1968), p. 25.
3. Rank (1959).
4. *All Star Comics* #8 (1941); *Wonder Woman* #1 (1987).
5. *All Star Comics* #8 (1941).
6. Rank (1959), p. 65.
7. Rank (1959).
8. *Wonder Woman* #1 (1987).
9. Rank (1959).
10. *All Star Comics* #8 (1941); *Wonder Woman* #1 (1987).
11. Campbell (1949/1968).
12. Campbell (1991).
13. Campbell (1949/1968).
14. Campbell (1949/1968).
15. *All Star Comics* #8 (1941); *Wonder Woman* #1 (1987).
16. Campbell (1949/1968).
17. *All Star Comics* #8 (1941); *Wonder Woman* #1 (1987).
18. *Wonder Woman* (2009 animated motion picture).
19. Campbell (1949/1968).
20. *Wonder Woman* #1 (1987).
21. Campbell (1949/1968).
22. Campbell (1949/1968).
23. *All Star Comics* #8 (1941); *Wonder Woman* #1 (1987).
24. *All Star Comics* #8 (1941; *Wonder Woman* #1 (1987).
25. Campbell (1949/1968).
26. *Wonder Woman* (2009 animated motion pictured).
27. Campbell (1949/1968).
28. Campbell (1949/1968), p. 82.
29. Campbell (1949/1968).

30. *Wonder Woman* (2009 animated motion picture).
31. *Sensation Comics* #2 (1942); *Wonder Woman* #9 (1987).
32. Campbell (1949/1968).
33. Campbell (1949/1968).
34. *Wonder Woman* #9 (1987); *Wonder Woman* #19 (1988).
35. Campbell (1949/1968).
36. Murdock (1990); Preister (2012).
37. Murdock (1990), p. 3.
38. Murdock (1990).
39. Campbell (1949/1968).
40. *Justice League* #12 (2012).
41. Campbell (1949/1968).
42. *Wonder Woman* #9 (1987).
43. Campbell (1949/1968).
44. Campbell (1949/1968).
45. *Wonder Woman* #10 (2012).
46. Campbell (1949/1968).
47. *Wonder Woman* #128 (1997).
48. Campbell (1949/1968).
49. *Sensation Comics* #6 (1942).
50. *Justice League* episode 1-10, "Paradise Lost," part 1 (January 21, 2002).
51. Campbell (1949/1968).
52. *Wonder Woman* #7 (1987).
53. Campbell (1949/1968).
54. *Wonder Woman* (2009 animated motion picture).
55. Campbell (1949/1968).
56. Campbell (1949/1968).
57. *All Star Comics* #8 (1941).

Wisdom and Knowledge

M A R A   W O O D

As one of the psychological virtues identified by positive psychologists, *wisdom and knowledge* involves the acquisition and use of knowledge to live a good life.[1] It is composed of these strengths: creativity, curiosity, open-mindedness, love of learning, and perspective. This virtue permeates Woman Woman stories both on the comic book page and in the creator's life. William Moulton Marston was a man of knowledge who sought to apply that knowledge to the world. Trained by Hugo Münsterberg, the founder of forensic psychology and applied psychology, Marston developed a psychological approach based on theory and research.[2]

Marston's contributions to psychology demonstrate his possession of the strengths associated with the virtue of wisdom and knowledge: curiosity, creativity, love of learning, open-mindedness, and perspective. For example, his *curiosity* was activated by the desire to know when a person was lying. He approached the problem by incorporating physical measures[3] and saw new ways in which his work could be used. Even though the systolic blood pressure measure and the lie detector test were not widely accepted as accurate,[4] that didn't stop Marston. He turned his focus to film and its psychological value.[5] Curiosity is significantly linked with life satisfaction and happiness and is one of the few "cognitive" strengths associated with life satisfaction.[6]

Marston was adaptable and *creative,* and he understood the potential for the use of psychology in popular culture. His work on films attempted to determine what viewers were interested in watching.[7] Marston later saw comics as vehicle for teaching children provided that they contained lessons worth sharing.[8] Wonder Woman, Marston's lasting contribution to comics, was a creative way to expose young readers to Marston's ideal woman.[9] He also used his knowledge of psychology to offer insight into male preferences for women. Rather than survey men's reactions to women, he used his systolic blood pressure tool to determine how men physically reacted to different women.[10]

Marston's *love of learning,* evidenced by his career in academia and his contributions to the field of psychology, was shared by the two women in his life: Elizabeth "Betty" Marston and Olive "Dotsie" Byrne. Marston's wife Betty held multiple degrees and served as an editor for *Encyclopedia Britannica.*[11] (For more on Elizabeth Holloway Marston's early life, education, and career in her own words, see chapter 4, "The Tale of a Manx Cat: A Memoir from the Woman who Gave Us Wonder.") Olive was a research assistant and journalist who became a member of the family. Though she primarily took care of the children, Olive continued to engage in learning. She contributed articles to *Family Circle* magazine,[12] and she, along with Betty, provided assistance on Marston's work.[13]

The character strength of *open-mindedness* is evident in Wonder Woman's journey to America. Though from a secluded culture, she readily engages with the new culture.[14] Diana learns a new language, a different way to dress, and the concerns of the larger world.[15] Instead of retreating to her familiar way of life, she seeks to understand how her new world operates and what she can do to aid it.[16] Marston felt bothered by limited, narrow-minded perspectives in psychology and took an open-minded view of psychology and human lifestyles.[17]

Perspective encompasses a person's ability to coordinate information and deliberately use it to improve a person's well-being.[18] It can be manifested in a person's ability to offer sage advice after taking stock of a situation. This strength was incorporated into Jung's archetype of the Sage, a universal feature across cultures.[19] The role of the Sage who embodies perspective is found in Athena, who in her wisdom guides Wonder Woman by giving her the eyes of a goddess.[20]

The strengths of wisdom and knowledge created the foundation for Wonder Woman. Through careful consideration, Marston used his experience and knowledge to create a character and world that could portray the same virtue he possessed. The result was a hero and a cast of characters that place value on understanding the world at large.

Comic Book References

Sensation Comics #1 (1942). "Wonder Woman Comes to America." Script: W. M. Marston. Art: H. G. Peter.

Wonder Woman #1 (1942). "The Origin of Wonder Woman." Script: W. M. Marston. Art: H. G. Peter.

Wonder Woman #98 (1959). "The Million-Dollar Penny." Script: R. Kanigher. Art: R. Andru & M. Esposito.

Wonder Woman #3 (1987). "Deadly Arrival." Script: G. Pérez & L. Wein. Art: G. Pérez & B. Patterson.

Wonder Woman #217 (2005). "The Bronze Doors, Conclusion." Script: G. Rucka. Art: R. Morales, M. Blair, & M. Propst.

Wonder Woman #4 (2016). "Year One, Part Two." Script: G. Rucka. Art: N. Scott.

Wonder Woman #6 (2016). "Year One, Part Three." Script: G. Rucka. Art: N. Scott.

Other References

Bunn, G. C. (2012). *The truth machine: A social history of the lie detector.* Baltimore, MD: Johns Hopkins University Press.

Committee to Review the Scientific Evidence on the Polygraph (2003). *The polygraph and lie detection.* Washington, DC: National Academic Press.

Daniels, L. (2000). *Wonder Woman: The complete history.* San Francisco, CA: Chronicle.

Davidson, T. (2015). *Profile: Elizabeth Holloway Marston.* Feminist Voices: http://www.feministvoices.com/elizabeth-holloway-marston/.

Kaczmarek, L. D., Kashdan, T. B., Kleiman, E. M., Baczkowski, B., Enko, J., Siebers, A., Szäefer, A., Król, M., & Baran, B. (2013). Who self-initiates gratitude interventions in daily life? An examination of intentions, curiosity, depressive symptoms, and life satisfaction. *Personality & Individual Differences, 55*(7), 805–810.

Kawamoto, T., Ura, M., & Hiraki, K. (2017). Curious people are less affected by social rejection. *Personality & Individual Differences, 105,* 264–267.

Lamb, M. (2001). *Who was Wonder Woman? Long-ago LAW alumna was the muse who gave us a superheroine.* Boston, MA: Boston University.

Marston, W. M. (1917). Systolic blood pressure symptoms of deception. *Journal of Experimental Psychology, 2*(2), 117–163.

Marston, W. M. (1928). Emotions of normal people. New York, NY: Harcourt, Brace.

Marston, W. M. (1947). Lie detection's bodily basis and test procedures. In P. L. Harriman (Ed.), *Encyclopedia of psychology* (pp. 354–363). New York, NY: Philosophical Library.

Olenina, A. (2015). The doubly wired spectator: Marston's theory of emotions and psychophysiological research on cinematic pleasure in the 1920s. *Film History, 27*(1), 29–57.

Park, N., Peterson, C., & Seligman, M. E. P. (2004). Strengths of character and well-being. *Journal of Social & Clinical Psychology, 23*(5), 603–619.

Peterson, C., & Seligman, M. E. P. (2004). *Character strengths and virtues: A handbook and classification.* Washington, DC: American Psychological Association.

Pitkin, W. B., & Marston, W. M. (1930). *The art of sound pictures.* New York, NY: Appleton.

Proctor, C., Maltby, J., & Linley, P. A. (2011). Strengths use as a predictor of well-being and health-related quality of life. *Journal of Happiness Studies, 12,* 152–169.

Richard, O. (1940, October 25). Don't laugh at the comics. *Family Circle,* pp. 10–11, 22.

Richard, O. (1944, August 14). Our women are our future. *Family Circle,* pp. 14–17, 19.

Notes

1. Park, Peterson, & Seligman (2004); Peterson & Seligman (2004).
2. Daniels (2000).
3. Marston (1917, 1947).
4. Bunn (2012); Committee to Review the Scientific Evidence on the Polygraph (2003).
5. Pitkin & Marston (1930).
6. Kaczmarek et al. (2013); Kawamoto et al. (2017); Proctor et al. (2011).
7. Olenina (2015).
8. Richard (1940).
9. Daniels (2000).
10. Daniels (2000).

11. Davidson (2015); Lamb (2001).
12. e.g., Byrne writing as Richard (1940, 1944).
13. Personal communication with Pete Marston (2016).
14. *Wonder Woman* #3 (1987).
15. *Sensation Comics* #1 (1942); *Wonder Woman* #3 (1987).
16. *Wonder Woman* #1 (1942); *Wonder Woman* #98 (1959); *Wonder Woman* #4 (2016); *Wonder Woman* #6 (2016).
17. Marston (1928).
18. Peterson & Seligman (2004).
19. Peterson & Seligman (2004).
20. *Wonder Woman* #217 (2005).

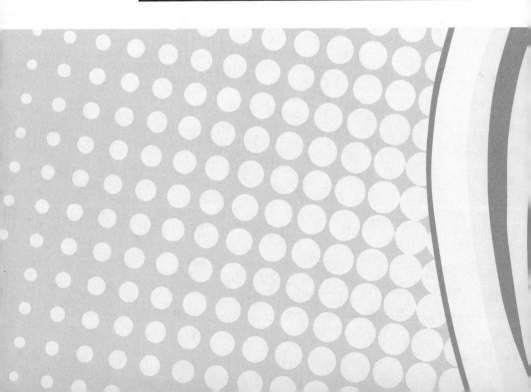

HEROISM DOES NOT DEPEND ON MEMBERSHIP IN A GENDER AND NEITHER SHOULD PSYCHOLOGICAL SCIENCE, AND YET BOTH HEROIC FICTION AND PSYCHOLOGY HAVE OFTEN FALLEN SHORT IN HOW THEY LOOK AT WOMEN.

PART III

WOMAN'S WORLD

CHAPTER EIGHT

A Mother's Magic: Parenting Issues in Paradise

MIKE MADRID AND REBECCA M. LANGLEY

"I know now that you are not just my daughter—you are a child of the world!"
—Hippolyta[1]

"Thus, the mother-child relationship is paradoxical and, in a sense, tragic. It requires the most intense love on the mother's side, and yet this very love must help the child to grow away from the mother, and to become fully independent."
—psychologist Erich Fromm[2]

It's often said that the bond between a mother and her child is one of the strongest in life. Raised by a loving mother, the Amazon queen Hippolyta,[3] Diana grows to adulthood with very secure attachment to her and to many other supportive mother figures on Paradise Island until war leads her away.[4]

War separates many families by means both voluntarily (such as when soldiers enlist on their own or when Diana makes a great sacrifice to fight against war itself) and involuntarily (such as when family members get drafted or many families' homes get bombed), and such separation and war-related chaos can alter family dynamics.

After World War II, changes to families produced wide-ranging results among youth that included a post-war increase in juvenile delinquency, psychological troubles, and altered relationships.[5] In the United States, Dr. Fredric Wertham and others blamed comic books for those changes (see chapter 3, "Marston, Wertham, and the Psychological Potential of Comic Books"), but in Europe, research on these changes led to the development of *attachment theory*, a view on the ways in which early child/caregiver bonds influence behavioral and emotional development throughout life. Researchers in this area assess different *attachment styles*, patterns of how children feel connected to their caregivers. The *secure* attachment style, in which separation can cause some distress but without impairing the individual's ability to trust and remain connected, is present in the healthiest parent–child relationships.[6] Securely attached children will explore their environment with enthusiasm, checking back with the parental figure often while exploring but showing initiative and freedom of movement while under the watchful eye of the attachment figure[7]—as Diana demonstrates even in adulthood once she discovers that she can return to Paradise Island after all.[8] Attachment style has been found to predict functioning in many areas, notably the ability to develop healthy relationships throughout life.

Attachment

The bond between Diana and her mother is especially close and can be attributed to the fact that, as originally depicted, Hippolyta shapes her daughter from clay with her own hands without the presence of a father.[9] Clearly, Diana has a very secure attachment to Hippolyta, which allows her the freedom and security to explore her environment and develop the many skills she acquires as the Amazon princess that she will use when she becomes Wonder Woman. Additionally, she was taught and developed a strong moral center that prompts her sense of duty to go out into the world, forfeit her immortality, and try to make the world outside of Paradise Island a better place.

Although mothers are a relative rarity in the superhero genre, they are a fundamental element in Wonder Woman's mythology. As mother to the Amazons, the goddess Aphrodite creates the race of immortal and invincible women to be her weapons against the forces of war and aggression.[10] This sacred mission entrusted to the Amazons shapes Diana, whose heroism appears to come from a high level of moral development. Kohlberg's studies on moral development in children and adults indicate three main stages of moral development: *pre-conventional* (early childhood, before learning conventional morality), *conventional* (later childhood into adulthood, gaining and continuing acceptance of moral conventions), and *post-conventional* (later if at all, following self-defined, more complex ethical principles).[11] For many superheroes, the focus is on the law and order morality of the conventional stage, in which the focus is primarily on obeying authority and following rules or laws with minimal attention to the overall ethics driving the hero or the villain. This view is considered more advanced than the pre-conventional stage, in which the primary focus is on either avoiding punishment or acting only to gain a reward.

This was especially prevalent in the period when Wonder Woman was originally written, before conflicted superheroes such as Spider-Man would see ethical gray areas that indicate higher levels of moral development.[12] In the post-conventional stage, the primary focus is on promoting the general welfare of others by fulfilling the so-called social contract of the "greatest good for the greatest number of people" or by stressing even higher moral functioning of the service of justice that is based on universal ethical principles—a level that, though influenced by the values with which she has been raised, is self-defined and distinguishes her from those who have influenced her.[13] This ties in with the Amazon belief that love can be a force to stop war and aggression, which Hippolyta instills in her daughter.[14]

Wonder Woman, more than most superheroes, works from post-conventional moral development.[15] She has powers that surpass those of most other superheroes, and her cultural upbringing focusing on the greater good drives her decision to leave Paradise Island. A vital lesson that Wonder Woman also learns from her mother is the importance of redemption. Using Amazon principles, Wonder Woman and her mother are able to reform the murderous Nazi agent Paula Von Gunther,[16] turning her from archenemy to ally. Hippolyta's wisdom helps Wonder Woman employ mercy in her mission in "Man's World,"[17] setting her apart from the male heroes who dispense judgment on evildoers in a more uncompromising style.

Finding a Place in the World

Though life in Hippolyta's kingdom is idyllic, on a certain level Diana must feel confined there while growing up. Among all the Amazons, she is the only one who has never experienced the world beyond the shores of Paradise Island because she is the only one whose life has begun on the island.[18] Within the stages of psychosocial development put forth by Erik Erikson, the idea of crises in each developmental stage drives people toward a life of fulfillment and meaning or into pathology and emptiness.[19] The foundations of an individual's morality appear to be laid down during the third of these stages. Developing a sense of trust during infancy (in the *basic trust vs. mistrust* crisis) and doing things for oneself between ages two and four (in the *autonomy vs. shame and doubt* stage) makes it easier for individuals to achieve the healthier account around the time many start school (ages four to six, the *initiative vs. guilt* stage): *initiative*, asserting power over the world around the child instead of *guilt,* preoccupation with a sense that such an assertion is morally wrong.[20] Because young Diana trusts her mother to look out for her while letting her explore and because Hippolyta encourages her to develop autonomy, Diana more readily develops a sense of initiative during the time when she is learning moral values.

The Amazons' immortality alters the meaning of several of the life stages Erikson refers to, and the struggles with what to do with oneself loom possibly even larger when one faces the endless passage of time. Hippolyta instructs Diana in all the arts, sciences, and languages of the ancient and modern worlds while also grooming her to become the ruler of the Amazons.[21] But as the heir apparent to a deathless queen, Diana seems unlikely ever to put much of this knowledge to use.[22] Ultimately, the question becomes: Does Diana want to live forever without meaning or forgo immortality and have generativity by joining the mortal world and making it a better place? She may feel that her life has no significance outside the roles placed upon her by her very powerful mother. This is described by Erikson as the crisis that "mortals" reach in midlife (in the *generativity vs. stagnation* stage) as they look for a reason to care about the larger world and make an impact on it. It would seem that living forever would give a person time to examine what she or he would want to be.

Submission versus Independence

The Amazons believe in loving submission, an unquestioning surrender to authority (*authoritarian obedience*).[23] As Diana's creator, queen, and military commander, Hippolyta controls almost every aspect of her daughter's life. In Erikson's theory of psychosocial development, Diana is struggling with the adolescent crisis of *identity vs. role confusion*. Her role is clear, perhaps, but she seems to have no self-chosen identity of her own as originally written, instead simply being the daughter of Hippolyta and princess of the Amazons, much as royals who are bound by their bloodline and duty still exist today and sometimes also choose to alter or abandon their duty altogether.

When Aphrodite commands Hippolyta to have her mightiest Amazon return Steve to Man's World and remain there to fight for peace and the rights of womankind, Diana sees this as her true purpose in life, defying her mother to define herself as a unique and separate human being.[24] Diana's personal dilemma of sacred duty to save the world[25] versus obedience to her mother would suggest that she experiences the psychosocial crisis of early adulthood called *intimacy vs. isolation*: the struggle to find love and be loved in an adult relationship. These issues could also suggest use of the Freudian defense mechanism *sublimation*, which is the act of taking a less acceptable urge or desire and transforming it into a socially acceptable behavior or activity.[26] Sublimation is suggested to be healthier and more mature than the defense mechanism displacement, which is the act of transferring emotions or desires deemed unacceptable into a new objective

Additionally, there is the issue of the isolation of being on Paradise Island, limiting opportunities to develop new intimate relationships. Ultimately, Diana's feelings of duty and love prove to be stronger than her obligation to obey her mother; this could indicate both the psychosocial crisis of early adulthood (*intimacy vs. isolation*) and the crisis of middle adulthood (*generativity vs. stagnation*).[27]

Parenting on Paradise Island

Psychologist Diana Baumrind developed a theory of parenting styles that in many ways corresponds with attachment styles.[28] Secure children more often have *authoritative* parents, those who exert authority over their children, but all those parents consider each child's wishes, give explanations for rules and expectations, and weigh and, when appropriate, accept each child's input.[29] Other parenting styles tend to produce a variety of insecure patterns of attachment to the parents. *Authoritarian* parents expect high levels of unquestioning obedience, are strict, focus on punishment rather than rewards, rarely explain rules and expectations, and give children little say in the home. The goddess Aphrodite stipulates that her daughters, the Amazons, must not submit to a man's dominance. After Hippolyta violates this rule, authoritarian parent Aphrodite's punishment is to send the Amazons to Paradise Island to live out their immortal lives isolated from the world they were created to save.[30] She even makes the Amazons continue to wear the shackles their captors previously enslaved them with as eternal reminders of the consequences of breaking one of their mother's rules.[31] The parenting style of Hippolyta seemingly goes back and forth between authoritarian and authoritative, although always with a loving undertone that can often be seen in authoritative parents and is not apparent in authoritarians.[32] Authoritative parenting is more consistently the case in Wonder Woman's early adventures, when Hippolyta offers her daughter loving support and encouragement as Diana develops into a mature, independent hero.[33] In later years the relationship between Hippolyta and her daughter is portrayed as more controlling and manipulative. This has an infantilizing effect on Wonder Woman, at which point Hippolyta varies between authoritative and authoritarian parenting.[34]

Both authoritarian and authoritative parents expect much from their children, but they differ in how much freedom and respect they show their children, as opposed to *permissive parents,* who expect little from their children, let them largely have and do what they want, and often act less like a parent and more like a friend to their children, or *uninvolved* or *neglectful* parents, who allow their children freedom as a consequence of simply not being involved with them.[35] Throughout most of her history, Wonder Woman is depicted as having no father, having been brought to life from clay, but in the "New 52" version of her history, Diana is actually the daughter of Zeus, who has been an uninvolved, neglectful parent.[36] Because she has one heavily involved parent and grows up unaware of Zeus's negligence, Diana shows secure attachment to her mother and should have the ability to develop stable, secure relationships in other areas of life. How a child's attachment correlates with future relationships appears to be shaped largely by the child's relationship with his or her primary caregiver—in this case Diana's mother.

As Wonder Woman, Diana uses her mother's lessons on equality and female empowerment to change the lives of the oppressed women of Man's World.[37] Hippolyta's leadership skills help Wonder Woman move into the role of mentor and mother figure herself, first when she transforms the members of a Holliday College sorority into a fighting force[38] and later when she trains Cassandra Sandsmark to become her young partner, Wonder Girl.[39] Hippolyta is always available to counsel her daughter, but the vast distance between them gives Wonder Woman the independence needed to evolve into her own adult persona. Jungian *individuation,* which has been described as the journey of transformation people experience as they integrate aspects of their personality, spirituality, and life experiences to become a functional whole, is one possible interpretation of the journey Diana takes to live in the mortal world.[40] Another, more well-known and researched possibility is the desire to reach the pinnacle of Maslow's hierarchy of needs: *self-actualization*, the highest point of human achievement in being all one can be.[41] Innate motivation to progress toward self-actualization could give Diana the drive to make an impact on the world at large and to use her Wonder Woman powers to further that desire.[42]

Gender roles are socially constructed expectations for what positions men and women can hold in society and how they ought to behave.[43] This is a different issue from gender itself in that subscribing to traditional masculinity or femininity can be separate from a person's concept of himself or herself as being male or female. Psychologist Sandra Bem postulated that gender role expectations are transmitted to children through their culture and society (*gender role socialization*) and that there are four main categories in which individuals identify: *sex-typed*, being the kind of person who accepts the "traditional" roles that were common when Bem conducted her initial research;[44] *cross-sex-typed*, meaning the opposite of "traditional" gender roles; *androgynous*, meaning that the person has characteristics of both genders; and *undifferentiated*, in which there are few signs of gender differentiation of any sort.[45]

In regard to Diana and the Amazon culture, gender roles in her society on Paradise Island are largely nonexistent. The fact that the island is populated only by females means that significant *androgyny*, the possession of characteristics of both males and females, is the norm, and that the women are not burdened with reproductive duties, which frees them to pursue many other interests including education, leadership roles, and military training. They have a level of freedom of choice virtually

unheard of in the 1940s, when Wonder Woman was originally written. Growing up on Paradise Island, young Diana is
taught that men are the source of the two forces the Amazons
have been created to battle: aggression and dominance.[46] The
Amazonian view of males as strongly sex-typed, one-note
beings of aggressive malevolence is often as negative and
stereotypical as the overriding, strongly sex-typed view of the
day when women were expected to fill their roles as essentially
one-note beings of passive nurturance.[47] As Wonder Woman,
Diana finally encounters real men and learns they are not all
evil. Diana is forced to question whether the Amazon teachings of her mother are as indisputable as she had believed.[48]
This marks another step in Wonder Woman's passage toward
maturity as she develops a personal worldview that is different
from that of her mother.

> *"Goodbye, mother. I am frightened—yet, I shall remember*
> *the power within me whenever I think of you!"*
> —Diana[49]

> *"It is easy for any mother to love her child before this process*
> *of separation has begun—but it is the task at which most*
> *fail, to love the child and at the same time to let it go—and*
> *to want to let it go."*
> —psychologist Erich Fromm[50]

Comic Book References

All-Star Comics #8 (1941). "Introducing Wonder Woman." Script: W. M. Marston. Art:
    H. G. Peter.
Sensation Comics #1 (1942). "Wonder Woman Comes to America." Script: W. M.
    Marston. Art: H. G. Peter.
Sensation Comics #2 (1942). "Wonder Woman Comes to America." Script: W. M.
    Marston. Art: H. G. Peter.
Sensation Comics #6 (1942). "Summons to Paradise Island." Script: W. M. Marston. Art:
    H. G. Peter.
Sensation Comics #22 (1943). "The Secret Submarine." Script: W. M. Marston. Art:
    H. G. Peter.

The Legend of Wonder Woman #1 (2015). Script: R. De Liz. Art: R. Dillon.

Wonder Woman #1 (1942). "Wonder Woman's Story." Script: W. M. Marston. Art: H. G. Peter.

Wonder Woman #2 (1987). "A Fire in the Sky." Script: G. Potter & G. Pérez. Art: G. Pérez.

Wonder Woman #4 (1943). "The Adventure of the Mole Men." Script: W. M. Marston. Art: H. G. Peter.

Wonder Woman #5 (1943). "Battle for Womanhood." Script: W. M. Marston. Art: H. G. Peter.

Wonder Woman #45 (1951). "The Second Life of the Original Wonder Woman." Script: R. Kanigher. Art: D. Heck

Wonder Woman #204 (1973). "The Wonder Woman Story." Script: R. Kanigher. Art: H. G. Peter.

Wonder Woman #5 (1987). "The Ares Assault." Script: G. Pérez & L. Wein. Art: G Pérez.

Wonder Woman #14 (1988). "For The Glory of Gaea." Script: G. Pérez & L. Wein. Art: G. Pérez.

Wonder Woman #158 (2000). "Initiation." Script: E. Luke. Art: S. Cariello & M. Clark.

Wonder Woman #171 (2001). "Cry Havoc." Script: P. Jimenez. Art: T. Moore & P. Jimenez.

Wonder Woman #2 (2011). "Home." Script: B. Azzarello. Art: C. Chiang.

Other References

Ainsworth, M. D. S., & Bell, S. M. (1970). Attachment, exploration, and separation: Illustrated by the behavior of one-year-olds in a strange situation. *Child Development, 41*(1), 49–67.

Ainsworth, M. D. S., Blehar, M. C., Waters, E., & Wall, S. (1978). *Patterns of attachment: A psychological study of the strange situation.* Hillsdale, NJ: Erlbaum.

Baumrind, D. (1967). Child care practices anteceding three patterns of preschool behavior. *Genetic Psychology Monographs, 75*(1), 43–88.

Baumrind, D. (2013). Authoritative parenting revisited: History and current status. In R. E. Larzelere, A. S. Morris, & A. W. Harrist (Eds.), *Authoritative parenting: Synthesizing nurturance and discipline for optimal child development* (pp. 11–34). Washington, DC: American Psychological Association.

Baumrind, D., Larzelere, R. E., & Owens, E. B. (2010). Effects of preschool parents' power assertive patterns and practices on adolescent development. *Parenting: Science & Practice, 10*(3), 157–201.

Bem, S. L. (1974). The measurement of psychological androgyny. *Journal of Consulting and Clinical Psychology, 42*(2), 155–162.

Bem, S. L. (1981a). The BSRI and gender schema theory: A reply to Spence and Helmreich. *Psychological Review, 88*(4), 369–371.

Bem, S. L. (1981b). Gender schema theory: A cognitive account of sex typing. *Psychological Review, 88*(4), 354–364.

Bem, S. L. (1983). Gender schema theory and its implications for child development: Raising gender-aschematic children in a gender-schematic society. *Signs, 8*(4), 598–616.

Bretherton, I. (1992). The origins of attachment theory: John Bowlby and Mary Ainsworth. *Developmental Psychology, 28*(5), 759–775.

Calder, A. (2003). *Myth of the Blitz.* London, UK: Pimlico.

Erikson, E. H. (1950). *Childhood and society.* New York, NY: Norton.

Erikson, E. H. (1968). *Identity, youth, and crisis.* New York, NY: Norton.

Erikson, E.H. (1980). *Identity and the life cycle.* New York, NY: Norton.

Erikson, E. H. (1998). *The life cycle completed* (extended version). New York, NY: Norton.

Freud, A. (1937/1966). *The ego and the mechanisms of defence.* London, UK: Hogarth.

Fromm, E. (1955). *The sane society.* New York, NY: Open Road.

Jung, C. G. (1939). *The integration of the personality.* Oxford, UK: Farrar & Rinehart.

Jung, C. G. (1968). *The archetypes and the collective unconscious.* New York, NY: Routledge.

Kohlberg, L. (1973). Stages and aging in moral development: Some speculations. *Gerontologist, 13*(4), 497–502.

Kohlberg, L., Levine, C., & Hewer, A. (1983). *Moral stages: A current formulation and a response to critics.* Basel, NY: Karger.

Maccoby, E. E., & Martin, J. A. (1983). Socialization in the context of the family: Parent–child interaction. In P. Mussen and E. M. Hetherington (Eds.), *Handbook of child psychology, Volume IV: Socialization, personality, and social development* (pp. 1–101). New York, NY: Wiley.

Maslow, A. H. (1943). A theory of human motivation. *Psychological Review, 50*(4), 370–96.

Maslow, A. H. (1968). *Toward a psychology of being.* New York, NY: Van Nostrand.

Morris, T., & Morris, M. (Eds.). (2005). *Superheroes and philosophy: Truth, justice, and the Socratic way.* Chicago, IL: Open Court.

Sorkhabi, N., & Mandara, J. (2013). Are the effects of Baumrind's parenting styles culturally specific or culturally equivalent? In R. E. Larzelere, A. S. Morris, & A. W. Harrist (Eds.), *Authoritative parenting: Synthesizing nurturance and discipline for optimal child development* (pp. 11–34). Washington, DC: American Psychological Association.

Van Dijken, S. (1998). *John Bowlby: His early life.* London, UK: Free Association.

Notes

1. *Wonder Woman* #14 (1988).
2. Fromm (1955), p. 42.
3. *Wonder Woman* #1 (1942).
4. *All-Star Comics* #8 (1941); *Wonder Woman* #1 (1942).
5. Bretherton (1992); Calder (2003); Van Dijken (1998).
6. Ainsworth (1970).
7. Ainsworth (1978).
8. *Sensation Comics* #6 (1942).
9. *Wonder Woman* #1 (1942).
10. *Wonder Woman* #1 (1942).
11. Kohlberg (1973).
12. Morris & Morris (2005).
13. Kohlberg (1973).
14. *Wonder Woman* #45 (1951).
15. Kohlberg (1983).
16. *Wonder Woman* #4 (1943).
17. *Sensation Comics* #22 (1943).
18. *Wonder Woman* #1 (1942).
19. Erikson (1950).
20. Erikson (1968, 1998).
21. *All-Star Comics* #8 (1941).

22. *The Legend of Wonder Woman* #1 (2015).
23. *Wonder Woman* #4 (1943).
24. *Wonder Woman* #1 (1942).
25. *Wonder Woman* #171 (2001).
26. Freud (1937/1966).
27. Erikson (1950).
28. Baumrind (1967, 2013); Baumrind et al. (2010).
29. Maccoby & Martin (1983).
30. *Wonder Woman* #1 (1942).
31. *All-Star Comics* #8 (1941).
32. Baumrind et al. (2010); Baumrind (2013).
33. e.g., *All-Star Comics* #8 (1941); *Sensation Comics* #1 and #6 (1942).
34. e.g., *Wonder Woman* #204 (1973).
35. Baumrind (1967); Maccoby & Martin (1983).
36. *Wonder Woman* #2 (2011).
37. *Wonder Woman* #5 (1943).
38. *Sensation Comics* #2 (1942).
39. *Wonder Woman* #158 (2000).
40. Jung (1939, 1968).
41. Maslow (1943).
42. Erikson (1950, 1980).
43. Bem (1981).
44. Bem (1974).
45. Bem (1981), pp. 369–371.
46. *Wonder Woman* #1 (1942).
47. Bem (1981, 1983).
48. *Wonder Woman* #5 (1987).
49. *Wonder Woman* #2 (1987).
50. Fromm (1955), pp. 42–43.

CHAPTER NINE

Multiple Identities, Multiple Selves? Diana's Actual, Ideal, and Ought Selves

WIND GOODFRIEND AND ANNAMARIA FORMICHELLA-ELSDEN

"I'm almost jealous of myself as Wonder Woman—nothing I do, as a normal woman, Diana Prince, ever impresses anybody. I have to become the sensational Wonder Woman before anybody notices me!"
—Diana[1]

> *"It is the difference between failing to meet our ideals versus failing to meet our oughts that provides the key to unlocking the mystery of why. . . ."*
> —psychologist Tory Higgins[2]

Superheroes often have multiple identities, but don't we all? Most people have fantasies, dreams, and goals for what they would like to achieve or become. We also all have anxieties and fears about what we could become but wish to avoid.

Many of us may additionally feel the pressure of what other people seem to wish for us, especially when their desires don't align with our own. These multiple conceptions of the self and the ways they interact are organized and explained by *self-discrepancy theory*, which predicts how we react when our selves do not align.[3] Perhaps, as in the case of Wonder Woman, our mothers want us to remain on a hidden island and benevolently rule the inhabitants while we want to go on adventures and fight Nazis instead. Wonder Woman certainly juggles her two identities. Does she also struggle with maintaining multiple psychological selves?

Three Simultaneous Selves

Psychologist E. Tory Higgins suggests that all of us at any given time have three separate but potentially overlapping self-concepts. Though Wonder Woman may represent those self-concepts more extremely, each of her selves aligns with what we see in real people.

Actual Self

The first is called the *actual self*, which is made up of the traits and characteristics that we actually, currently possess.[4] Higgins fine-tunes this concept by dividing the actual self into the "actual/own self" and the "actual/other self" to distinguish between the characteristics a person believes he or she possesses and the characteristics that others attribute to that person. Either way, the actual self consists of both the positive and negative qualities a person has right now.

One way to apply the concept of the actual self to Wonder Woman is to consider how she is when she is *not* Wonder Woman but is instead simply Diana. Perhaps without her costumed public figure, the more private role of who she is at home on Paradise Island and with her family reflects her natural and current self. Even Diana, however, is "wonderful" in the colloquial sense. She is intelligent and athletic but also kind and full of moxie. While many of the other Amazons quietly observe Steve Trevor's plane crashing on Paradise Island, Diana smiles and runs toward it, saying, "Let's find out what it is!"[5] After Diana ventures into the external world, she is more restrained in her Diana Prince identity than she is as Wonder Woman. The difference is so great that people don't even recognize her; when Steve Trevor first sees her as Diana Prince, he jokes with his supervisor that he will never be tempted by this reserved and demure person.

Ideal Self

A second self that Higgins theorizes exists in all of us is the ideal self. As the name implies, the *ideal self* includes what we would like to become in the future: our goals, desires, and dreams for the type of person we'd like to become. One way to apply the concept of the ideal self is to consider Diana's alter ego, Wonder Woman, to be the embodiment of her ideals.

In the earliest Wonder Woman comics, each strip opens with a character description, and in most of them her portrayal is insistently idealized: "As lovely as Aphrodite—as wise as Athena . . . Wonder Woman brings to America a new hope for salvation!"[6] By giving her godlike powers and pitting her against human corruption, Marston makes Wonder Woman an almost infallible ideal, someone who has already achieved self-actualization. As Wonder Woman, Diana embodies her ideal self.

Higgins suggests that our ideal selves reflect a *promotion focus*, meaning that we strive toward goals in a positive manner.[7] In short, by living out our ideals, we attempt both to promote the best version of ourselves and to promote our goals for the type of world in which we'd like to live. Throughout her time as Wonder Woman, Diana clearly attempts to promote a world in which all people are given respect and life is valued. This comes across most clearly in her fight against the Nazi regime and in her feminism. Both ideals are noted when Marston introduces her in an early strip: "Like the crash of thunder from the sky comes the Wonder Woman, to save the world from the hatreds and wars of men in a man-made world!"[8] Similar ideals come from Wonder Woman herself when she compares Paradise Island with the outside world and notes, "On Paradise Island there are only women. Because of this pure environment, we are able to develop our minds and our physical skills, unhampered by masculine destructiveness."[9] Her costume highlights the American flag, a clear symbol of her political ideals of freedom and justice.

Ought Self

Although Diana's actual and ideal selves are very closely aligned, there is still a third self to be considered. Higgins's self-discrepancy theory[10] suggests that the *ought self* is our representation of the traits and characteristics that we believe we ought to possess if we want to live up to *other people's* desires. Whereas the ideal self is focused on "promotion" or striving toward a goal, the ought self has a *prevention focus*. Here, we have fear, anxiety, or guilt if we disappoint these other people in our lives. For Diana, her conception of the ought self seems to come from two primary sources: her mother and the cultural mores of society away from Paradise Island.

Diana's mother, Queen Hippolyta, is proud of her daughter's abilities, and little conflict exists between them. An exception is that the queen doesn't want Diana to leave the island with Steve Trevor to fight the Nazis; we thus first see Diana's ought self emerge through her mother's wishes.[11] After Diana takes on the alter ego of nurse and secretary Diana Prince, she is again aware that her mother may not approve, which makes her ought self salient. She reflects, "If Mother could see me now . . . as a very feminine woman . . . a nurse, no less, in a world full of men, and in love, too—with myself for a rival!"[12] Diana seems to be experiencing her first coming-of-age crisis as she must decide which is more important to her: the ideal self she has constructed for herself or the ought self that her mother would prefer.

Diana also finds it amusing that the ought-self expectations thrust upon her by cultural standards do not match her ideal self. In America, she is subjected to a new set of social expectations and pressures. When she first walks down a city street in her costume, two women remark, "The hussy! She has no clothes on!" and "The brazen thing!"[13] Instead of allowing this version of her ought self to become important, however, Diana seems more amused than embarrassed; society's ought self doesn't seem to weigh on her in the same way that her mother's ought self does. She consistently rejects the ought self imposed upon her by sexist double standards.[14]

In fact, Steve himself frequently reinforces the socially prescribed ought self in terms of what both Diana and Wonder Woman "should" be. After Wonder Woman warns Steve that an upcoming mission could be dangerous, he simply laughs and responds, "You know what your trouble is? Too much work and not nearly enough play."[15] Steve seems protective of her "innocence," thus putting his conceptions of what she ought to be on Diana.[16] Steve does appear to have sexist notions about how Diana should behave, and yet he applies his old-fashioned double standards to Wonder Woman.

When Selves Don't Align: Discrepancy

In Higgins's conceptualization, the three selves simultaneously co-exist. If each self were represented as a circle, a Venn diagram could show all three and their differing degrees of overlap.

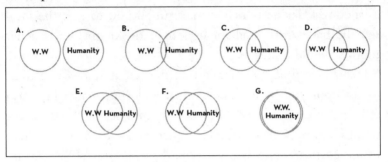

Note that if all three selves were in perfect alignment, the diagram would show a single circle. The person would be "self-actualized" according to Maslow. However, not even Diana can fully embody this impossibility.

Actual versus Ideal Discrepancy

Within self-discrepancy theory is the idea that different emotions result from different discrepancies among the three selves. Higgins suggests that when the actual self and ideal self don't match—in other words, when we don't live up to our own ideals or fail to achieve our dreams—we will experience *dejection-related emotions*.[17] These feelings of dejection include disappointment, dissatisfaction, shame, embarrassment, and potentially depression. Fortunately for Diana, it is rare for her to feel any of these negative emotions because of the heroic efforts she has made to accomplish her ideals. We might say that one way of understanding what it means to be super (a prefix that derives from the Latin for "above," "over," or "beyond"), as in *superhuman*, is to be above the kinds of self-conflict most humans experience.

Emotionally, the closest Diana comes to dejection is when she experiences a paradoxical rivalry between her two personae. In the early comics, a kind of rivalry develops between Diana and Wonder Woman as Steve Trevor pays attention only to the latter. In one moment of self-discrepancy, she notes, "Steve Trevor is so busy talking about this 'beautiful angel' Wonder Woman that he pays no attention to me whatsoever! I wonder if I am getting jealous of my other self."[18] She is aware that the difference between her selves is causing negative emotions, just as Higgins would predict. In another rare moment of acknowledging her conflict between selves, Diana reflects on a temporary situation in which she allowed herself to be put in bondage.[19] Afterward she reflects, "What a fool I was to let a man weld chains upon" her bracelets.[20]

Actual versus Ought Discrepancy

While still rare, it is more common for Diana to experience discrepancies between her actual self and ought self. Higgins suggested that this discrepancy would lead to *agitation-related emotions*, including fear, guilt, self-contempt, and anxiety. Although it might be exaggeration to state that Diana ever truly feels fear—at least for herself—she does appear to feel anxiety about not satisfying her mother. Diana explicitly goes against her mother's wishes by competing in a tournament to determine which Amazon will take Steve Trevor home.[21] Her anxiety about disappointing her mother and her ought self is clearer than ever when she tells Hippolyta, "You're my mother, and even now, if you tell me to stay, I'll stay."[22] She appears to be torn between her ideal self, wanting to follow Trevor home, and her ought self, wanting to satisfy her mother's wishes. Fortunately for Diana, Hippolyta is supportive and reassures Diana that she will be proud of her regardless of her choice.

The "Women Are Wonderful" Effect

Higgins's theory proposes that we all struggle with not living up to our ideal or ought self. While Diana may or may not experience this kind of doubt and disappointment, perhaps the most fascinating way to apply self-discrepancy theory to the world of Wonder Woman is not to think about how it fits Diana but how others are affected by her presence. Perhaps the question should be: How does exposure to Wonder Woman change other people's ideal or ought self?

In her world, encountering Wonder Woman seems to make others reflect on their values and goals. An example of this occurs in the comics when she challenges the deplorable conditions at an exploitive department store and uses her magic lasso to persuade the owner to change her ways. Now the owner sees how her previous actual self was flawed, and her new ideals and oughts are improved. The owner tells her workers, "Girls, starting now your salaries are doubled, your hours and working conditions will be improved! Wonder Woman made me work like you and now I understand!"[23] She also persuades a Nazi woman to switch sides and join the Allies.[24]

Importantly, she also successfully decreases sexism and double standards for men and women. Both Steve Trevor and his son, Steve Trevor. Jr., hold on to their benevolently misogynistic view of the world, but both simultaneously revere Wonder Woman for her strength and moxie. She is successful at changing Steve Jr.'s beliefs even more than his father's (perhaps because he lives in a culture more accepting of women's rights, one generation later). In one episode, when a villain sneers at Steve and Wonder Woman and states, "You see what you get when you trust a woman?" Steve smiles and replies, "Yeah, you get the job done."[25]

Perhaps the most important question to ask is whether readers of the Wonder Woman comics and viewers of the tele-

A FEARED SELF?

Higgins suggested only three selves, but other psychologists have offered ideas for additional self-concepts. One is the *feared self*, the embodiment of what we definitely do *not* want for ourselves.[26] The feared self could be the combined opposites of our ideal and ought selves, the constellation of traits we think would disappoint both ourselves and the important others in our lives. Research has shown that when one's actual self becomes closer to the feared self, both depression and anxiety occur (we experience both dejection-related and agitation-related emotions).[27] But again, what constitutes our fears will vary from person to person. If we compare ourselves with the superheroic Wonder Woman, do we fear that we will never live up to that kind of ideal? Other research reveals that perhaps striving for perfection is not all it's cracked up to be; people who think that they need to be perfect rate themselves as more depressed.[28] Even though Wonder Woman may help us imagine a better world or a better self, remembering that she is both fictional and in possession of superpowers may be good for our mental health.

vision show were influenced by her character. Even now, as Wonder Woman continues to be reinvented and reintroduced, does exposure to her change our ideas of what ideal women ought to be? Does it change what women audience members want for their own ideals, goals, and dreams? In psychology, the *"women are wonderful" effect*[29] is the concept that in general, the stereotype of women is that they possess more positive traits (e.g., kind, nurturing) than men do but that those traits also make them weak. Wonder Woman's greatest legacy may be that she changed the world's view of what ideal and ought women could be or should be by redefining what wonderful really means. Maybe instead of nice but weak, women can be athletic, intelligent, sarcastic feminists who stand up for what's right. Then again, perhaps the idealized picture of a woman who has enough time and energy to work, take care of children, be beautiful, and still have time to destroy Nazis and lobby Washington for equal rights is an ideal no real woman could ever accomplish. Although Wonder Woman may have changed our views of women and of ourselves in a complex way, it is clear that she has left an enduring impact on what we imagine women can—and perhaps should—be.

Comic Book References

Sensation Comics #1 (1942). "Wonder Woman Comes to America." Script: W. M. Marston. Art: H. G. Peter.
Sensation Comics #2 (1942). "Dr. Poison." Script: W. M. Marston. Art: H. G. Peter.
Sensation Comics #3 (1942). "A Spy in the Office." Script: W. M. Marston. Art: H. G. Peter.
Sensation Comics #4 (1942). "School for Spies." Script: W. M. Marston. Art: H. G. Peter.
Sensation Comics #7 (1942). "The Milk Swindle." Script: W. M. Marston. Art: H. G. Peter.
Sensation Comics #8 (1942). "Department Store Perfidy." Script: W. M. Marston. Art: H. G. Peter.
Wonder Woman #1 (1942). "The Origin of Wonder Woman;" "Wonder Woman Goes to the Circus!" Script: W. M. Marston. Art: H. G. Peter.

Other References

Carver, C. S., Lawrence, J. W., & Scheier, M. F. (1999). Self-discrepancies and affect: Incorporating the role of feared selves. *Personality & Social Psychology Bulletin, 25*(7), 783–792.
Eagly, A. H., & Mladinic, A. (1994). Are people prejudiced against women? Some answers from research on attitudes, gender stereotypes, and judgments of competence. *European Review of Social Psychology, 5*(1), 1–35.
Flett, G. L., Besser, A., & Hewitt, P. L. (2005). Perfectionism, ego defense styles, and depression: A comparison of self-reports versus informant ratings. *Journal of Personality, 73*(5), 1355–1396.

Higgins, E. T. (1987). Self-discrepancy: A theory relating self and affect. *Psychological Review, 94*(3), 319–340.

Higgins, E. T. (2012). Regulatory focus theory. In P. Van Lange, A. W. Kruglanski, & E. T. Higgins (Eds.), *Handbook of theories of social psychology* (vol. 1, pp. 483–504). Thousand Oaks, CA: Sage.

Notes

1. *Sensation Comics* #7 (1942).
2. Higgins (2012).
3. Higgins (1987, 2012).
4. Higgins (1987).
5. *The New Original Wonder Woman* (1975 television movie).
6. *Sensation Comics* #2 (1942).
7. Higgins (2012).
8. *Sensation Comics* #1 (1942).
9. *Wonder Woman* episode 1–2, "The Nazi Wonder Woman" (April 28, 1976).
10. Higgins (1987).
11. *The New Original Wonder Woman* (1975 television movie).
12. *Sensation Comics* #1 (1942).
13. *Sensation Comics* #1 (1942).
14. *Wonder Woman* episode 2–4, "The Bermuda Triangle Crisis" (October 7, 1977).
15. *Wonder Woman* episode 1–12, "The Bushwackers" (January 29, 1977).
16. *Wonder Woman* episode 2–4, "The Bermuda Triangle Crisis" (October 7, 1977).
17. Higgins (1987).
18. *Sensation Comics* #3 (1942).
19. *Sensation Comics* #4 (1942).
20. *Sensation Comics* #4 (1942).
21. *Wonder Woman* #1 (1942).
22. *Wonder Woman* episode 2–1, "The Return of Wonder Woman" (September 16, 1977).
23. *Sensation Comics* #8 (1942).
24. *Wonder Woman* episode 1–2, "The Nazi Wonder Woman" (April 28, 1976).
25. *Wonder Woman* episode 2–13, "Light-Fingered Lady" (January 6, 1978).
26. Carver et al. (1999).
27. Carver et al. (1999).
28. Flett et al. (2005).
29. A phrase coined by Eagly & Mladinic (1994).

CHAPTER TEN

Growing a Goddess: Child Development and Wonder Woman

MARA WOOD

"You always make me proud, daughter."
—Hippolyta[1]

> *"The predictable outcome of a child's attachment behavior is to bring him into closer proximity with other people, and particularly with that specific individual who is primarily responsible for his care."*
> —psychologist Mary Ainsworth[2]

Diana's childhood is marked by a loving, present mother and a host of women who form an environment conducive to growth, discovery, and adventure, all of which contribute to her eventual role as Wonder Woman. Psychologists such as Mary Ainsworth, Jean Piaget, and Lev Vygotsky have studied how the journey from childhood to adulthood is marked by cognitive and behavioral milestones that shape the way children develop into the adults they will become.[3] Even the way people handle their interpersonal relationships in adulthood corresponds with early parent-child relations to a considerable degree.[4] Heroism in adulthood has its roots in childhood. Diana's mother and fellow Amazons help foster Diana's journey to adulthood, and the same elements can foster the growth of children anywhere.

Making Sense of the World

Most children undergo a process of cognitive development that shapes their outlook on the world around them. Children make sense of the world by forming *schemas*, patterns of associated concepts about the world around them.[5] Schemas (a.k.a. *schemata*) are typically thought of as the building blocks for intelligence. For example, the *gender schema* develops as a young child not only differentiates between boys and girls but also adds many ideas associated with what gender means (e.g., differences in bodies, clothing, haircuts, choices of toys).

On Themyscira, Diana's gender schema reflects her childhood. Born on an island occupied solely by women, she hears about men, but her knowledge of them is limited to what the others tell her. Stories about Man's World include greed, war, pain, and death.[6] These elements are common to gender schemas throughout the world: Violence and destruction are more often associated with men than with women.[7] Diana's gender schema includes a vast understanding of what it means to be female and an extremely narrow understanding of what it means to be male. Although real-life examples tend not to be this extreme, anyone with unusually limited contact with individuals of any particular group is likely to have a narrow range of expectations regarding that group.[8] Therefore, some-

FITNESS SCHEMA

Diana's perception of women has to be accommodated during her time in Man's World. Previously, her knowledge of the female physical form was limited to what is considered peak perfection. The women of Themyscira were physically fit and engaged in athletic competitions regularly. The women of Man's World, in contrast, varied greatly in size and physical ability. Diana is not alone in this limitation; it has been a significant amount of time since any of the women of Themyscira have seen a person who is less than fit. When the delegates from Man's World are brought to Themyscira at the beginning of the nation's reemergence in the world, one man questions the reaction of the women to his paralysis. Like Diana, the Amazons accommodate their knowledge of physical well-being to include the wheelchair-bound man.[9]

one who does not know men will likely have a less elaborate schema for what it means to be male.

When Diana first meets Steve Trevor, she makes assumptions about him that are based on her existing gender schema. Adding information to a specific schema without changing the schema is *assimilation*. She initially assimilates Steve into the schema. Her limited knowledge of men is challenged when she learns more about Steve and is challenged even more after she delivers him to the outside world. When a schema is changed by new information, that is *accommodation*. Diana's schema of men changes to accommodate everything she learns through her interactions with men across all strata. Men are no longer greedy rapists like the Hercules she learned of; rather, they are just as varied and nuanced as women.

Attachment

Mary Ainsworth theorized that the birth-to-toddler years are crucial to the overall development of the child. During this time, the child learns the response pattern of the mother or primary caregiver. The behavior of the child is shaped by this dependent interaction. If the mother is responsive and available to meet the needs of the baby, the child is likely to be *securely attached* to the parent. Parents who are ambivalent or unavailable typically have avoidant or ambivalent/anxious children.[10] The type of attachment between the parent and the child is not solely a product of the parent's reaction to the child: The child's temperament can either facilitate or hinder the attachment between the parent and the child.[11] A child with an easy temperament is easier to develop a secure attachment to than is a child with a difficult temperament. The response of the child is a behavioral shaper for the parent's reaction.

Diana shows many signs of secure attachment to her mother in terms of trust, security, and the ability to become independent from her mother while maintaining warm relationships when they are reunited. Securely attached children have developed trust in their primary caregivers. Observations of young, securely attached children show that they may become upset at first when the primary caregiver leaves the vicinity.[12] These children are able to recoup and engage in other activities without the primary caregiver present. Upon the caregiver's return, these children acknowledge the presence of the parent. Conversely, children who are not securely attached undergo great stress when the parent leaves and returns or do not notice the presence of the parent at all.

Securely attached children also have greater ability to explore their environments. The primary caregiver is referred to as a *secure base* (or a secure haven when the child has a sense of wariness)[13] from which the child can branch out. In fear experiments, the child is exposed to a fearful stimulus in the presence of the primary caregiver. Children who were securely attached stood in proximity to the parents in order to observe the stimulus. Children who were not securely attached did not attempt to explore the stimulus to overcome the initial fear.[14] Exploration in general is hampered in these children; children with an avoidant attachment have a rigid exploration pattern, and children with an anxious/ambivalent attachment are distracted during exploration.[15]

Early accounts of Diana as a child show her to be an inquisitive girl. In the safety of her home on Paradise Island, the Silver Age Wonder Tot (a very young Diana) explores her environment and goes on many adventures.[16] Wonder Tot's mother encourages growth and exploration—for example, when Hippolyta teaches her how to ride air currents and even lets Wonder Tot have a particularly scary experience before saving her.[17] Like teaching a baby bird to fly, Hippolyta acts as a safety net for her young daughter. As she grows into young adulthood, Diana's curiosity extends beyond the shores of her home. In nearly every account of her origin story, Diana desires to journey to Man's World.[18] She also, when permitted, returns home often to the secure base her mother provides.

The benefits of secure attachment extend to adulthood. Children with a secure attachment have an accurate assessment of their self-worth, insecurely attached children tend to lack self-worth, and children with an anxious/avoidant attachment try to portray themselves as perfect.[19] As children age, the quality of their early attachment to the primary caregiver impacts their overall approach to others. Adult attachment is conceptualized along two dimensions: avoidance and anxiety.[20] High avoidance indicates a defensive dismissal and avoidance of close relationship, whereas low avoidance correlates with comfort with closeness and dependency on others.[21] Adults who rate high on the anxiety dimension have an anxious/fearful preoccupation with relationships, and adults who rate low on this dimension have confidence in being accepted in relationships.[22] Adults who had a secure attachment as infants typically display low avoidance and low anxiety. Additionally, these adults display a high need for achievement and a low fear of failure.[23] Goal achievement also is correlated with securely attached adults.[24]

Prosocial Environments

Positive interactions with others go a long way in terms of a child's development. Themyscira is uniquely situated as an ideal place for a child to grow up. The Amazons in most accounts are immortal and childless, except for Hippolyta. Whether Diana is bestowed to the Amazons as a gift or through more natural means, she is cherished by many other women on the island. Diana grows up in a prosocial environment in which the women care for, share with, and help others and social relationships are cherished.[25]

Sharing in positive events with others can prolong or increase positive moods.[26] It is commonly thought that positive attitudes and moods can increase longevity, though there is a lack of solid evidence for causality.[27] That is, does a positive mood lead to good health or does good health lead to a positive mood? Regardless of the causality of positivity, negative stressors in life can exacerbate health problems.[28] The Amazons are known for unnaturally, god-given long lives that they aim to fill with peaceful, happy, positive experiences. The women share their happiness with each other through shared activities, most notably festivals such as Diana's Day and the very contest that sends Diana to Man's World.[29]

Children respond to positivity in their caregivers. Positive children are able to express their emotions, and they are responsive and warm.[30] Positive emotions in general foster social connectedness with others, which in turn further deepens positive emotions.[31] The community of the Amazons creates a cradle of positive interactions and emotions for Diana. Prosocial behaviors in a child's community can lead to lower levels of problem behaviors in school.[32] These prosocial behaviors include cooperation, caring, and empathy, hallmarks of the Themysciran society Diana hails from.

Although community plays a part in the development of the child, it is a small effect compared to that of the primary caregiver. The mother's well-being, physically and mentally, has a significant impact on the child's prosocial behavior. A mother can help increase positive mood in her child through touch, displays of positive emotion, and engagement in leisure activities with the child.[33] Hippolyta and Diana engage in touch throughout the decades, from Hippolyta picking up a grown Diana in greeting to sitting side by side and sharing a moment of quiet contemplation.[34] As a child, Diana is shown seeking comfort from Hippolyta through physical touch, and Hippolyta responds warmly and reaffirms that secure attachment.[35] Hippolyta's display of positive emotion is restrained due to her status as a queen, but she finds time to share smiles and laughter with Diana. Her positive display of emotions is also present during Diana's childhood through smiles and words of affection.[36] Leisure activities are shared between the two women, as well as between many of the Amazons and Diana.[37] Notably,

Diana feels isolated because she is the only child on an island of grown women. Hippolyta, unable to fulfill the peer role Diana seeks, enlists the help of Amazon scientists to create a playmate for Diana. Diana is accompanied by a robot playmate at one point (who proves to be disastrous) and a mirror clone-copy of Diana (who later is retconned to be Donna Troy).[38] Hippolyta recognizes the importance of leisure in Diana's life and, when her presence is not enough, facilitates a peer relationship. If Diana grew up in a community where there were young girls her age, we can imagine Hippolyta encouraging her to befriend them all.

Like attachment styles, the degree and intensity of prosocial interactions in early childhood affect behaviors over the course of a lifetime. Experiencing high prosocial interactions during early childhood is linked with reduced aggression and deviant behaviors in late childhood and adolescence.[39] Interactions with antisocial children are correlated with antisocial behaviors as the child grows.[40] Diana is in a unique situation, being the only child on Themyscira in several accounts. There have been more recent stories featuring a young Diana with peers, though she is different from her peers by birth.[41] A cruel nickname, "Clay," is used by Aleka in Diana's young adulthood to distance Diana from the other Amazons[42] by belittling her and effectively *dehumanizing* her. Diana's reaction to the insult indicates that in this atypical and darker version of her history, she has heard it throughout her childhood.

A prosocial environment can be a source of an individual's internalized prosocial outlook as an adult. Additionally, the sensitivity of a mother such as Hippolyta helps foster lifelong prosocial behaviors. Without the prosocial environment in early childhood, a person possessing the level of power that Diana does could develop antisocial tendencies and become a villain.

The Woman Today

Diana is the summation of her entire childhood, much in the same way that everyone else is. Her childhood is not too different from any we see from person to person—with the exception of some mythological creatures and the whole made-from-clay thing. The elements that are present, such as cognitive development, attachment, and prosocial interactions, are all said to have an impact on the way an adult thinks and interacts with her environment. In Diana's case, her childhood has led to her status as a compassionate, strong, empathetic human being who seeks out positive, prosocial relationships with others. There is no magic to her growth into adulthood; what is effective in her childhood is also effective in the childhood of other people.

Comic Book References

Legend of Wonder Woman #1 (2016). Script: R. De Liz. Art: R. De Liz & R. Dillon.
Legend of Wonder Woman #3 (2016). Script: R. De Liz. Art: R. De Liz & R. Dillon.
Wonder Woman #3 (1943). "A Spy on Paradise Island." Script: W. M. Marston. Art: H. G. Peter.
Wonder Woman #113 (1960). "Wonder Girl's Birthday Party." Script: R. Kanigher. Art: R. Andru & M. Esposito.
Wonder Woman #114 (1960). "Wonder Girl's Robot Playmate!" Script: R. Kanigher. Art: R. Andru & M. Esposito.
Wonder Woman #123 (1961). "Amazon Magic-Eye Album!" Script: R. Kanigher. Art: R. Andru & M. Esposito.
Wonder Woman #126 (1961). "Wonder Tot and Mister Genie!" Script: R. Kanigher. Art: R. Andru & M. Esposito.
Wonder Woman #2 (1987). "A Fire in the Sky!" Script: G. Potter & G. Perez. Art: G. Perez & B. Patterson.
Wonder Woman #37 (1989). "Strangers in Paradise." Script: G. Perez & M. Newell. Art: C. Marrinan & S. Montano.
Wonder Woman #134 (1998). "Who is Donna Troy?" Script: J. Byrne. Art: J. Byrne.
Wonder Woman #3 (2012). "Clay." Script: B. Azzarello. Art: C. Chiang.
Wonder Woman #2 (2016). "Year One Part 1." Script: G. Rucka. Art: N. Scott.
Wonder Woman #4 (2016). "Year One Part 2." Script: G. Rucka. Art: N. Scott.
Wonder Woman Earth One (2016). Script: G. Morrison. Art: Y. Paquette.

Other References

Adesokan, A. A., Ullrich, J., van Dick, R., & Tropp, L. R. (2011). Diversity beliefs as moderator of the contact–prejudice relationship. *Social Psychology, 42*(4), 271–278.

Ainsworth, M. D. S. (1985). Attachments across the life span. *Bulletin of the New York Academy of Medicine, 61,* 792–812.

Ainsworth, M. D. S., Blehar, M. C., Waters, E., & Wall, S. (1978). *Patterns of attachment: A psychological study of the strange situation.* Hillsdale, NJ: Lawrence Erlbaum.

Bai, S., Repetti, R. L., & Sperling, J. B. (2015). Children's expressions of positive emotions are sustained by smiling, touching, and playing with parents and siblings: A naturalistic observational study of family life. *Developmental Psychology, 52*(1), 88–101.

Baugher, A. R., & Gazmararian, J. A. (2015). Masculine gender role stress and violence: A literature review and future directions. *Aggression & Violent Behavior, 24,* 107–112.

Diener, E., & Chan, M. Y. (2011). Happy people live long: Subjective well-being contributes to health and longevity. *Applied Psychology: Health & Well-Being, 3*(1), 1–43.

Elliot, A. J., & Reis, H. T. (2003). Attachment and exploration in adulthood. *Journal of Personality & Social Psychology, 85*(2), 317–331.

Feeney, J. A. (1996). Attachment, caregiving, and marital satisfaction. *Personal Relationships, 3*(4), 401–416.

Flouri, E., & Sarmadi, Z. (2016). Prosocial behavior and childhood trajectories of internalizing problems: The role of neighborhood and school contexts. *Developmental Psychology, 52*(2), 253–258.

Fuller, T. L., & Fincham, F. D. (1995). Attachment style in married couples: Relation to current marital functioning, stability over time, and method of assessment. *Personal Relationships, 2*(1), 17–34.

Laible, D., Carlo, G., Davis, A. N., & Karahuta, E. (2016). Maternal sensitivity and effortful control in early childhood as predictors of adolescents' adjustment: The mediating roles of peer group affiliation and social behaviors. *Developmental Psychology, 52*(6), 922–932.

Myers, D. G. (2013). *Psychology* (10th ed.). New York, NY: Worth.

Sable, P. (2000). *Attachment and adult psychotherapy.* Northvale, NJ: Jason Aronson.

Notes

1. *Wonder Woman* #4 (2016).
2. Ainsworth et al. (1978).
3. Myers (2013).
4. Feeney (1996); Fuller & Fincham (1995); Sable (2000).
5. Myers (2013).
6. *Wonder Woman* #2 (1987).
7. Baugher & Gazmararian (2015).
8. Adesokan et al. (2011).
9. *Wonder Woman* #37 (1989).
10. Myers (2013).
11. Laible et al. (2016).
12. Ainsworth et al. (1978).
13. Ainsworth et al. (1978).
14. Ainsworth et al. (1978).
15. Elliot & Reis (2003).

16. e.g., *Wonder Woman* #126 (1961).
17. *Wonder Woman* #123 (1961).
18. *Legend of Wonder Woman* #3 (2016); *Wonder Woman* #2 (2016).
19. Ainsworth (1985).
20. Elliot & Reis (2003).
21. Elliot & Reis (2003).
22. Elliot & Reis (2003).
23. Elliot & Reis (2003).
24. Elliot & Reis (2003).
25. Flouri & Sarmadi (2015).
26. Bai et al. (2015).
27. Diener & Chan (2011).
28. Diener & Chan (2011).
29. *Wonder Woman Earth One* (2016).
30. Bai et al. (2015).
31. Bai et al. (2015).
32. Flouri & Sarmadi (2016).
33. Bai et al. (2015).
34. *Wonder Woman* #4 (2016).
35. *Wonder Woman* #114 (1960).
36. *Wonder Woman* #113 (1960).
37. *Wonder Woman* #3 (1943).
38. *Wonder Woman* #114 (1960); *Wonder Woman* #134 (1998).
39. Laible et al. (2016).
40. Laible et al. (2016).
41. *Legend of Wonder Woman* #1 (2016).
42. *Wonder Woman* #3 (2012).

CHAPTER ELEVEN

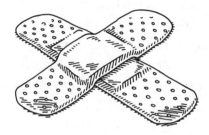

Compassion is My Superpower

JENNA BUSCH AND JANINA SCARLET

"Because of who my adversaries are, they only see my love as a defect in the armor. . . . But they don't know it's also what gives me my strength."
—Wonder Woman[1]

"Compassion may have ensured our survival because of its tremendous benefits for both physical and mental health and overall well-being."
—psychologist Emma Seppälä[2]

Charles Darwin, the English geologist and evolutionist, wrote about "survival of the fittest," meaning survival of those who are strongest and most resilient accompanied by the extinction of those who are weak.[3] This seems to imply that humans and other mammals need to be selfish and be "on the lookout" for their kin to survive.[4] However, Darwin also encouraged people to be kind and compassionate to one another, arguing that the most compassionate communities would be the ones most likely to flourish.[5] Although Wonder Woman has superior physical strength and longevity, it is her sense of compassion that seems to drive her strength and resilience.[6] In fact, some research studies suggest that compassion can lead to greater physiological and psychological resilience as well as increased longevity.[7] What are the benefits of compassion, and how does compassion work?

The Elements of Compassion

Compassion consists of several elements: mindfulness, empathy, the desire to help others, and (usually) a form of an altruistic action.[8] For example, when she comes upon a little girl who has been tossed out of a sword-fighting game because of her gender, Wonder Woman sees her pain, feels a kinship with her, and teaches her to sword fight better than the boys.[9] Similarly, when Wonder Woman sees how Green Lantern is suffering because of his hatred of the alien race that killed his family, she feels his pain. She chooses to both protect the alien race the Green Lantern is trying to kill and refuse to fight him, offering her open hand to him.[10]

The first component of compassion, *mindfulness*, is the ability to notice the present moment rather than worrying about the future or regretting the past.[11] As an example of this, Wonder Woman says, "Kal looks to the future, Batman looks to the past . . . and I reside in the present, securely bridging the two," when she decides to give up the fantasy of having a normal life and relationship. Instead, she chooses to live in her current reality, helping others and dealing with the current crisis.[12]

Mindfulness is especially important to compassion practice

Compassion makes Wonder Woman stronger. *Brave and the Bold* #140 (1978). Art: Jim Aparo. ®DC Comics.

as it involves noticing the individuals (including oneself) who may be struggling and need compassion and support.[13] For example, in *Kingdom Come*,[14] Wonder Woman sees an older Clark Kent who has given up being Superman because of the terrible losses he has sustained. She listens to his feelings kindly and helps him see that he cannot turn his face from the world, giving him new purpose.

The numerous benefits of practicing mindfulness include reduction in depression,[15] reduction of chronic pain,[16] and an overall improved mood and happiness.[17] In addition, mindfulness practice seems to serve as a protective factor against developing the flu[18] and reduce the negative effects of cancer and chemotherapy on the body.[19]

The second component of compassion is *empathy*, or the ability to understand and to some degree feel the emotional or physical suffering of another being.[20] Unlike mindfulness, empathy is not always beneficial as a distinct process. In fact, extensive empathy without the other elements of compassion can lead to depression[21] and *empathic distress* (emotional burnout after taking on the suffering of another).[22] For example, Wonder Woman faces crisis after crisis and the pain of others around the world. She is so exhausted after dealing with the emotions and fear of other people that she has to return to Themyscira to revive herself. She says, "I certainly understand the power of comfort. Every so often, I need some myself."[23]

The last two components of compassion are the desire to help and taking action to help others. Similar to the effects of mindfulness, these elements have been associated with increased physical and psychological benefits.[24] In fact, people who are altruistic are less likely to be depressed, demonstrate less neuroticism, experience lower empathic distress, and are more likely to help strangers.[25] In fact, Wonder Woman frequently helps strangers, such as the group of Middle Eastern women who were being used as human shields.[26] In addition, she fights her fellow Amazons in a contest to be given the right to help strangers in Man's World in most versions of her origin story.[27] Such acts of helping others can elevate positive emotions and mood[28] and reduce loneliness.[29]

Compassion and Health

Compassion practices seem to have multiple positive effects on physical and psychological health.[30] Specifically, compassion practices, as well as their constituent elements, seem to lead to reduced inflammation in the body.[31] This is especially important since inflammation can lead to the onset or an increase in the symptoms of lupus, arthritis, and other types of chronic pain[32] as well as cancer.[33] It is therefore not surprising that compassion practices also reduce chronic pain.[34] For instance, in a fight with Medousa, Wonder Woman is forced to blind herself to save a young child. Each time the goddess Athena offers her a blessing, she chooses to help others instead of getting her sight back; her compassionate actions make the pain of her blindness more bearable. Her continued selflessness and compassion not only cause Athena to restore her sight but allow her to bind her sight with the goddess's, thereby sharing her wisdom.[35] Moreover, empathy may produce increases in brain grey matter, a reduction of which is typically associated with dementia.[36] Finally, mindfulness and compassion practices have also been associated with an increased life span.[37]

In addition to improved physical health, individuals can benefit from compassion practices in terms of psychological resilience and healing. Specifically, compassion practices have been shown to be helpful in reducing anxiety and depression[38] and posttraumatic stress disorder (PTSD)[39] as well as in creating meaning after a tragedy[40] and overcoming the fear of death.[41] An example of this occurs when Zeus asks Diana to be his champion but tells her to let the world be destroyed in the process. Diana looks at our world with compassion and thus makes a choice to save the world. Although she loses her God-given powers in the process, she gains new and better ones because of her choice,[42] proving that her love of humans is indeed her strength and not her weakness, as Ares claims.[43] In fact, compassion seems to create feelings similar to love,[44] thus increasing happiness[45] and reducing suffering[46] in those who practice it. Finally, compassion creates a sense of connection to others, which reduces loneliness and enhances overall physical and psychological well-being.[47]

Love Is All You Need

Wonder Woman fights for love and equality for all people.[48] Even when Ares accuses her of being weak because of her love for others, she reminds herself that love gives her strength.[49] Indeed, compassionate love toward others can build resilience.[50] Specifically, compassion is associated with more grey matter, less inflammation, and healthier telemeres,[51] all of which are markers of improved health and longevity. In addition, compassion can reduce the symptoms of depression, anxiety, and PTSD[52] and increase positive mood.[53] Overall, it seems that Wonder Woman is on the right track in terms of her belief that her compassion is her strength, as compassion seems to provide people with improved physical and psychological health.

Comic Book References

All Star Comics #8 (1941). "Two New Members Win Their Spurs." Script: G. Fox. Art: E. E. Hibbard,.

Kingdom Come (1996). Script: M. Waid. Art: A. Ross & T. Klein.

The Legend of Wonder Woman #1–9 (2015–2016). Script: R. De Liz. Art: R. Dillon.

Wonder Woman #19 (2008). "Expatriate, Part 2: Lifeblood." Script: G. Simone. Art: B. Chang.

Wonder Woman #37 (2009). "Warkiller," part 2 of 4: "Of Two Minds." Script: G. Simone. Art: B. Chang.

Wonder Woman #141 (1999). "Trinity 98 Part II." Script: E. Luke. Art: A. Hughes, Y. Paquette, B.

Wonder Woman #200 (2004). "Down to Earth—Conclusion." Script: G. Rucka. Art: R. Snyder & D. Johnson.

Wonder Woman #210 (2005). "Stoned, Conclusion." Script: G. Rucka. Art: D. Johnson, & R. Snyder.

Wonder Woman #217 (2005). "The Bronze Doors, Conclusion." Script: G. Rucka. Art: R. Morales, M. Bair, & M. Propst.

Wonder Woman: Spirit of Truth (2001). Script: P. Dini & A. Ross. Art: A. Ross.

Other References

Brown, K. W., & Ryan, R. M. (2003). The benefits of being present: Mindfulness and its role in psychological well-being. *Journal of Personality & Social Psychology, 84*(4), 822–848.

Carlson, L. E., Beattie, T. L., Giese-Davis, J., Faris, P., Tamagawa, R., Fick, L. J., Degelman, E. S., & Speca, M. (2015). Mindfulness based cancer recovery and supportive expressive therapy maintain telomere length relative to controls in distressed breast cancer survivors. *Cancer, 121*(3), 476–484.

Cole, S. W., Hawkley, L. C., Arevalo, J. M., Sung, C. Y., Rose, R. M., & Cacioppo, J. T. (2007). Social regulation of gene expression in human leukocytes. *Genome Biology, 8*(9), R189.

Coussens, L. M., & Werb, Z. (2002). Inflammation and cancer. *Nature, 420*(6917), 860–867.

Darwin, C. (1979). *The origin of species by means of natural selection: Or, The preservation of favored races in the struggle for life.* New York, NY: Avenel.

Darwin, C. (1989). *The descent of man, and selection in relation to sex.* New York, NY: New York University Press.

Davidson, R. J., Kabat-Zinn, J., Schumacher, J., Rosenkranz, M., Muller, D., Santorelli, S. F., Urbanowsi, F., Harrington, A., Bonus, K., & Sheridan, J. F. (2003). Alterations in brain and immune function produced by mindfulness meditation. *Psychosomatic Medicine, 65*(4), 564–570.

Dawkins, R. (2016). *The selfish gene.* Oxford, UK: Oxford University Press.

Desrosiers, A., Vine, V., Klemanski, D. H., & Nolen-Hoeksema, S. (2013). Mindfulness and emotion regulation in depression and anxiety: Common and distinct mechanisms of action. *Depression & Anxiety, 30*(7), 654–661.

Epel, E., Daubenmier, J., Moskowitz, J. T., Folkman, S., & Blackburn, E. (2009). Can meditation slow rate of cellular aging? Cognitive stress, mindfulness, and telomeres. *Annals of the New York Academy of Sciences, 1172*(1), 34–53.

Graff, L. A., Walker, J. R., & Bernstein, C. N. (2009). Depression and anxiety in inflammatory bowel disease: A review of comorbidity and management. *Inflammatory Bowel Diseases, 15*(7), 1105–1118.

Hoge, E. A., Chen, M. M., Orr, E., Metcalf, C. A., Fischer, L. E., Pollack, M. H., De Vivo, I., & Simon, N. M. (2013). Loving-kindness meditation practice associated with longer telomeres in women. *Brain, Behavior, & Immunity, 32,* 159–163.

Jinpa, T. (2016). *A fearless heart: How the courage to be compassionate can transform our lives.* New York, NY: Avery.

Kabat-Zinn, J. (1982). An outpatient program in behavioral medicine for chronic pain patients based on the practice of mindfulness meditation: Theoretical considerations and preliminary results. *General Hospital Psychiatry, 4*(1), 33–47.

Kearney, D. J., Malte, C. A., McManus, C., Martinez, M. E., Felleman, B., & Simpson, T. L. (2013). Loving-kindness meditation for posttraumatic stress disorder: A pilot study. *Journal of Traumatic Stress, 26*(4), 426–434.

Killingsworth, M. A., & Gilbert, D. T. (2010). A wandering mind is an unhappy mind. *Science, 330*(6006), 932–932.

Klimecki, O. M., Leiberg, S., Lamm, C., & Singer, T. (2012). Functional neural plasticity and associated changes in positive affect after compassion training. *Cerebral Cortex, 23*(7), 1552–1561.

Klimecki, O., & Singer, T. (2012). Empathic distress fatigue rather than compassion fatigue? Integrating findings from empathy research in psychology and social neuroscience. In B. Oakley. A. Knafo, G. Madhavan, & D. S. Wilson (Eds.), *Pathological altruism* (pp. 368–383). New York, NY: Oxford University Press.

Leung, M. K., Chan, C. C., Yin, J., Lee, C. F., So, K. F., & Lee, T. M. (2012). Increased gray matter volume in the right angular and posterior parahippocampal gyri in loving-kindness meditators. *Social Cognitive & Affective Neuroscience, 8*(1), 34–39.

O'Connor, L. E., Berry, J. W., Weiss, J., & Gilbert, P. (2002). Guilt, fear, submission, and empathy in depression. *Journal of Affective Disorders, 71*(1), 19–27.

O'Connor, L., Langan, R., Berry, J., Stiver, D., Hanson, R., Ark, W., & Li, T. (2015). Empathy, compassionate altruism and psychological well-being in contemplative practitioners across five traditions. *Psychology, 6*(8), 989–1000.

Park, C. L., & Ai, A. L. (2006). Meaning making and growth: New directions for research on survivors of trauma. *Journal of Loss & Trauma, 11*(5), 389–407.

Piff, P. K., Dietze, P., Feinberg, M., Stancato, D. M., & Keltner, D. (2015). Awe, the small self, and prosocial behavior. *Journal of Personality & Social Psychology, 108*(6), 883–899.

Poulin, M. J., Brown, S. L., Dillard, A. J., & Smith, D. M. (2013). Giving to others and the association between stress and mortality. *American Journal of Public Health, 103*(9), 1649–1655.

Rudd, M., Vohs, K. D., & Aaker, J. (2012). Awe expands people's perception of time, alters decision making, and enhances well-being. *Psychological Science, 23*(10), 1130–1136.

Ryan, R. M., Huta, V., & Deci, E. L. (2008). Living well: A self-determination theory perspective on eudaimonia. *Journal of Happiness Studies, 9*(1), 139–170.

Seppälä, E. (2013). The compassionate mind: Science shows why it's healthy and how it spreads. *Observer, 26*(5). http://www.psychologicalscience.org/index.php/publications/observer/2013/may-june-13/the-compassionate-mind.html.

Stellar, J. E., John-Henderson, N., Anderson, C. L., Gordon, A. M., McNeil, G. D., & Keltner, D. (2015). Positive affect and markers of inflammation: Discrete positive emotions predict lower levels of inflammatory cytokines. *Emotion, 15*(2), 129–133.

Yalom, I. (2008). *From staring at the sun: Overcoming the terror of death.* San Francisco, CA: Jossey-Bass.

Zhang, J. M., & An, J. (2007). Cytokines, inflammation and pain. *International Anesthesiology Clinics, 45*(2), 27–37.

Notes

1. *Wonder Woman* #37 (2009).
2. Seppälä (2013).
3. Darwin (1979).
4. Dawkins (2016).
5. Darwin (1989).
6. *Wonder Woman* #37 (2009).
7. Fredrickson et al. (2008); Hoge et al. (2013); Kearney et al. (2013).
8. Jinpa (2016).
9. *Batman: The Brave and the Bold* episode 3–4 "Scorn of the Star Sapphire!" (July 26, 2009).
10. *Wonder Woman* #19 (2008).
11. Brown & Ryan (2003).
12. *Wonder Woman* #141 (1999).
13. Jinpa (2016).

14. *Kingdom Come* #4 (1996).
15. Morgan (2003).
16. Kabat-Zinn (1982).
17. Brown & Ryan (2003); Killingsworth & Gilbert (2010).
18. Davidson et al. (2003).
19. Carlson et al. (2015).
20. O'Connor et al. (2002).
21. O'Connor et al. (2002).
22. Klimecki & Singer (2012).
23. *Wonder Woman: Spirit of Truth* (2010).
24. Fredrickson et al. (2008); O'Connor et al. (2015).
25. O'Connor et al. (2015).
26. *Wonder Woman: Spirit of Truth* (2010).
27. *All Star Comics* #8 (1941), *The Legend of Wonder Woman* #1–9 (2015–2016).
28. Klimecki et al. (2012).
29. Jinpa (2016).
30. Cole et al. (2007); Hoge et al. (2013); Kearney et al. (2013).
31. Cole et al, (2007); Stellar et al. (2015).
32. Zhang & An (2007).
33. Coussens & Werb (2002).
34. Zhang & An (2007).
35. *Wonder Woman* #210, #217 (2005).
36. Leung et al. (2012).
37. Carlson et al. (2015); Epel et al. (2009); Hoge et al. (2013).
38. Graff et al. (2009).
39. Kearney et al. (2013).
40. Park & Ai (2006).
41. Yalom (2008).
42. *The Legend of Wonder Woman* #7–9 (2016).
43. *Wonder Woman* #37 (2009).
44. Klimecki et al. (2012).
45. Ryan et al. (2008).
46. Klimecki et al. (2012).
47. Jinpa (2016); Piff et al. (2015); Poulin et al. (2013); Rudd et al. (2012).
48. *Wonder Woman* #200 (2004).
49. *Wonder Woman* #37 (2009).
50. Cole et al. (2007); Hoge et al. (2013); Kearney et al. (2013).
51. Cole et al. (2007); Epel et al. (2009); Leung et al. (2012).
52. Desrosiers et al. (2013); Kearney et al. (2013).
53. Fredrickson et al. (2008).

CHAPTER TWELVE

Feminist Psychology: Teaching How to Be Wonderful

MARA WOOD

*"A woman is every bit as good as a man if given the chance!
And you're going to be given the chance!"*
—Wonder Woman[1]

*"Not even girls want to be girls so long as our feminine
archetype lacks force, strength, and power. Not wanting to be
girls, they don't want to be tender, submissive, peace-loving
as good women are. Women's strong qualities have become
despised because of their weakness. The obvious remedy is to
create a feminine character with all the strength of Superman
plus all the allure of a good and beautiful woman."*
—psychologist William Moulton Marston[2]

Feminist psychology is best understood as the explicit understanding and recognition of the ways in which women
behave.[3] The history of psychology, and therefore the history

of psychological research, has been limited to the understanding and experiences of men. Our early understanding of many psychological phenomena was filtered through the minds of male psychologists, and gender differences were rarely reported or considered.[4] Gender differences reported by psychologists were androcentric and discounted the abilities of women and the similarities between the genders. Feminist psychology instead took into account the unique experiences of women. William Moulton Marston, creator of *Wonder Woman*, had views on women that differed from much public opinion, notably in the natural superiority he felt women possess. Although his views are not commonly held as feminist (the superiority of women rather than the equality of the sexes), his superheroine embodies the culmination of the first feminist movement as well as feminist psychology. After this period, Wonder Woman continues to be both a reflection of and commentary on feminism in America.

Feminist Psychology Origins

Sigmund Freud, one of the early developers of psychology as we know it today, is an unlikely inspiration for feminist psychology. His theory of psychoanalysis often centered on the male perspective. For example, his theory of the Oedipal complex and the presence of penis envy in women are decidedly masculine and excluding in that these theories are tied to child psychosocial development and the idea that every woman secretly wants a penis.[5] In Freud's theory, boys come out of their childhood development with a superego, a part of the subconscious that dictates morality. The development of the superego is a result of the conflict between the boy and the father for the attention and love of the mother. The female equivalent, the

Electra complex, was not nearly as developed. Proposed by Carl Jung, the Electra complex involves young girls supposedly falling in love with their fathers and competing with their mothers for the fathers' attention.[6] Additionally, Freud believed that the outcome of childhood development for girls was passivity and masochism. These two tendencies grew from the daughter's desire to be impregnated by the father (to be acted upon by another person and willingly experience pain).[7] With a far less developed superego and the end goal of passivity, Freud portrayed woman as psychologically inferior to men.

The Female Response to Freud

Women in the field of psychology tended to find Freud's understanding of psychological forces in women lacking. Much of the early understanding of psychological forces operating within women were defined by men, implying a theory of psychology that better represented the desires and disappointments of men rather than unbiased insight.[8] As a response to Freud, Karen Horney and other female psychologists developed theories of psychology that did not exclude women.[9] Horney did not believe that the envy of a penis was part of the growth and development of a female child. Rather, she considered the source of envy to be the social status and recognition given to men over women.[10] She rejected Freud's theory in 1926 and later introduced the term *womb envy*,[11] her idea that men envy women's power of creation and direct connection to their children. Horney had taken a Freudian concept and framed it within the understanding of women and the female experience.

It is no surprise that the buildup to the beginning of feminist psychology occurred at the same time as the buildup to the creation of Wonder Woman. The first wave of feminism, which included women's right to vote, coincided with the early growth of psychology. The best-known first wave work occurred between 1900 and 1920 and ended when women were granted the right to vote. During that period, psychologists developed theories of intelligence and intelligence testing, classical conditioning, and behaviorism.[12] Many of those psychological theories are still relevant today. Though some notable women were involved in the early growth of psychology, such as Mary Whiton Calkins (the first female president of the American Psychological Association) and Margaret Floy Washburn (the first woman to receive a PhD in psychology), women were generally excluded from academia.[13] Elizabeth Holloway, the wife of William Moulton Marston, held a degree in psychology but was not permitted to attend college with men, where much of the cutting edge psychological research was being conducted. She was, however, invited to be a lecturer at her alma mater.[14]

Marston's "Feminist" Perspective

In 1937 Marston proclaimed that women would begin to establish a matriarchy within a hundred years.[15] It was not merely equality that Marston predicted; he believed that women would be the dominant gender in place of men. Because women have twice the number of love-generating organs as men, he argued, it made biological sense for women to rule the world.[16] His belief evolved from his theory of emotions, published in 1928. Human emotion, Marston explained, came from four main factors: dominance, compliance, submission, and inducement. Inducement is an encouraging force to submit to the will of the inducer. It is the most desirable trait to use, producing pleasantness in the submissive person and in the inducer. It is also the trait Marston observed most often in women. Wonder Woman, who first graced the pages of All-Star Comics in 1941, appeared to be the cumulative exemplar of Marston's theory of female superiority.

Marston initially created the character to teach readers—especially boys and men—that women are capable.[17]

Wonder Woman is depicted as more than just capable in her early appearances. Described "as lovely as Aphrodite—as wise as Athena—with the speed of Mercury and the strength of Hercules"[18] (though at times noted to be stronger than Hercules and swifter than Mercury[19]), she was Marston's vehicle for showing what women were capable of doing. Wonder Woman is shown caring for an injured man, competing in athletic events, and gaining the approval of her mother.[20] Further, she came from a society in which love and justice provided freedom and strength through matriarchal leadership.[21] With the vote for white women secured in America, it seemed that a change in politics was on the horizon. Paradise Island, ruled and populated by women, was Marston's model government. Wonder Woman, an emissary from Paradise Island, is sent to America, the last citadel for equal rights for women.[22] It is easy to see that Marston had high hopes for political advances if women provided the right model.

Marston's view of women as leaders is explicitly played out when he describes the world a thousand years in the future in *Wonder Woman* #7. The world is led by a woman who has "taught people to elect officials who serve the public while expecting nothing for themselves."[23] As president, she has reduced the influence of men. Men in this future embody corruption in politics that ended only when women took control of the government. Marston also writes of women who are unsuited for leadership, both in his futuristic ideal (Queen Andra) and in his present-day world (Queen Clea).[24] It is interesting to note that in Marston's ideal future, men still hold positions of influence in both the military and the police.[25] Marston's ideal society still has a place for men, albeit those willing to submit to a matriarchal leader.

More Alike Than We Know

Early psychological studies discounted the effect of psychological phenomena on women and the way they experienced their lives. Differences were attributed to biology rather than social influences, and this furthered stereotypes of gender behaviors.[26] Early influencers and pioneers of psychology such as William James believed that women possessed inferior characteristics, such as being "tender-minded."[27] Gender was not given much attention in the early years of psychology. The first wave of feminism at the turn of the twentieth century laid the foundation for feminist psychology, and then the second wave (1960s–1980s) seriously challenged the androcentric nature of psychology.[28] In doing so, researchers found that men and women are often more alike than different.[29]

In studies, there may be differences in the average results of men and women. However, because scores on a bell curve (any variable that is normally distributed, such as intelligence or height) fall in a range above and below the average, the majority of results for men and women overlap, indicating that there are far more similarities than differences between the sexes.[30] The differences that are observed can be controlled for to determine a correlation. For example, in academic achievement research, the majority of research studies do not show a difference between men and women. Initial research in achievement claimed that women had a fear of success; in reality, differences between men and women can be attributed to socially held stereotypes.[31]

One of Marston's core beliefs about women was their potential as leaders. He believed women's disposition to be less aggressive and less acquisitive than men's.[32] Marston was likely referring to social stereotypes in which aggression is less tolerated in women as well as his belief that men engaged more often in dominance than in inducement. Research reveals that there are no significant differences in aggression between girls and boys; however, social learning theory suggests that boys are more likely to learn aggressive tendencies by modeling themselves after grown men.[33] In society, women are expected to be less aggressive.[34] Marston's belief that women are naturally nonaggressive shows how influential perceptions of stereotypes and gender roles were during the time of his research.

Social Learning Theory and Social Structural Theory

Many of the psychological differences seen in men and women can be traced to theories of development. In feminist psychology, a popular theory of development is *social learning theory*.[35] This theory posits that boys and girls are rewarded by their parents or guardians differently. For instance, girls would be rewarded for playing cooperatively with other children and boys would be rewarded for independence. Social learning theory also includes the child's imitation and observation of others, particularly those the child feels connected to.[36] This theory posits that girls with reinforced feminine characteristics will tend to imitate their mothers on the basis of observation; masculine boys will tend to imitate their fathers. Beyond early childhood, gender stereotypes are reinforced by other caregivers, peers, and media. What may have originated as minimal differences become generalizations of how men and women should behave. Social learning theory became more acceptable in the field of feminist psychology because it deemphasized inherent gender differences that suggested that men had greater capacity for morality than women because of the male anatomy, as Freud suggested.[37]

Social structural theory builds upon social learning theory in that it considers that sex differences are built by accommodation to the sexual division of labor.[38] Although the division of labor may have been critical in evolutionary history, it is less important in modern society. However, division of labor based on sexual differences has had a lasting impact: Men traditionally have held roles that enable them to have greater status, wealth, and power, leading to dominance of men and submission of women.[39] Women, whose role in society is often domestic, develop communal skills, which in turn become stereotypical of women in general.[40] And because of the stereotype, women are relegated to certain sex-specific roles in society, thus disenfranchising them even more. Social structure reflects culture and the patterns of behaviors between people and the positions they occupy.[41]

Marston believed men and women to be inherently different, but his belief about the superior nurturing tendencies of women can be contested with today's knowledge. There are no significant differences between the nurturing ability of men and that of women; however, like other gender stereotypes, social learning can account for differences. As children, women are rewarded for engaging in nurturing play, such as holding and playing with dolls.[42] Studies of altruism show that women are more likely to provide help with "feminine" tasks, such as helping a new mother with a baby or cooking a meal for a needy family.[43] Men are altruistic but tend to provide different, more physical services, such as changing a tire for someone or helping people who have fallen down.[44] Once again, the primary differences between men and women can be attributed to what they are socialized to learn and what they feel experienced in performing. Further, jobs that require nurturing skills have been feminized, discouraging men from entering those fields.

Marston's *Wonder Woman* seeks to establish how similar men and women are to each other. Though he may have advocated for the superiority of women, the first step was to demonstrate the similarities between the genders. Wonder Woman consistently matches or exceeds any male competition she encounters. She attributes her success not to the blessings of the gods and goddesses but to the rigors of Amazon training. That training is an option for every woman, and those who undergo the intense program emerge with increased confidence, strength, clarity of mind, and love.[45] Diana carries this viewpoint with her into Man's World. When she meets Olive, a young girl excluded from baseball games with boys, Wonder Woman explains to her the reason she is no match for the boys: Olive has not practiced or developed her muscles. "You can be strong as any boy if you'll work hard and train yourself in athletics, the way boys do. We train little Amazon girls on Paradise Island to be stronger than your grown-up men!"[46] Stripping away gender norms and stereotypes and training in a similar manner gives Olive an opportunity to stand on equal ground with the boys in her neighborhood.

The Holliday Girls are another example of Marston demonstrating innate, equal ability between men and women through fiction. The Holliday Girls are members of a sorority that both Wonder Woman and Diana Prince befriend. Under their tenacious leader Etta Candy, the girls demonstrate incredible bravery, innovation, and loyalty. Often, they are called upon to join the army in missions or to perform important assignments for Wonder Woman.[47] In some stories, the ability of the Holliday Girls is doubted, usually by a man.[48] With the help of Wonder Woman, they prove that women are just as capable as men.

Suprema

Though Marston's view of women may be outdated in light of today's research, it is important that he saw innate ability in women and felt it should be unleashed. He witnessed the inequality of treatment between men and women. Living

WOMEN AS LEADERS

One lens through which feminist psychology can be examined in the *Wonder Woman* comics is leadership, specifically, the leadership styles men and women exhibit and how those styles impact those who follow. Social learning theory and social structural theory explain that the differences between men and women are due to socialization in different ways. Marston's belief in women's capacity for love and compassion was the source of his rationale for their capacity for leadership.[49]

Leadership roles have typically been coded masculine, implying that only men have the natural capacity for leading others. Research shows otherwise. Women, who stereotypically embody cooperation, mentoring, and collaboration, tend to have a different leadership style.[50] These communal skills have become part of the gender stereotype according to social structural theory. *Transformational leadership* is a style in which the leader works to gain the trust and confidence of the followers. She makes herself a role model for others. Transformational leadership is associated with greater effectiveness than are other types of leadership.[51]

Explaining women's leadership styles is not simple. Culture has an impact on how women behave, and there are women who have used their environments and expectations to cultivate a more masculine approach to leadership.[52] Often, leadership roles demand the same from men and women, meaning that differences in sex are moot. As with most observed sex differences, men and women are more similar than different. Generally speaking, however, men exhibit leadership skills that are less effective, such as attending to subordinates' failures and being absent or uninvolved during critical times.[53] All being said and done, the leadership styles women typically exhibit are significantly, if only slightly, correlated with effective leadership.[54]

Marston's view on female leadership differed in that he believed that women would induce men to carry out their desires.[55] More specifically, women would sexually enslave men, who in turn would happily—and lovingly—submit to their control. To do so, women would embody their feminine characteristics and couple it with dominance, a trait that often is associated with men and male roles. When Wonder Woman collaborates with the Justice League International, Guy Gardner doubts her capacity as a leader. He criticizes her pacifist tendencies and warm heart. Rather than argue, Wonder Woman demonstrates her tactical thinking and decision-making, winning Guy over as a follower.[56] Wonder Woman may not be the dominant leader of all the superheroes Marston envisioned, but she is an able leader of both men and women and can achieve success.

in a household with two very capable and brilliant women furthered his ideas of female superiority. Marston's original name for the character, Suprema, reflected his view of such superiority. His high opinion of women extended to his work on *Wonder Woman*; several women worked with Harry G. Peter on the art, Joye Murchison provided secretarial assistance and writing after Marston contracted polio, Alice Marble did editorial assists and contributed to the *Wonder Women of History* feature, and Lauretta Bender consulted and supported the comic series.[57] These women helped shape the Wonder Woman we know today. Marston promoted the idea that women were superior to men, and his Wonder Woman stories featured a female character who stood on equal ground with the men she encountered.

Comic Book References

All-Star Comics #8 (1941). "Introducing Wonder Woman." Script: W. M. Marston. Art: H. G. Peter.

Sensation Comics #2 (1942). "Dr. Poison." Script: W. M. Marston. Art: H. G. Peter.

Sensation Comics #9 (1942). "The Return of Diana Prince." Script: W. M. Marston. Art: H. G. Peter.

Sensation Comics #58 (1946). "The Bog Trap." Script: W. M. Marston. Art: H. G. Peter.

Sensation Comics #89 (1949). "Amazon Queen for a Day." Script: R. Kanigher. Art: H. G. Peter.

Wonder Woman #6 (1943). "The Conquest of Paradise." Script: W. M. Marston. Art: H. G. Peter.

Wonder Woman #7 (1943). "America's Wonder Women of Tomorrow!" Script: W. M. Marston. Art: H. G. Peter.

Wonder Woman #8 (1944). "Queen Clea's Tournament of Death." Script: W. M. Marston. Art: H. G. Peter.

Wonder Woman #38 (1949). "The Five Tasks of Thomas Tighe." Script: R. Kanigher. Art: H. G. Peter.

Wonder Woman #25 (1988). "The Burning School." Script: G. Perez. Art: C. Marrinan & W. Blyberg.

Other References

Daniels, L. (2000). *Wonder Woman: The complete history*. San Francisco, CA: Chronicle.

Denmark, F. L., & Fernandez, L. C. (1993). Historical development of the psychology of women. In F. L. Denmark & M. A. Paludi (Eds.), *Psychology of women: A handbook of issues and theories* (pp. 4–22). Westport, CT: Greenwood.

Eagly, A. H. (2007). Female leadership advantage and disadvantage: Resolving the contradictions. *Psychology of Women Quarterly, 31*, 1–12.

Eagly, A. H., & Wood, W. (1999). The origins of sex differences in human behavior: Evolved dispositions versus social roles. *American Psychologist, 54*(6), 408–423.

Hall, C. S., & Lindzey, G. (1957). *Theories of personality* (pp. 114–152). Hoboken, NJ: Wiley.

Held, L. (2010). Karen Horney. In A. Rutherford (Ed.), *Psychology's feminist voices multimedia internet archive*. Retrieved from http://www.feministvoices.com/karen -horney/.

Horney, K. (1967). *Feminine psychology*. New York, NY: Norton.

Hyde, J. S., & Rosenberg, B. G. (1976). *Half the human experience: The psychology of women*. Lexington, MA: DC Heath.

Kupfersmid, J. (1995). Does the Oedipal complex exist? *Psychotherapy: Theory, Research, Practice, Training, 32*(4), 535–547.

Marston, W. M. (1928). *Emotions of normal people*. New York, NY: Harcourt, Brace.

Marston, W. M. (1943). Why 100,000,000 Americans read comics. *American Scholar, 13*(1), 35–44.

Matlin, M. W. (1987). *The psychology of women*. Fort Worth, TX: Holt, Rinehart, & Winston.

Minton, H. L. (2000). Psychology and gender at the turn of the century. *American Psychologist, 55*(6), 613–615.

Myers, D. G. (2013). *Psychology* (10th ed.). New York, NY: Worth.

Scott, J. (2005). *Electra after Freud*. Ithaca, NY: Cornell University Press.

Notes

1. *Sensation Comics* #89 (1949).
2. Marston (1943).
3. Denmark & Fernandez (1993).
4. Denmark & Fernandez (1993).
5. Kupfersmid (1995).
6. Scott (2005).
7. Hyde & Rosenberg (1976).
8. Horney (1967).
9. Hall & Lindzey (1957).
10. Held (2010).
11. Hyde & Rosenberg (1976).
12. Myers (2013).
13. Myers (2013).
14. Daniels (2000).
15. Daniels (2000).
16. Daniels (2000).
17. Daniels (2000)
18. *All-Star Comics* #8 (1941).
19. *Sensation Comics* #9–10 (1942).
20. *All-Star Comics* #8 (1941).
21. *Sensation Comics* #2 (1942).
22. *All-Star Comics* #8 (1941).
23. *Wonder Woman* #7 (1943).
24. *Wonder Woman* #7 (1943); *Wonder Woman* #8 (1944).

25. *Wonder Woman* #7 (1943).
26. Daniels (2000).
27. Minton (2000).
28. Minton (2000).
29. Matlin (1987).
30. Matlin (1987).
31. Matlin (1987).
32. Daniels (2000).
33. Matlin (1987).
34. Matlin (1987).
35. Hyde & Rosenberg (1976).
36. Hyde & Rosenberg (1976).
37. Hyde & Rosenberg (1976).
38. Eagly & Wood (1999).
39. Eagly & Wood (1999).
40. Eagly & Wood (1999).
41. Eagly & Wood (1999).
42. Hyde & Rosenberg (1976).
43. Matlin (1987).
44. Matlin (1987).
45. *Wonder Woman* #6 (1943).
46. *Sensation Comics* #58 (1946).
47. *Sensation Comics* #2 (1942).
48. *Wonder Woman* #38 (1949).
49. Marston (1928).
50. Eagly (2007).
51. Eagly (2007).
52. Eagly (2007).
53. Eagly (2007).
54. Eagly (2007).
55. Daniels (2000).
56. *Wonder Woman* #25 (1988).
57. Daniels (2000).

Temperance

TRAVIS LANGLEY

Though commonly perceived as inactive, the virtue of *temperance* is more about restraint combined with actions. Its defining feature lies in managing temptation and finding a better way of doing things. A temperate person seeks balance while taking action. Wonder Woman exemplifies the *Character Strengths and Virtues* handbook's[1] temperate strengths of forgiveness and mercy, humility and modesty, prudence, and self-regulation, and she is clearly a person of action.

Forgiveness and mercy, for example, might seem to be only about choosing not to punish, seek revenge, or bear a grudge. Great strength may be required to feel forgiving inwardly when bestowing mercy outwardly. While fleeing her village during an air raid, nine-year-old Phan Thi Kim Phuc encountered falling napalm. Screaming in agony, the badly burned girl tore her napalm-covered clothes from her body and inadvertently became the subject of a Pulitzer Prize–winning photograph.[2]

After many surgeries and more years, she became an advocate for peace, speaking before crowds of thousands around the world. Upon meeting with one tearful veteran who said he had planned the bombing, she reassured him that she forgave him and hoped they could work together to help others.[3] Forgiveness is active.

Though the Amazons in Wonder Woman's stories value forgiveness and mercy, all wear bracelets as reminders that they should never again let men enslave them and a number of them distrust all men because of that history,[4] and yet they dedicate the entirety of Reform Island to helping wrongdoers become better people instead of punishing them.[5] Showing forgiveness and mercy becomes more difficult when transgressions are apparently deliberate and the consequences severe.[6] Diana, the Amazon who ventures out into Man's World to help, believes in these values. A person who is empathic, optimistic about people, and better at *perspective taking* (seeing others' points of view)[7] tends to show a more forgiving nature. Diana helps enemies reform, testifies on their behalf in court, helps people who have performed villainous acts try to turn over a new leaf, forgives others whether they ask for it or not, and will befriend people who have tried to kill her.[8]

The temperate strength of *modesty and humility* involves an honest, authentic assessment of oneself without arrogance, with greater interest in other people's better qualities than in their own; *modesty* referring to the person's external manner, with *humility* being the underlying, internal characteristic.[9] The modest person does not act like he or she is the center of the universe, and the truly humble person knows he or she is not. Although Wonder Woman's bathing suit attire may seem immodest through much of her history, there is nothing immodest about it by the standards of the Amazons who created it for her.[10] The essence of this temperate strength, showing greater interest in other people's strengths and well-being than in her own, is a consistent core part of her personality.

Prudence is about making smart choices. This temperate strength can be mistaken for paralysis when it is in fact about taking action judiciously, with responsibility, caution, and critical thought.[11] More so than many other personality trait, prudence may depend on the individual's intelligence because it can require abilities to analyze information, imagine alternatives (*divergent thinking*[12]), narrow down options (*convergent thinking*[13]), form long-term plans, and act with foresight.[14] When another Amazon criticizes her cautious nature, Diana tries to explain, "Patriarch's world is a complex place, Artemis. I've been trying to learn its ways before—" but impatient Artemis interrupts, calling her incapable of real action.[15] In the end, though, Artemis's impatience, impulsivity, hostility, and "my ambition and arrogance" get her killed, and the dying Artemis acknowledges that the more temperate Diana is the Amazon who should be Wonder Woman.[16]

Self-regulation (self-control or self-discipline) lets a person control his or her own actions in order to live up to personal standards and pursue goals.[17] This person has an *internal locus of control*,[18] seeing each individual as being in control of his or her own life (as opposed to an *external locus of control*, believing that factors outside the individual's control determine what happens[19]). Even though Wonder Woman might seem to be an obvious paragon of discipline and restraint, one of the later Marston stories indicated that Diana is not naturally self-restrained but instead will run wild if her bracelets are removed. When an enemy removes the bracelets, thinking that will make her weak, Diana announces that they helped her restrain herself because she is too strong, and she turns reckless, aggressive, and boastful until the bracelets are back in place.[20] This reflects her creator's views on using a compliance-related stimulus (in this case the bracelets) to help a person

Wonder Woman #3 (1943). Art: H. G. Peter. ©DC Comics.

exert restraint. Marston believed that "the moment" the person is no longer subjected to the stimulus, "the natural reflex equilibrium automatically re-establishes itself, and dominance emotion inevitably supplants compliance."[21] It is an unusual depiction of Diana, rare for Marston's stories and not seen in others.

Quintessence of temperance that she may be, her humility keeps Diana from taking her temperate qualities for granted. Caution, self-control, and mercy can require mindfulness and practice.[22] Honest self-appraisal includes being honest about dishonesty and recognizing the potential for self-deception.[23] The magic lasso she wears on her hip keeps Diana honest with herself[24] at all times and lets her compel herself to resist selfish temptation.[25] Although the strengths of temperance may receive less praise and endorsement in Western culture than do other positive qualities, virtually all religious and philosophical views value temperance as a virtue and feel that it helps people enjoy healthy, less chaotic lives.[26] In her first live-action theatrical appearance, it is Wonder Woman whose temperance makes her seem the most heroic[27] when other superheroes act rashly, choose poorly, get deceived, and come into conflict that could be avoided.[28] A level head can prevail.

Comic Book References

All-Star Comics #8 (1941). "Introducing Wonder Woman." Script: W. M. Marston. Art: H. G. Peter.

Wonder Woman #1 (1942). "The Origin of Wonder Woman." Script: W. M. Marston. Art: H. G. Peter.

Wonder Woman #3 (1943). "A Spy on Paradise Island." Script: W. M. Marston. Art: H. G. Peter.

Wonder Woman #4 (1943). "The Treachery of Mavis." Script: W. M. Marston. Art: H. G. Peter.

Wonder Woman #19 (1946). "Invisible Terror." Script: W. M. Marston. Art: H. G. Peter.

Wonder Woman #98 (1995). "Sisters." Script: W. Messner-Loebs. Art: M. Deodata, Jr.

Wonder Woman #100 (1995). "Blank Madness." Script: W. Messner-Loebs. Art: M. Deodata, Jr.

Wonder Woman #170 (2001). "She's a Wonder!" Script: P. Jimenez & J. Kelly. Art: P. Jimenez & A. Lanning.

Other References

Adams, G. S., & Inesi, M. E. (2016). Impediments to forgiveness: Victim and transgressor attributions of intent and guilt. *Journal of Personality & Social Psychology*, epub ahead of print. http://psycnet.apa.org/psycinfo/2016-40097-001/.

Alban Metcalfe, R. J. (1978). Divergent thinking "threshold effect": IQ, age, or skill? *Journal of Experimental Education, 47*(1), 4–8.

Baumann & Kuhl (2005). How to resist temptation: The effects of locus of control versus autonomy support on self-regulatory dynamics. *Journal of Personality, 73*(2), 443–470.

Berman, E. (2016, March 24). *How Wonder Woman steals the spotlight in Batman v Superman.* Time: http://time.com/4271356/wonder-woman-batman-v-superman/.

Brandtstädter, J. (1989). Personal self-regulation of development: Cross-sequential analyses of development-related control beliefs and emotions. *Developmental Psychology, 25*(1), 96–108.

Bowman, T. (1997, December 14). *Veteran's admission to napalm victim a lie; minister says he never meant to deceive with "story of forgiveness."* Baltimore Sun: http://articles.baltimoresun.com/1997-12-14/news/1997348085_1_plummer-napalm-phuc.

Cropley, A. (2006). In praise of convergent thinking. *Creativity Research Journal, 18*(3), 391–404.

Gearan, A. (1997, April 20). *Embrace silence decades of nightmares for ex-pilot.* Los Angeles Times: http://articles.latimes.com/1997-04-20/news/mn-50586_1_helicopter-pilot.

Giammarco, E. A., & Vernon, P. A. (2014). Vengeance and the Dark Triad: The role of empathy and perspective taking in trait forgivingness. *Personality & Individual Differences, 67*, 23–29.

Golden, N. (2013, November 20). *Vietnamese bombing survivor came from war, now preaches peace.* Catholic Philly: http://catholicphilly.com/2013/11/us-world-news/national-catholic-news/vietnamese-bombing-survivor-came-from-war-now-preaches-peace/.

Hallinan, J. (2014). *Kidding ourselves: The hidden power of self-deception.* New York, NY: Crown.

Halevy, R., Shalvi, S., & Verschurere, B. (2014). Being honest about dishonesty: Correlating self-reports and actual lying. *Human Communication Research, 40*(1), 54–72.

Kim, K. H. (2008). Meta-analyses of the relationship of creative achievement to both IQ and divergent thinking test scores. *Journal of Creative Behavior, 42*(2), 106–130.

Lannamann, N. (2016). *Batman v Superman doesn't have enough Wonder Woman.* The Portland Mercury: http://www.portlandmercury.com/film/2016/03/23/17775919/batman-v-superman-doesnt-have-enough-wonder-woman.

Marston, W. M. (1928). *Emotions of normal people.* London, UK: Kegan Paul, Trench, Trubner.

Nuzzo, R. (2015). Fooling ourselves. *Nature, 526*(7572), 182–185.

Peterson, C., & Seligman, M. E. P. (2004). *Character strengths and virtues: A handbook and classification.* Washington, DC: American Psychological Association.

Pulitzer Prizes (n.d.). *The 1973 Pulitzer Prize winner in spot news photography.* Pulitzer: http://www.pulitzer.org/winners/huynh-cong-ut.

Rotter, J. B. (1966). Generalized expectancies for internal versus external locus of control of reinforcement. *Psychological Monographs, 80*(1, whole no. 609).

Ruisel, I. (2006). Is prudence a bridge between intelligence and personality? *Studia Psychologica, 48*(3), 197–206.

Sandage, S. J., & Worthington, E. L., Jr., (2010). Comparison of two group interventions to promote forgiveness: Empathy as a mediator of change. *Journal of Mental Health Counseling, 31*(1), 35–57.

Takaku, S., Weiner, B., & Ohbuchi, K. (2001). A cross-cultural examination of the effects of apology and perspective-taking on forgiveness. *Journal of Language & Social Psychology, 20*(1–2), 144–166.

Twenge, J. M., Zhang, L., & Im, C. (2004). It's beyond my control: A cross-temporal meta-analysis of increasing externality in locus of control, 1960–2002. *Personality & Social Psychology Review, 8*(3), 308–319.

Visci, M. (2016, April 7). *Wonder Woman was the best part of Batman v Superman: Dawn of Justice.* The Saint: http://www.thesaint-online.com/2016/04/wonder-woman-was-the-best-part-of-batman-v-superman-dawn-of-justice/.

Vigilla, H. (2016, March 28). *Batman v Superman: Wonder Woman could have been more heroic if the guys weren't such meatheads.* Flixist: http://www.flixist.com/batman-v-superman-wonder-woman-could-have-been-more-heroic-if-the-guys-weren-t-such-meatheads-major-spoilers--220445.phtml.

World Press Photo (n.d.). *Nick Ut.* World Press Photo: http://www.worldpressphoto.org/collection/photo/1973/world-press-photo-year/nick-ut.

Xu, H., Kou, Y., & Zhong, N. (2012). The effect of empathy on cooperation, forgiveness, and "returning good for evil" in the prisoner's dilemma. *Personnel Management, 41*(5), 105–115.

Notes

1. Peterson & Seligman (2004).
2. Pulitzer Prizes (n.d.); World Press Photo (n.d.).
3. Gearan (1997); Golden (2013). The veteran's later admission that he lied and had not been involved (Bowman, 1997) does not detract from the genuine nature of Kim Phuc's forgiveness and expression of mercy at the time.
4. *Wonder Woman* #1 (1942).
5. a.k.a. Transformation Island, first seen in *Wonder Woman* #4 (1943).
6. Adams & Inesi (2016); Takaku et al. (2001).
7. Giammarco & Vernon (2014); Sandage & Worthington (2010); Xu et al. (2012).
8. *Justice League* episode 4–5, "The Balance" (May 28, 2005).
9. Peterson & Seligman (2004).
10. *All-Star Comics* #8 (1941).
11. Peterson & Seligman (2004).
12. Alban Metcalfe (1978); Kim (2008).
13. Cropley (2006).
14. Ruisel (2006).
15. *Wonder Woman* #98 (1995).
16. *Wonder Woman* #100 (1995).
17. Peterson & Seligman (2004).
18. Baumann & Kuhl (2005); Brandtstädter (1989); Twenge et al. (2004).
19. Rotter (1966).
20. *Wonder Woman* #19 (1946).
21. Marston (1928), p. 195.
22. Nuzzo (2015).
23. Halevy et al. (2014); Hallinan (2014).
24. *Wonder Woman* #170 (2001).
25. *Wonder Woman* #3 (1943).
26. Peterson & Seligman (2004).
27. Berman (2016); Lannamann (2016); Vigilla (2016); Visci (2016).
28. *Batman v. Superman: Dawn of Justice* (2016 motion picture).

IN MALE-DOMINATED CULTURE, WHERE DOES THE HERO WHO IS NOT A MAN FIT IN WHILE REMAINING FULLY WOMAN? AND WHY IS THAT EVEN AN ISSUE?

PART IV

MAN'S WORLD

CHAPTER THIRTEEN

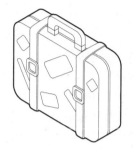

An Amazon in a World of Men

LARA TAYLOR KESTER
AND NINA TAYLOR KESTER

"In America you'll indeed be a 'Wonder Woman,' for I have taught you well!"
—Hippolyta[1]

> *"The effective integration of immigrants in educational, work, and community settings is essential to the well-being of this country and its future."*
> —former American Psychological Association president Melba J. T. Vasquez[2]

Cross-cultural psychology understands that an individual's behavior is influenced by his or her cultural surroundings and experiences.[3] New connections are established every day from one end of the globe to the other. Media will use a greater variety of cultural references, expanding each individual's exposure to multiple cultures. The need to negotiate multicultural experiences becomes a greater part of daily life. Multicultur-alism itself becomes more multifaceted. It is now understood that culture is any set of shared knowledge, beliefs, values, and customs that facilitate building connections between individu-als for mutual benefit. *Acculturation*—the process of change that arises when two cultures come into contact with one another—occurs not just when encountering a new race or ethnicity, but also when encountering any number of cultures centered on our social experiences or passions, like hip-hop music or geeky comic books, in addition to the cultures of countries from all over the world.[4]

Princess Diana of Themyscira, Wonder Woman, is a repre-sentation of this modern-day experience with acculturation. From the depth and variety of the stories written about her, Diana goes through almost every different process and role an individual finds herself in when encountering a new culture. She is both an immigrant, someone who leaves her coun-try with the purpose of establishing residency in a new land, and a sojourner, someone who visits a foreign country with a distinct purpose and role for a limited amount of time. Wonder Woman experiences every method of adapting or acculturating to a new culture, whether from the perspective of the new girl in town or of a member of the dominant culture in her own homeland of Themyscira. She is an Amazon, an American, an Amazon-American, and neither.

Diana provides a safe, fun way to explore issues of diver-sity and cultural differences by providing insight from every angle. She leads us through the acculturation process of first impression, negotiating the conflict that often ensues and find-ing a solution to benefit all.[5] Wonder Woman is an ambassador, mediator, immigrant, outcast, princess, warrior, angel, and hero of multiculturalism.

Cultural Identity

If culture is the set of knowledge, beliefs, values, and customs one shares with a group of other like-minded people, one's *cultural identity* can be viewed as one's self-defined culture and internal connection to that group of people.[6] Until Steve Trevor crash-lands on Themyscira, Diana has only known one culture that has shaped her cultural identity: the Amazon culture of her mother and sisterhood. Diana does not yet identify herself as the Wonder Woman of the man's world, but instead as one of many brave and empowered Amazon women inhabiting Paradise Island where men are neither wanted nor allowed and where truth is highly valued. There, she is well educated as a scientist, diplomat, and honorable warrior under the protection of the Amazons' patrons, Aphrodite and Athena, sharing many customs of dress, ceremony, and democracy with ancient Greece and early feminism.[7]

There are three parts that make up an individual's cultural identity—cultural knowledge, category label, and social connections.[8] *Cultural knowledge* comprises what the individual knows about the practices, beliefs, and values of his or her culture. It also consists of a shared understanding of symbolic meanings, and characteristics that are important to the group, much like the Amazons' reverence for treasures given to them by the Greek gods and their appreciation of wisdom and strength in battle. *Category labels* are how a person labels the group he or she belongs to. These labels can be self-chosen, or imposed by others. Though to others she has been known as freak, princess, goddess, child of clay, and ambassador, among many other labels, on Wonder Woman's own book of essays and speeches she requires that her authorship be credited simply as Diana of Themyscira.[9]

The last part of cultural identity, *social connections*, refers to relationships an individual has with others within a culture.[10] Humans are social creatures by nature, and social relationships help build an emotional connection and attachment to the culture and those within the group. Family serves as the most significant relationship in forming opinions about and connection to culture, being a person's first social experience. Diana forges social connections in each new culture she encounters as part of her diplomatic nature, be it her relationship with Steve Trevor, fellow super friends in the Justice League, her staffers as an ambassador, or UN soldiers during a quick overthrow of a tyrant halfway around the world.[11]

These components, when combined, give individuals not only their own cultural identity, but also a frame of reference for what is appropriate and acceptable behavior, where they fit into the group, and a sense of belonging or feeling at home with others within the group.[12] Belonging to a group can help group members feel safe, accepted, and valued.[13] Wonder Woman establishes strong cultural ties to the Justice League, which help her define her cultural identity away from her original home.[14] This can be especially important when one comes in contact with a new culture, or moves out of his or her own culture entirely.

Diana's cultural experiences imperceptibly form the framework that motivates her behavior and helps her to judge and evaluate the actions of others, without her even realizing it.[15] In some versions of Wonder Woman's origin story, she is quick to judge Steve Trevor and the rest of his military unit and to accuse him of trying to attack Themyscira.[16] Without the influence of her sisters and their descriptions of men, she may have seen his actions as explorative or peace-loving. Her culture and her personal cultural identity are the lenses through which all of her future experiences are seen.

Cognitive Changes

A transition, such as when Diana comes in contact with Americans for the first time, causes the mind to lose its equilibrium, and creates a need for it to regain that balance. When a person encounters something new, whether it be an object, a phrase, or an experience, the mind has to find a way to accept the new information, using schemas. *Schemas* are the mental representations individuals use to define and understand the world.[17] There are two ways that new information can be interpreted and stored away into schemas: assimilation and accommodation.

Assimilation utilizes the current schemas in the mind to make sense of new experiences.[18] In this cognitive process, a new object or experience is similar enough that it can be compared to a previous experience. Diana uses assimilation when she calls our planes "metal birds," an army commander a "high priestess of war," or pinup girls painted on the sides of planes "goddesses of our people."[19] *Accommodation*, on the other hand, is when an entirely new schema is created. When the Flash introduces Wonder Woman to the American delicacy of iced mochas, Wonder Woman's experience drinking it fails to fit into her existing schemas and she simply replies, "Mmm . . . They don't have these on Themyscira," as she internally develops a new schema explicitly for iced mochas.[20]

When faced with a new experience or object, the mind can incorporate it into an already known category or create a new category altogether. The first time someone sees a motorcycle, that individual might think of it as a large bicycle or a two-wheeled car, much like Diana's assimilation of planes. Someone else may see it and create a whole new category for motorcycle, in the way that Diana does for iced mochas. These internal processes allow a person such as Diana to make sense of her experiences and pave the way for her to reflect on her values.

Acculturation

When two cultures come into contact, as a result of either a permanent move or a temporary visit, individuals in both the dominant host culture and the minority culture begin to go through a shift. Strange, new customs are experienced, new figures of speech are overheard, new fashion trends are worn, and new values are presented. While the mind is taking all of this information in and trying to work it into schemas, individuals also have to decide how much these new ideas are going influence their way of life and their behavior—an example of acculturation.[21]

Acculturation is the major challenge that those coming into contact with new cultures have to grapple with.[22] While Wonder Woman has many other (sometimes literal) demons to battle, she also has to contend with the fact that she is now living in a world very different from Themyscira. These experiences of change can be stressful, as well as part of a process of learning and growth that provides an expansion of worldviews, cultural competence, and adaptability.[23] Oftentimes, Diana is depicted as a bridge between the Amazons and the world of men, curious about the outside world, and more adaptable than her sisters, making her ripe for these kinds of learning experiences and suitable for her job as an ambassador to America.

During the acculturation process, the individual has to answer two questions, usually subconsciously: Is it important to maintain one's cultural identity and characteristics? Is it important to create or maintain relationships with other groups? How these questions are answered defines how an individual fits into

Table 1: Four Modes of Acculturation		
	Maintain cultural identity?	Create/Maintain outside relationships?
Assimilation	No	Yes
Integration	Yes	Yes
Separation	Yes	No
Marginalization	No	No

one of four modes of acculturation—assimilation, integration, separation, and marginalization.[24] See Table 1 for how these questions break down into modes of acculturation.

Cultural assimilation is different from the cognitive assimilation described earlier. In cultural assimilation, individuals immerse themselves in the new culture entirely and give up the customs from their home culture.[25] In a controversial storyline, Diana values her romance with Steve Trevor over her connection to Themyscira. She gives up her uniform, powers, and coveted lasso of truth to live only as Diana Prince and no longer Wonder Woman.[26] In general, members of both the host culture and the immigrant culture (and some Wonder Woman fans) see assimilation as a loss of identity.[27] (For writer Dennis O'Neil's recollections about that writing storyline, see his interview in chapter 16, "Snapping Necks and Wearing Pants: Symbols, Schemas, and Stress Over Change.")

Integration involves adapting to the new culture by mixing it with the home culture to make it one's own—for example, by making a gun, a weapon from man's world, part of an Amazon competition to see who can deflect bullets.[28] As the contemporary world incorporates more and more multicultural influences with a focus on globalization, this has become the preferred mode of acculturation.[29] This could be partly because of the desire for people to feel strong about who they are, but also take some positive learning experience away from being part of a new culture.

Individuals can choose to blend cultures, create a new multi-cultural identity altogether, or keep them separate. In fact, some people identify with the host culture in one setting (at work or school, for example), and maintain their own culture in another (such as at home).[30] In the early *Wonder Woman* comics, Diana is able to slip seamlessly between her alter ego as army nurse Diana Prince and Wonder Woman.[31] In a way, it could be argued that most superheroes go through their own type of integration by leading dual lives.

When an individual decides that it is more important to keep to the old ways than it is to be part of the larger society, *separation* occurs. Separation can also happen when the domi-nant culture is unaccepting of multiculturalism.[32] Diana has an adventurous spirit and is curious about the world of men, so she isn't often depicted as someone who engages in separation. However, in some versions of her story, she becomes burned out and decides she wants to go home to Themyscira, where she can recharge and revisit her roots before later returning to the world of men.[33]

Marginalization occurs either when individuals reject both the dominant group and their own culture, or when they feel rejected by both of those groups.[34] In the rebirth era, Diana finds herself cut off from Themyscira, literally rejected by her homeland.[35] With so many versions of her story that contradict one another, having been told at times that she was created from clay, and at others that Zeus is her father, she feels no connection to her life in America and seeks to reforge a connection with her home and her people (as well as the truth).[36] This mode of acculturation is least preferred by immigrants and hosts alike, due to its association with more negative outcomes, such as low self-esteem, loneliness, and acculturative stress (see sidebar).[37]

Sojourner Adjustment

Sojourners are those who travel to a new place for a short-term purpose, such as work or school, usually with the intent of returning home.[38] In some versions of Wonder Woman's story, Diana is unable to return home to Themyscira.[39] In others, she is expected to return home and teach the Amazons about the world of men.[40] In the latter version, she could be considered a sojourner. Diana's experiences abroad help her build cultural awareness and acceptance of differences between the Amazons and the rest of the world. She serves as a bridge between worlds in many versions of her story, and is able to navigate both worlds due to her personal connection to those on both sides.

Sometimes being away from home can give an individual an even stronger connection to the home culture, as they become more aware of what they believe, in relation to the values, customs, and beliefs of the host culture. Batman and Superman's dueling American approaches to heroism often cause strong reactions and greater self-assuredness in Wonder Woman that the values of the Amazons are hers as well.[41] While being away from home gives the traveler a better connection to home, it may also cause place strain relationships with those left behind.[42] It may be difficult to stay in contact with those who are far away, even in today's world. For Diana, it isn't as easy as just picking up a phone and calling her mother.

As a result of lack of contact with those back home, new relationships in the host country are developed. Diana makes friends everywhere she goes, including among those she rescues as well as members of the Justice League. These new relationships help her make her way in the world, much as her family helped shape her ideas and cultural identity in her home culture.[43] After coming in contact with a new culture and building new friendships, a person's sense of self can become altered, forcing that person to try to understand himself or herself all over again.[44] Such changes may cause trouble upon returning home.

Repatriation

When people who have been abroad return home after an extended period, they go through the process of *repatriation*.[45] The repatriation experience has been described as more stressful than the original acculturation process. Travelers might find that, after coming home from a long journey, they have become different than they were when they left. Home then feels foreign to them. The customs may feel outdated. They may have an accent when speaking their native language. Family members and friends may see them as outsiders. Even Wonder Woman's Amazon sisters feel that Diana has stayed too long in the world of men or is more committed to what they perceive as her American duty than her Amazon duty.[46]

America's Response to Wonder Woman

The experience of members of the host culture who come in contact with immigrants is just as important as the experience of the immigrants themselves, as the responses of those in the host culture directly affect how immigrants are seen in the world. People tend to like things they understand and can relate to, and those who look like them.[47] If Diana looked more like a minotaur or cyclops, it might be more difficult for America to accept her. Because she looks human, and (in some versions) can speak the language, it makes it easier for others to relate to her. Dominant groups also tend to respond negatively when

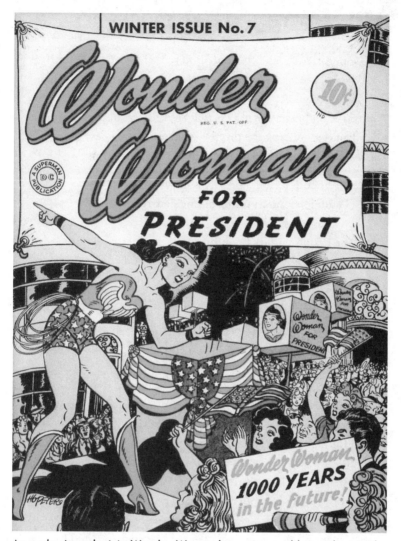

An early story depicts Wonder Woman becoming world president in the future. *Wonder Woman* #7 (1943). Art: H. G. Peter ©DC Comics.

they feel that their way of life is threatened by minorities trying to change the status quo.[48] In the story "Down to Earth," the founder of a conservative family values group chides Wonder Woman for espousing the views of her Amazon culture, which

CULTURE SHOCK

The negative shock often encountered when we find ourselves in an unfamiliar culture has aptly been named *culture shock*.[49] It is part of what psychology refers to as *acculturative stress*—the positive and negative effects that result from both excitement and anxiety during the process of adapting to a new culture.[50]

Many things cause acculturative stress, including:

- Encountering a new culture that cannot be understood in terms of one's current cultural frame of reference.
- Living within a dominant culture that does not align with your acculturation method.

These situations and more can make a traveler feel lost, confused, unwelcome, and downright lonely. Developing social connections in a new culture helps assuage acculturative stress, promote social well-being, and can be found by looking for similarities to one's culture of origin.[51]

When she arrives in the United States, Wonder Woman is overwhelmed with American culture and how much it differs from her Amazon culture. The emotions that overwhelm her may be positive, like the first time she witnesses children at play since there are no children on Themyscira. They may also be negative, such as when boys might exclude a girl from playing a heroic role in their games because they "need someone to save," which surprises Diana because no girl in her homeland would ever find herself relegated to such a helpless role.[52] However, when she focuses on similarities, she begins to make social connections with fellow warriors like Superman and Batman.[53] Justice League members share a culture of knowledge about combat, beliefs in the goodness of the human race, values of liberty and justice, and customs, including secret identities and costumes.

he claims "attack our ways of life." Wonder Woman's representative reminds him that the job of an ambassador like her is precisely to share her culture with America.[54]

In all versions of her origin story, when Diana first arrives in America she is seen as odd. She speaks strangely, doesn't understand American sarcasm, and misses social cues.[55] In her first origin story, she is even called a "hussy" for how she dresses.[56] People tend to ignore her oddness, and embrace her differences, though, due to her heroic acts and hope for the goodness of humankind.[57] Because of her perseverance, strength, wisdom, patience, and heroism, she is able to bridge the cultural divide and gain the love of the world.[58]

Comic Book References

All-Star Comics #8 (1941). "Introducing Wonder Woman." Script: W. M. Marston. Art: H. G. Peter.

Batman/Superman/Wonder Woman: Trinity #1–3 (2003). "Trinity." Script/Art: M. Wagner.

DC Comics: Bombshells #1 (2015). "Enlisted, Part One." Script: M. Bennett. Art: M. Sauvage.

DC Comics: Bombshells #4 (2015). "Combat, Part One." Script: M. Bennett. Art: B. Evely, M. Andolfo, & L. Braga.

Sensation Comics #1 (1942). "Wonder Woman Comes to America." Script: W. M. Marston. Art: H. G. Peter.

Wonder Woman #178 (1968). "Wonder Woman's Rival." Script: D. O'Neil. Art: M. Sekowsky.

Wonder Woman: Hiketeia (2002). Script: G. Rucka Art: J. G. Jones

Wonder Woman #195 (2003). "The Mission." Script: G. Rucka. Art: D. Johnson.

Wonder Woman #195–200 (2003–2004). "Down to Earth." Script: G. Rucka. Art: D. Johnson.

Wonder Woman #198 (2004). "Down to Earth, Part Three." Script: G. Rucka. Art: D. Johnson.

Wonder Woman #201 (2004). "Ripples." Script: G. Rucka. Art: S. Davis.

Wonder Woman #201–205 (2004). "Bitter Rivals." Script: G. Rucka. Art: S. Davis.

Wonder Woman #1 (2016). "The Lies, Part One." Script: G. Rucka. Art: L. Sharp.

Wonder Woman #2 (2016). "Year One, Part One." Script: G. Rucka. Art: N. Scott.

Wonder Woman #3 (2016). "The Lies, Part Two." Script: G. Rucka. Art: L. Sharp.

Wonder Woman #4 (2016). "Year One, Part Two." Script: G. Rucka. Art: N. Scott.

Wonder Woman #9 (2016). "The Lies, Part Five." Script: G. Rucka. Art: L. Sharp.

Wonder Woman: Rebirth #1 (2016). "Wonder Woman Rebirth." Script: G. Rucka. Art: M. Clark & L. Sharp.

Other References

Berry, J. W. (2005). Acculturation: Living successfully in two cultures. *International Journal of Intercultural Relations, 29*(6), 697–712.

Church, A. T. (1982). Sojourner adjustment. *Psychological Bulletin, 91*(3), 540–572.

Daniels, L. (2000). *Wonder Woman: The complete history.* San Francisco, CA: Chronicle.

Mana, A., Orr, E., & Mana, Y. (2009). An integrated acculturation model of immigrants' social identity. *Journal of Social Psychology, 149*(4), 450–473.

Nesdale, D. (2002). Acculturation attitudes and the ethnic and host-country identification of immigrants. *Journal of Applied Social Psychology, 32*(7), 1488–1507.

Oberg, K. (1954). *The social economy of the Tlingit Indians of Alaska* [doctoral dissertation]. Chicago, IL: University of Chicago.

Sussman, N. M. (2000). The dynamic nature of cultural identity throughout cultural transitions: Why home is not so sweet. *Personality & Social Psychology Review, 4*(4), 355–373.

Vasquez, M. T. (2011). *Crossroads: The psychology of immigration in the new century. Report of the APA Presidential Task Force.* Washington, DC: American Psychological Association.

Vivero, V. N., & Jenkins, S. R. (1999). Existential hazards of the multicultural individual: Defining and understanding "cultural homelessness." *Cultural Diversity & Ethnic Minority Psychology, 5*(1), 6–26.

Wan, C., & Chew, P. Y. G. (2013). Cultural knowledge, category label, and social connections: Components of cultural identity in the global, multicultural context. *Asian Journal of Social Psychology, 16*(4), 247–259.

Ying, Y. W. (2002). The effect of cross-cultural living on personality: Assimilation and accommodation among Taiwanese young adults in the United States. *American Journal of Orthopsychiatry, 72*(3), 362–371.

Yoon, E., Lee, R. M., & Goh, M. (2008). Acculturation, social connectedness, and subjective well-being. *Cultural Diversity & Ethnic Minority Psychology, 14*(3), 246–255.

Zimmermann, J., & Neyer, F. J. (2013). Do we become a different person when hitting the road? Personality development of sojourners. *Journal of Personality & Social Psychology, 105*(3), 515–530.

Notes

1. *All-Star Comics* #8 (1941).
2. Vasquez (2011).
3. Berry (2005).
4. Wan & Chew (2013).
5. Berry (2005).
6. Wan & Chew (2013).
7. *Wonder Woman* #195–200 (2003–2004); *Wonder Woman* #201–205 (2004).
8. Wan & Chew (2013).
9. *Wonder Woman* #195 (2003); *Wonder Woman* #178 (1968); *Wonder Woman: Hiketeia* (2002).
10. Wan & Chew (2013).
11. Wonder Woman #195 (2003); Wonder Woman #2 (2016).
12. Vivero & Jenkins (1999).
13. Vivero & Jenkins (1999).
14. *Justice League Unlimited* episode 1–2, "For the Man Who Has Everything" (August 7, 2004).

15. Sussman (2000).
16. *DC Comics Bombshells* #1 (2015).
17. Ying (2002).
18. Ying (2002).
19. *DC Comics Bombshells* #4 (2015).
20. *Justice League*, episode 1–3: "Secret Origins," part 3 (November 17, 2001).
21. Mana et al. (2009).
22. Nesdale (2002).
23. Yoon et al. (2008).
24. Mana et al. (2009).
25. Berry (2005).
26. *Wonder Woman* #178 (1968); Daniels (2000).
27. Mana et al. (2009).
28. *Wonder Woman* #4 (2016).
29. Mana et al. (2009).
30. Mana et al. (2009).
31. *Sensation Comics* #1 (1942).
32. Berry (2005).
33. *Justice League Unlimited* episode 2–5: "The Balance" (May 28, 2005); *Wonder Woman: Hiketeia* (2002).
34. Vivero & Jenkins (1999).
35. *Wonder Woman* #1 (2016).
36. *Wonder Woman: Rebirth* #1 (2016); *Wonder Woman* #1 (2016); *Wonder Woman* #3 (2016).
37. Mana et al. (2009); Nesdale (2002).
38. Sussman (2000).
39. *Wonder Woman* #4 (2016).
40. *Wonder Woman* (2009 animated motion picture).
41. *Batman/Superman/Wonder Woman: Trinity* #1–3 (2003).
42. Zimmermann & Neyer (2013).
43. Zimmermann & Neyer (2013).
44. Sussman (2000).
45. Sussman (2000).
46. *Wonder Woman* #201 (2004).
47. Nesdale (2002).
48. Mana et al. (2009).
49. Oberg (1954).
50. Berry (2005).
51. Yoon et al. (2008).
52. *Wonder Woman* (2009 animated motion picture).
53. *Batman/Superman/Wonder Woman: Trinity* #1–3 (2003).
54. *Wonder Woman* #198 (2004).
55. *Justice League*, episode 1–14: "Fury," part 1 (April 7, 2002).
56. *Sensation Comics* #1 (1942).
57. *Wonder Woman Rebirth* #1 (2016).
58. *Wonder Woman* #9 (2016).

CHAPTER FOURTEEN

It's a Man's World: Wonder Woman and Attitudes Toward Gender Roles

ERIN CURRIE

"How thrilling! I see you're chaining me to the cookstove.
What a perfect caveman idea!"
—Wonder Woman[1]

"Despite widespread cultural messages suggesting that sexist
discrimination is a thing of the past, systematic data show
that it remains pervasive in the lives of many women."
—psychologists Ann Fischer and Kenna Bolton Holz[2]

L ife as a woman in Man's World isn't always easy. Current cultural norms and laws in places such as the United States formally prohibit obvious forms of discrimination and injustice toward women.[3] However, atrocities like domestic and sexual violence are still perpetrated against women throughout the world with staggering frequency, even in the United States, and women are still discriminated against when they seek positions of power.[4] Work toward true equality can seem like a feat requiring superhero strength. Conquering modern sexism in all its subtle forms seems to require goddesslike levels of love and wisdom. Luckily, Wonder Woman exists to guide us toward equality for all genders, even though by entering Man's World, she finds herself to be an object of sexism.

Gender Roles

Gender roles refer to the division of essential characteristics and tasks on the basis of gender.[5] In a binary perception of gender, the result is two opposing and complementary sets of stereotypic traits: feminine and masculine. Appropriate tasks are prescribed based on the natural strengths associated with each set of traits. For women, these strengths include a communal mind-set focused on being warm and nurturing and pleasing others even at the cost of self-sacrifice.[6] Wonder Woman's emphasis on sisterhood and her mission to teach peace and love fit that nurturing trait.[7] Her willingness to put herself in danger to save the lives of others reflects the extent of that love.[8]

For men, those strengths are focused on competence and the accrual of power/influence over self, others, and environment.[9] One means to achieve domination is through large physical size, speed, strength, and fighting skills.[10] Wonder Woman has the means to act out this form of domination. The gods gave her strength greater than that of Hercules and speed to rival that of the god Hermes, and as an Amazon she is extensively trained in combat.[11]

Gender roles have a corresponding ideal physical manifestation for women as well. The ideal female physique is small and slight to complement the large male.[12] Wonder Woman misses the ideal here. Aside from a few run-ins with shrinking rays,

Wonder Woman is never portrayed as short, and though she is slender, she has impressive muscle definition.[13] Women also are supposed to be visually pleasing to men.[14] The gift of the beauty of Aphrodite serves Princess Diana well in that regard.[15]

In addition to the prescription of traits, certain tasks often are prescribed to each gender. Jobs that correspond to the feminine strengths focus on supporting and caring for others, including the domestic, nursing, and education fields.[16] Golden Age Wonder Woman fulfills this expectation when she takes the place of Diana Prince as a military nurse.[17]

The corresponding tasks prescribed to fit masculine strengths of domination focus on leadership, accrual of financial resources, and protection. Politics, the corporate executive suite, and military service are fields that showcase these skills.[18] The category of superhero, as it is traditionally defined, also fits the masculine career path. Regardless of gender, Princess Diana is well suited to the superhero role by her strength, speed, and flight and fighting skills. Some villains dislike this role switch and her associated dominance over them, and so they try to stop Princess Diana from being a superhero while shouting for their minions to "put her in her place."[19] The "bad guys" aren't the only ones limiting women to gender stereotypes; the "good guys" can be just as biased.[20] Soon after the Justice Society of America forms, Jay Garrick (the original Flash) relegates Wonder Woman to an honorary role as secretary, leaving her out of numerous battles even after she proves herself by fighting side by side with the other superheroes against the Nazis.[21]

Sexism

If traditional gender role traits are supposed to be separate, opposite, and complementary, what happens to individuals who do not conform to their assigned gender roles? What happens to someone like Wonder Woman, who is a combination: both physically strong and beautiful? She is a fierce and skilled fighter but uses those skills to promote communal values of peace and love. Unfortunately, the belief that gender roles are natural means that anyone who defies them is considered unnatural. Further, defying the traditional gender role arrangement can be perceived as a threat by the people who benefit from the existing power structure.[22]

Hostile Sexism

Hostile sexism is the expectation that women will conform to prescribed gender roles and the withdrawal of protection and the justification of punishment/discrimination for those who don't conform.[23] The main expectation is that women will submit to the domination of men. This could entail submission to romantic or sexual advances or be manifested in women's traditionally lower status roles in the workplace.[24] The main feelings associated with hostile sexism are negative and include anger and contempt.[25] The villain Doctor Psycho reacts to rejection by women for his small stature with hatred and violence.[26] From the very beginning, the god Mars repeatedly uses the anger of men like Doctor Psycho to try to take out the Amazons and Wonder Woman for the audacity of challenging the domination of men and the wars they cause.[27]

Domestic violence is a tool of dominance that some men use to maintain ongoing control in relationships and as punishment when their partners displease them.[28] Thus, it is beautifully ironic that the Amazons are created by the Greek goddesses from the souls of women previously killed by men. The soul of the Queen of the Amazons is that of a pregnant woman killed by her mate, and the soul of her unborn baby becomes her daughter, Princess Diana.[29]

Benevolent Sexism

Recent research on sexism has shown that when people are asked about their stance toward women, they generally report more positive than negative attitudes. This benevolent reaction includes feelings of affection, attraction, and protectiveness.[30] In contrast to hostile sexism, this *benevolent sexism* is the expectation that women conform to traditional gender roles and the promise of protection and special treatment for doing so.[31] This plays out regularly for Wonder Woman as her famed beauty gets her positive attention throughout the world.[32] It also helps her get what she wants, for example, when she tries to get the police to let her help investigate her publicist's death.[33]

Despite the positive tone of the term, benevolent sexism is a double-edged sword. Benevolent sexism includes the promise of protection for women who defer to the authority of the men in their lives, whether father, boss, or romantic partner. There is nothing wrong with being nurturing, beautiful, or protected by those with greater power. However, implicit in these characteristics is the dependence of women on men. In U.S. culture, in which autonomy is highly prized and rewarded, dependence is seen as weakness.[34] Wonder Woman is anything but weak, and by publicly using strength greater than that of most mortal men, she relinquishes the protection promised to women in Man's World who fulfill the feminine ideal.

In spite of promises of protection, women are often punished for reaping the benefits promised by benevolent sexism.[35] In the fair set up by Wonder Woman's publicist, the mission to help needy children is overshadowed by an emphasis on Wonder

Woman's beauty. Although the purpose of hiring a publicist is to help Princess Diana spread her message of peace and love, not self-promotion, the publicist uses her beauty to bring in the crowds.[36] This emphasis is cast by the villain Silver Swan as evidence of Wonder Woman's character as conceited and her motives as self-serving.[37]

Ambivalent Sexism

An *ambivalent sexist* holds both hostile and benevolent sexist attitudes.[38] This seems counterintuitive because of the difference of feelings for the target. After all, how can one idealize and want to protect women but hate and want to harm them at the same time? The answer is found in research showing that benevolent sexism and hostile sexism work together to create two different categories of women. "Good women" conform to conventional gender roles and deserve to be rewarded. "Bad women" defy conventional gender roles by enacting male traits and roles and need to be punished until they revert to "their place."[39] Two characters who exemplify these opposing roles are Myndi Mayer, Wonder Woman's publicist, and Myndi's sister, Lili.

Research shows that women who are seen as power- or success-driven are perceived more negatively than are similarly driven men.[40] Hostile sexism is used to punish women who seek success in traditionally male fields.[41] In spite of this, Myndi Mayer tenaciously fights to make her public relations firm a success. As a consequence, Myndi has an unsavory reputation. Even Diana's friend Julia Kapatelis knows of Myndi and initially dismisses her when she offers to be Wonder Woman's publicist, assuming there will be trouble.[42]

Women's sexuality is also regulated by hostile sexism. Sexual prowess is generally is seen as a positive trait in the male gender role only. Therefore, women like Myndi who actively seek out and enjoy sex outside of committed relationships are subject to

PREJUDICE EVERYWHERE

Research shows that prejudice is widespread throughout the world and across time. It can start with conscious and unconscious exposure to stereotypes.[43] Subtle and not so subtle stories repeatedly send messages about how certain groups think, feel, and act. For instance, racism is perpetuated by the frequency with which individuals of specific racial and cultural groups are portrayed as criminals in movies and on television.[44] Repeated exposure to these stereotypes can create what prejudice researchers call *habitual thinking*.[45] Just as with any other bad habit, when we are under stress or otherwise distracted, those thinking habits pop up and cause us to act accordingly. This is true even for people who report holding strong values for equality and against bigotry.[46] The good news is that like other bad habits, it is possible to replace stereotypes with more accurate, multifaceted ideas about people over time through continual effort.[47]

scorn.[48] People refer to Myndi several times as a "tramp." This slang term referring to promiscuity is used primarily against women as an insult, whereas slang terms for promiscuous men, such as "stud," are complimentary.[49] Also, when she is a young woman, Myndi's father kicks her out of his house when Lili tells him about her sexual exploits.[50]

If benevolent sexism is used to reward conformity to traditional gender roles, it is no surprise that Myndi's father idealizes Lili, granting her the love he denies Myndi by refusing to see her or responding to her with sullen silence. According to

Myndi, Lili plays the role of the perfect daughter, taking care of their father after their mother passes away. Further, she marries young and has children, presumably bypassing the exploits of her older sister.[51]

Gender Roles Harm Men

Women aren't the only ones who experience the harmful effects of pressure to conform to gender roles. Men are expected to be dominant, successful, and physically large. Men who do not meet these expectations experience negative consequences. For instance, research shows that men of small stature, such as Doctor Psycho, are more likely to experience discrimination in dating, at the workplace, and in other situations in which power is awarded.[52] Doctor Psycho attributes his hatred of Wonder Woman and his life of crime to mistreatment by women because he is short and unattractive.[53] If it weren't for the narrowness of traditional gender roles, would Mars be without one of his most trusted minions?

Enacting Equality

The presence of traditional gender role stereotypes is hard to eliminate while they are part of the cultural psyche.[54] However, recent research is showing evidence of protective attitudes that some women use to fend off the cumulative effects of sexism.[55] Wonder Woman is able to thrive in Man's World because she uses some of them. For instance, one major protective factor is a person's sense of personal control over her environment.[56] It is clear that Wonder Woman has confidence in her ability to have a positive impact on difficult situations. When fighting

Ares to prevent global nuclear war, Wonder Woman has faith in the training she receives and the resources available to her, including the brave women and men fighting at her side.[57]

It is difficult to challenge pervasive stereotypes, but research shows that repeated interactions with people who challenge stereotypes and elicit empathy reduce bias.[58] Wonder Woman's presence in the world in all her feminine and masculine glory is the perfect challenge to traditional gender roles. Her visible, public use of strength—not as a tactic for domination but to help people in need—endears her to most people, creating the empathy that is key to fighting negative bias.

Although superhero strength helps, one cannot overlook the importance of the people of Man's World who support Wonder Woman without regard for her gender presentation. Steve Trevor supports Wonder Woman without feeling threatened by the fact that she is exponentially stronger and faster than he.[59] Julia Kapatelis contributes her own strengths to Wonder Woman's cause without feeling diminished by her beauty.[60] Ideally, the people of Man's World will learn from their example and gain the strength to fight everyday battles against subtle and not so subtle forms of sexism. The sooner that happens, the sooner we can all be the most heroic version of ourselves.

> *"If the prospect of living in a world where trying to respect the basic rights of those around you and valuing each other simply because we exist are such daunting, impossible tasks that only a superhero born of royalty can address them, then what sort of world are we left with?"*
> —Wonder Woman[61]

> *"Raising daughters more like sons is a good thing. But how about raising our sons more like our daughters?"*
> —activist/author Gloria Steinem[62]

Comic Book References

All Star Comics #13 (1942). "Shanghaied into Space." Script: G. Fox. Art: J. Burnley, S. Moldoff, C. Young, S. Aschmeier, J. Gallagher, B. Baily, & H. G. Peter.

Sensation Comics #9 (1942). "The Return of Diana Prince." Script: W. M. Marston. Art: H. G. Peter.

Wonder Woman #5 (1943). "Battle for Womanhood." Script: W. M. Marston. Art: H. G. Peter.

Wonder Woman #159 (1966). "Doom Island." Script: R. Kanigher. Art: R. Andru & M. Esposito.

Wonder Woman #160 (1966). "Doctor Psycho's Revenge." Script: R. Kanigher. Art: R. Andru & M. Esposito.

Wonder Woman #161 (1966). "Battle Inside of a Brain." Script: R. Kanigher. Art: R. Andru & M. Esposito.

Wonder Woman #162 (1966). "The Startling Secret of Diana Prince." Script: R. Kanigher. Art: R. Andru & M. Esposito.

Wonder Woman #1 (1987). "The Princess and the Power." Script: G. Pérez & G. Potter. Art: B. Patterson.

Wonder Woman #5 (1987). "The Ares Assault." Script: L. Wein. Art: G. Pérez.

Wonder Woman #6 (1987). "Power Play." Script: L. Wein. Art: G. Pérez.

Wonder Woman #15 (1988). "Swan Song." Script: G. Pérez. Art: G. Pérez.

Wonder Woman #16 (1988). "Bird of Paradise/Bird of Prey." Script: G. Pérez. Art: G. Pérez.

Wonder Woman #17 (1988). "Traces." Script: G. Pérez. Art: G. Pérez.

Wonder Woman #20 (1988). "Who Killed Myndi Mayer?" Script: G. Pérez. Art: G. Pérez.

Wonder Woman #54 (1991). "Mind Games." Script: G. Pérez. Art: J. Thompson & R. Tanghal.

Wonder Woman #170 (2001). "She's a Wonder." Script: P. Jimenez & J. Kelly. Art: P. Jimenez, A. Lanning.

Wonder Woman Annual #1 (1988). "Amazons." Script: G. Pérez. Art: C. Marrinan, A. Adams, J. Bolton, J. L. Garcia-Lopez, C. Swan, R. Andru, & B. Bolland.

Other References

Banaji, M. R., Hardin, C., & Rothman, A. J. (1993). Implicit stereotype in person judgment. *Journal of Personality & Social Psychology, 65*(2), 272–281.

Black, M. C., Basile, K. C., Breiding, M. J., Smith, S. G., Walters, M. L., Merrick, M. T., Chen, J., & Stevens, M. R. (2011). *The National Intimate Partner and Sexual Violence Survey: 2010 summary report.* Atlanta, GA: National Center for Injury Prevention and Control, Centers for Disease Control and Prevention.

Brescoll, V., & Uhlmann, E. L. (2008). Can angry women get ahead? Status conferral, gender, and workplace emotion expression. *Psychological Science, 19*(3), 268–275.

Cralley, E. L. & Ruscher, J. B. (2005). Lady, girl, female or woman: Sexism and cognitive business predict use of gender biased nouns. *Journal of Language & Social Psychology, 24*(3), 300–314.

Cuddy, A. J. C., Wolf, E. B., Glick, P., Crotty, S., Chong, J., & Norton, M. I. (2015). Men as cultural ideals: Cultural values moderate gender stereotype content. *Journal of Personality & Social Psychology, 109*(4), 622–635.

Devine, P. G. (2001). Stereotypes and prejudice: Their automatic and controlled components. *Journal of Personality & Social Psychology, 56*(1), 5–18.

Dovidio, J. F., Kawakami, K., Johnson, C., Johnson, B., & Howard, A. (1997). On the nature of prejudice: Automatic and controlled processes. *Journal of Experimental Social Psychology, 33*(5), 510–540.

Fischer, A. R. & Holz, K. B. (2010). Testing a model of women's personal sense of justice, control, well-being, and distress in the context of sexist discrimination. *Psychology of Women Quarterly, 34*(3), 297–310.

Glick, P. & Fiske, S. T. (2001a). An ambivalent alliance: Hostile and benevolent sexism as complementary justifications for gender inequality. *American Psychologist, 56*(2), 109–118.

Glick, P. & Fiske, S. T. (2011b). Ambivalent sexism revisited. *Psychology of Women Quarterly, 35*(3), 530–535.

Lukaszewski, A. W., Simmons, Z. L., Anderson, C., & Roney, J. R. (2015). The role of physical formidability in human social status allocation. *Journal of Personality & Social Psychology, 110*(3), 385–406.

Okimoto, T. G., & Brescoll, V. L. (2010). The price of power: Power seeking and backlash against female politicians. *Personality & Social Psychology Bulletin, 36*(7), 923–936.

Plant, E. A., & Devine, P. G. (1998). Internal and external motivation to respond without prejudice. *Journal of Personality & Social Psychology, 75*(3), 811–832.

Richeson, J. A., & Ambady, N. (2001). Who's in charge? Effects of situational roles on automatic gender bias. *Sex Roles, 44*(9/10), 493–512.

Ridgeway, C. (1992). Gender, interaction, and inequality. New York: Springer-Verlag.

Rudman. L. A., & Kilianski, S. E. (2000). Implicit and explicit attitudes toward female authority. *Personality & Social Psychology Bulletin, 26*(11), 1315–1328.

Salska, I., Frederick, D. A., Pawlowski, B., Reilly, A. H., Laird, K. T., & Rudd, N. A. (2008). Conditional mate preferences: Factors influencing preference for height. *Personality & Individual Differences, 44*(1), 203–215.

Salusso-Deonier, C. J., Markee, N. L., & Pederson, E. L. (1993). Gender differences in the evaluation of physical attractiveness ideals for male and female body builds. *Perceptual & Motor Skills, 76*(3, pt. 2), 1155–1167.

Sibley, C. G., & Wilson, M. S. (2004). Differentiating hostile and benevolent sexist attitudes toward positive and negative sexual female subtypes. *Sex Roles, 51*(11/12), 687–696.

Steinem, G. (2004). *Leaps of consciousness.* Speech delivered at the Women and Power Conference, New York, NY. Transcript: http://www.feminist.com/resources/artspeech/genwom/leaps.html.

Vicki, G. T., Abrams, D., & Hutchinson, P. (2003). The "true romantic": Benevolent sexism and paternalistic chivalry. *Sex Roles, 49*(9/10), 533–537.

Notes

1. *Sensation Comics* #9 (1942).
2. Fischer & Holz (2010), p. 297.
3. Glick & Fiske (2001).
4. Black et al. (2011); Okimoto & Brescoll (2010).
5. Rudman & Kilianski (2000).
6. Glick & Fiske (2001).
7. *Wonder Woman Annual* #1 (1987).

8. *Wonder Woman* #6 (1988).
9. Okimoto & Brescoll (2010).
10. Lukaszewski et al. (2015).
11. *Wonder Woman* #1 (1987).
12. Salusso-Deonier et al. (1993); Vicki et al. (2003).
13. *Wonder Woman* #161 (1966).
14. Vicki et al. (2003).
15. *Wonder Woman* #1 (1987).
16. Rudman & Kilianski (2000).
17. *Wonder Woman* #162 (1966).
18. Okimoto & Brescoll (2010); Rudman & Kilianski (2000).
19. *Wonder Woman* #159 (1966).
20. Vicki et al. (2003).
21. *All Star Comics* #13 (1942).
22. Richeson & Ambady (2001).
23. Glick & Fiske (2011).
24. Richeson & Ambady (2001).
25. Glick & Fiske (2011).
26. *Wonder Woman* #5 (1943); *Wonder Woman* #160 (1966); *Wonder Woman* #54 (1991).
27. *Wonder Woman* #5 (1943).
28. Glick & Fiske (2011).
29. *Wonder Woman* #1 (1987).
30. Glick & Fiske (2011).
31. Sibley & Wilson (2004).
32. *Wonder Woman* #17 (1988).
33. *Wonder Woman* #20 (1988).
34. Ridgeway (1992).
35. Okimoto & Brescoll (2010).
36. *Wonder Woman* #15 (1988).
37. *Wonder Woman* #16 (1988).
38. Glick & Fiske (2011).
39. Brescoll and Uhlmann (2008).
40. Okimoto & Brescoll (2010).
41. Brescoll and Uhlmann (2008).
42. *Wonder Woman* #5 (1987).
43. Banaji et al. (1993).
44. Dovidio et al. (1997).
45. Devine (2001).
46. Cralley & Ruscher (2005).
47. Plant & Devine (1998).
48. Sibley & Wilson (2004).
49. Sibley & Wilson (2004).
50. *Wonder Woman Annual* #1 (1988).
51. *Wonder Woman Annual* #1 (1988).
52. Lukaszewski et al. (2015); Salska et al. (2008).
53. *Wonder Woman* #5 (1943).
54. Cuddy et al. (2015); Plant & Devine (1998)
55. Fischer & Holz (2010).
56. Fischer & Holz (2010).

57. *Wonder Woman* #6 (1987).
58. Devine (2001).
59. *Wonder Woman* #16 (1988).
60. *Wonder Woman* #5 (1987).
61. *Wonder Woman* #170 (2001).
62. *Steinem* (2004).

CHAPTER FIFTEEN

From Wing Chun to Wonder Woman: Empowerment through Martial Skill

E. PAUL ZEHR
AND JEFF PISCIOTTA

"She is an Amazon, a superheroine, an ambassador, a spy, and a warrior.
An avatar of truth, champion of the gods, and an emissary of peace.
A loving daughter, trusted friend, steadfast protector, and formidable foe.
She is Diana, Princess of Themyscira. Wonder Woman. Icon."
—artist George Pérez[1]

> *"Be gentle, kind and beautiful, yet firm and*
> *strong, both mentally and physically."*
> —judo practitioner Keiko Fukuda[2]

Having confidence about ourselves, based on our capabil-ities and capacity, is a good feeling. Confidence creates a feeling of agency and empowerment—a cognitive state wherein we perceive control over ourselves and our place in the world.[3] In the context of social cognitive theory, social psychologist Albert Bandura suggests that an essential quality of humanity is "the capacity to exercise control over the nature and quality of one's life."[4] Bandura further states that social cognitive theory considers agency in three modes: direct personal, proxy (where others act on our behalf), and collective agency (achieved through integrated social networks).[5] In many ways, Wonder Woman epitomizes agency and empowerment by focusing on her tremendous fighting skills.

Martial arts training and associated competence may have a positive effect on psychological health[6] and overall sense of ability and well-being.[7] Through training in martial arts, such as karate, kickboxing, and Thai boxing, women gain physical strength and skill that leads to confidence in personal safety and a feeling of power and ability.[8]

The powerful Wonder Woman that William Moulton Marston created has "the beauty of Aphrodite, the wisdom of Athena, the strength of Hercules, and the speed of Mercury."[9] In the early *Wonder Woman* comics, she is often described as "a woman to whom the problems and feats of men are mere child's play . . . whose sensational feats are outstanding . . . with a hundred times the agility and strength of the best male athletes and strongest wrestlers . . . she is known only as Wonder Woman . . ."[10]

In addition to her sensational strength and agility, Wonder Woman has amazing fighting skills both in hand-to-hand combat and while using weapons. The latter includes her effective use of her lasso, her bracelets, and her sword and shield. Here we consider the role of empowerment through martial arts training and skill development. This vision of Wonder Woman as empowered agent due to acquisition of martial skills is heavily influenced by a pivotal story in the 1960s.

Diana begins martial arts training in the controversial *Wonder Woman* #181 (1969). Art: M. Sekowsky & D. Giordano. TM & ®DC Comics.

In 1968, writer Dennis O'Neil explored what would happen if Wonder Woman gave up her powers in the "awesome Amazon rite of renunciation"[11] on Themyscira. Back in the States, she encounters a mysterious martial arts teacher, I Ching, who knows she has ". . . lost strength, swiftness, and magic . . ." He tells her that she "must learn skills! Abilities to replace your lost Amazon traits!" So he starts her "with a course in simple fighting—Karate!"[12] The narrative tells us that, as time passes, her "weeks are filled with strenuous physical and mental labor! Diana's body stretches, strains, acquires uncanny reflexes—her mind is forced to unbelievable discipline!" This is all due to her daily practice of "the deadly battle arts of the Orient."[13]

When the assignment for Wonder Woman came along, O'Neil "was really interested in martial arts and wanted to use them in his writing." Although he writes about Diana learning karate and other martial arts, he himself was primarily interested in tai chi and judo.[14] Here we first consider real-life examples of women in martial arts, fighting, and martial sport traditions that parallel the concept of Diana Prince—Wonder Woman warrior. We then consider how these experiences relate to Bandura's core tenets of human agency.[15]

Wing Chun Kung Fu

A "youngster" when contrasted with other styles of Chinese martial arts (some of which report a thousand-year history), Wing Chun techniques stress practical, simple movements instead of "flowery" ones. Wing Chun's fellow Chinese martial arts may typically have ten or more open hand forms and include multiple weapon forms and two-person forms. By contrast, the Wing Chun system has only three main "forms" (extended patterns of movement), a "wooden dummy" training form, and two weapon forms.

Wing Chun's technical canon, like Wonder Woman herself, is direct and to the point. And, reminiscent of Wonder Woman's early years on Themyscira, Wing Chun was founded and practiced widely by women. It is the only Asian martial art created by women or developed from the female perspective. As with any historical recollections, there are a few different versions of origins of Wing Chun. The version below is based mainly on that related by the teacher of Bruce Lee, Ip Man (this chapter's co-author Jeff Pisciotta is a direct-lineage student of Ip Man) and follows that of other sources.

About three centuries ago, a Buddhist nun named Ng Mui escaped from the Shaolin Temple in Henan, China when it was attacked and burned by the Manchurians. She escaped to the White Crane Temple on Daliang Mountain and there observed a fight between a snake and a crane.

Ng Mui had prior martial arts training and integrated what she saw between the snake and crane to formulate a new system of kung fu. She passed this knowledge on to a young woman named Yim Wing Chun (for whom the style was eventually named).

Yim Wing Chun had fled with her father to southwestern China and met Ng Mui, who was willing to train her. A warlord wanted to marry Yim and eventually attempted to take her by force. Wing Chun defeated the warlord in a public fight and won the right to choose her own husband. She married a skilled martial artist, and together they further developed the art of Wing Chun.

The entire system of Wing Chun kung fu reflects influences from female martial artists/warriors. Wing Chun is considered an extremely effective fighting system. The style is aggressive and known for economical attacks and defense. There is little emphasis on techniques that rely on brute strength.

Instead, the individual learns to "flow" with the opponent's techniques and redirect their force, rather than attempting to overcome physical force. The stances and postures of the Wing Chun system can be observed to reflect subtle elements more conducive to female anatomy and biomechanics. In Taoism, yin represents femaleness, passiveness, darkness, expansion, and softness, while yang represents maleness. Wing Chun consistently emphasizes the yin in its principles and philosophy.[16]

All of the above make Wing Chun difficult for many males to learn and apply. Many of Wing Chun's better male practitioners are slight of build with minimal muscle mass, Grandmaster Ip Man being one of the modern examples.

The system was passed down for many generations and in the 1900s to Grandmaster Ip Man. Ip Man is known for introducing Wing Chun to Hong Kong. Ip's senior students, along with their fellow student Bruce Lee, popularized Wing Chun throughout the world.[17] And it all started with a woman who founded an enduring martial arts style.

The Judo Vision of Jigoro Kano and the Story of Keiko Fukuda

From UFC and MMA we now turn to an art that inspired them—that of the "gentle way," judo. Founded by Japanese jujutsu master and educator Dr. Jigoro Kano in 1882, judo is considered a modern martial art.[18] Judo was the first Japanese martial art to gain widespread international recognition, and the first martial art to become an Olympic sport.[19] The main objective in judo is to either throw or take an opponent to the ground. Immobilization and submission techniques, such as "pinning" the opponent to the ground or utilizing joint locks and chokes, are key. Strikes and kicks are part of judo, but are found only in the forms—they are not allowed in free sparring and competition.

Kano established for judo basic principles based on "mottos," such as "maximum efficiency with minimum effort" and "mutual welfare and benefit."[20] As an educator, Kano certainly believed in equality—everyone had the right to an education,

Keiko Fukuda throwing a junior trainee (Jessie) while biographer Yuriko Romer films. From *Project Superhero*, with permission © E. Paul Zehr (2014).

regardless of gender. As a martial artist, his system was accessible to women. Similar to the Wing Chun system, judo stressed efficiency and minimal use of simple muscular force. Instead, judo trains the user to employ the opponent's force against him or her.

Although Kano welcomed and taught female students, historians have shown that he retained some of the biases of his culture and the times. For example, women were not supposed to perform free sparring, nor practice with men.[21] From a feminist perspective, the way women were taught judo could be viewed as conservative and/or restrictive. However, at that time, Japanese society regarded women as entirely submissive to their family and males.[22] Women were not allowed to learn traditional jujutsu, the prevailing Japanese martial art. Just to include women in judo was actually well outside the normal practice at the time and was a major breakthrough.

As late nineteenth-century society changed in both East and West, the "role" and eventually the "rights" of women began to

Teen Jessie empowered by learning evasive movement from her martial arts teacher From *Project Superhero*, with permission © E. Paul Zehr (2014).

change. Kano's original premise for judo as a way of "empowerment" for all had an opportunity to expand. It was during this time that the incredible story of Keiko Fukuda began.

Keiko Fukuda was the highest-ranked female judo practitioner in history and the last surviving student of Kano Jigoro. Keiko was considered a pioneer of women's judo and began her training in the late 1920s. The first female dojo was only created in 1923, forty-one years after the creation of judo. Women were still made to focus on kata and avoid "harm" and activities that had the potential for injury, such as sparring. Judo classes for women emphasized self-defense, while classes for their male counterparts emphasized free fighting and competition.[23]

While access to training was available, there remained an atmosphere of isolation as Keiko began her judo training. Despite standing at only four-foot-eleven inches (150 cm) and weighing less than one hundred pounds (45 kg), Keiko excelled and became a judo instructor in 1937. She learned some English and was considered a very good teacher. So much so that Kano asked her to travel abroad and spread judo to other countries shortly before his death in 1938.[24] Sometime in 1953, Keiko finally did travel to the United States to demonstrate and teach judo, returning in 1966 to live in San Francisco.

Keiko was the first woman to be promoted to fifth dan but was not promoted again for thirty years. Eventually, she held the rank of ninth dan from the Japanese Kodokan in 2006 and tenth dan in July 2011 from the United States Judo Federation. She is also the first and only woman to have been promoted to tenth dan in the art of judo.[25]

She continued to teach her art in the San Francisco Bay area until her death in 2013 at the age of ninety-nine. Her life was used to inform and inspire the empowerment through martial arts training of protagonist Jessie in this chapter's co-author E. Paul Zehr's book *Project Superhero* (see illustrations).[26] As documented in the excellent biography by Yuriko Romer *Mrs Judo*, Keiko used to always say "be gentle, kind and beautiful, yet firm and strong, both mentally and physically."[27] Fitting words for a real-life martial arts pioneer as well as the fictional Amazon warrior Wonder Woman.

Back to Bandura: Empowerment and Agency

We suggest that the training and practice of physical skills in the form of martial arts bestow on Wonder Woman (and real-life women) agency that dovetails with Bandura's "capacity to exercise control"[28] over herself and her environment. The agency and empowerment that Wonder Woman experiences in the story from *Wonder Woman* #179 is revealed when she uses her skills in combat. In a major panel, her thought bubble reveals, "My first real test of Ching's training—so far so good!"[29] She makes quick work of many attackers and is shown moving with great confidence, evidencing her new physical skills.

The empowerment and mode of agency Wonder Woman uses most is direct personal agency.[30] This is also found in the real-life historical (e.g., Ng Mui and Wing Chun), recent (e.g., Keiko Fukuda and judo), and contemporary (e.g., Sarah Kaufman and UFC) figures discussed here. With respect to social cognitive theory, the examples used in this chapter (including that of Wonder Woman) show aspects of Bandura's core features of human agency,[31] namely: intentionality (acts done on purpose); forethought (setting goals and anticipating outcomes); self-reactiveness (ability to shape appropriate actions and be motivated for successful execution); and, self-reflectiveness (metacognitive capacity to reflect on adequacy of thoughts and actions).

Can We Take Wonder Woman a Bridge Too Far?

Wonder Woman and empowerment of women through direct personal agency due to acquisition of martial skills should be rightly celebrated. Yet, some suggest that such things could also swing too far. In James Garbarino's *See Jane Hit*, he suggests that girls are steadily growing more violent. Garbarino points to criminal statistics and violence and aggression in sport to support his allegation that the empowerment of young women can also have a potential downside.[32] However, the karate pioneer and scholar Gichin Funakoshi wrote, "Karate without courtesy is violence."[33] Funakoshi was implying that control and decorum are critical parts of self-defense skill and ability.

The feelings of agency and competence that come with physical skill are well represented by the nun Jigme Konchok, who said that "Kung fu helps us to develop a certain kind of confidence to take care of ourselves and others in times of need."[34] Skill at martial arts has the powerful ability to empower—

whether it be a process called "pushing hands" on Paradise Island or kung fu kicking in Kathmandu. Long before her controversial period of studying under I Ching, Wonder Woman trains intensively as a warrior skilled in many combat techniques, emphasizing nonlethal methods with the kind of confidence, discipline, and grace required in martial arts.

Comic Book References

All Star Comics #8 (1941). "Introducing Wonder Woman." Script: W. M. Marston. Art: H. G. Peter.

Wonder Woman #179 (1968). "Wonder Woman's Last Battle." Script: D. O'Neil. Art: M. Sekowsky & D. Giordano.

Other References

Bandura, A. (2001). Social cognitive theory: An agentic perspective. *Annual Reviews of Psychology, 52*, 1–26.

Channon, A. G. (2013). Enter the discourse: Exploring the discursive roots of inclusivity in mixed-sex martial arts. *Sport in Society, 16*(10), 1293–1308.

Channon, A., & Jennings, G. (2014). Exploring embodiment through martial arts and combat sports: A review of empirical research. *Sport in Society, 17*(6), 773–789.

Fuller, J. R. (1988). Martial arts and psychological health. *British Journal of Medical Psychology, 61*(part 4), 317–328.

Funakoshi, G. (2003). *The twenty guiding principles of karate: The spiritual legacy of the master.* New York, NY: Kodansha USA.

Garbarino, J. (2006). *See Jane hit: Why girls are growing more violent and what can be done about it.* New York, NY: Penguin.

Greenberger, R., Pérez, G., McDonnell, C., & Marston, W. M. (2010). *Wonder Woman: Amazon, hero, icon* (1st ed.). New York, NY: Universe.

Hayhurst, L. M. C. (2014). The 'girl effect' and martial arts: Social entrepreneurship and sport, gender and development in Uganda. *Gender, Place, & Culture, 21*(3), 297–315.

Jain, S. (2016). *The kung fu nuns of Nepal.* BBC: http://www.bbc.com/travel/story/20160916-the-kung-fu-nuns-of-nepal?ocid=ww.social.link.email.

Kufuda, K. (2004). Ju-No-Kata: *A Kodokan textbook.* Berkeley, CA: North Atlantic.

Lowry, D. (2013). *The life of Keiko Fukuda, last surviving student of judo founder Jigoro Kano.* Black Belt Magazine: http://www.blackbeltmag.com/daily/traditional-martial-arts-training/judo-traditional-martial-arts/the-life-of-keiko-fukuda-last-surviving-student-of-judo-founder-jigoro-kano/.

Miarka, B., Marques, J. B., & Franchini, E. (2011). Reinterpreting the history of women's Judo in Japan. *The International Journal of the History of Sport, 28*(7), 1016–1029.

Romer, Y. (2012). *Mrs Judo: Be strong, be gentle, be beautiful.* Mrs. Judo: http://www.mrsjudomovie.com/.

Velija, P., Mierzwinski, M., & Fortune, L. (2013). "It made me feel powerful": Women's gendered embodiment and physical empowerment in the martial arts. *Leisure Studies, 32*(5), 524–541.

Watanabe, J., & Avakian, L. (1984). *The secrets of judo* (vol. 20). Rutland, VT: Tuttle.

Weaving, C. (2014). Cage fighting like a girl: Exploring gender constructions in the Ultimate Fighting Championship (UFC). *Journal of the Philosophy of Sport, 41*(1), 129–142.

Wing Chun Kung Fu (n.d.). *Introduction to Wing Chun (1952).* Wing Chun Kung Fu: http://wingchun.nu/en/wing-chun/history/grandmaster-wang-kiu/introducing-wang-kiu/.

Woodward, T. W. (2009). A review of the effects of martial arts practice on health. *Wisconsin Medical Journal, 108*(1), 40–43.

Xuan, D., & Little, J. (2015). The tao of Wing Chun. New York, NY: Skyhorse.

Zehr, E. P. (2014). *Project superhero.* Toronto, Ontario, Canada: ECW.

Notes

1. Greenberger et al. (2010), p. 10.
2. Romer (2012).
3. Velija et al. (2013); Weaving (2014).
4. Bandura (2001).
5. Bandura (2001).
6. Fuller (1988); Woodward (2009).
7. Channon & Jennings (2014).
8. Velija et al. (2013).
9. *All-Star Comics* #8 (1941).
10. Greenberger et al. (2010), p. 20.
11. *Wonder Woman* #179 (1968).
12. *Wonder Woman* #179 (1968).
13. *Wonder Woman* #179 (1968).
14. Personal communication (2014).
15. Bandura (2001).
16. Xuan & Little (2015).
17. Wing Chun Kung Fu (n.d.).
18. Watanabe & Avakian (1984).
19. Miarka et al. (2011).
20. Miarka et al. (2011).
21. Lowry (2013).
22. Miarka et al. (2011).
23. Miarka et al. (2011).
24. Kufuda (2004).
25. Lowry (2013).
26. Zehr (2014).
27. Romer (2012).
28. Bandura (2001).
29. *Wonder Woman* #179 (1968).
30. Bandura (2001).
31. Bandura (2001).
32. Garbarino (2006).
33. Funakoshi (2003).
34. Jain (2016).

Courage

MARA WOOD

Courage is a person's strength of will to accomplish a goal despite opposition.[1] The strengths of the virtue of courage are unique in that they aim to counteract a temptation or a part of human condition such as fear or exhaustion. The virtue courage is correlated with good physical and mental health,[2] and this may indicate that these strengths are adaptive to the individual and operate as protective factors.

Bravery entails doing something despite fear. It is not a matter of acting without fear, though. A person can feel fear but still perform the task, thus displaying bravery and courage.[3] Wonder Woman has numerous moments of bravery, like other superheroes, but one moment stands out as particularly brave and courageous. Medousa threatens to turn millions of people into stone via a live broadcast. Diana witnesses firsthand the dangerousness of Medousa shortly after a boy is turned to stone.[4] Regardless of the personal danger, Diana dons her armor and heads into battle against Medusa.[5] Bravery in a person can be developed through practice and example as well as through social (or communal) skills.[6] The Amazons, who come from a communal society, are poised to foster bravery in their princess.[7]

Whereas bravery is acting in the face of fear, *persistence* is acting in the face of boredom and tedium.[8] People are tempted to act on easier, more pleasurable tasks rather than the tasks that must be done.[9] Persistence is a quieter strength than bravery but is essential to performance and accomplishment.[10] Diana spends time as an ambassador for her country. Diana could easily engage with Man's World solely through superheroics, but she performs the harder task of engaging in politics and living her life as an example to others.[11] Persistence is correlated with high work performance and low counterproductive work behaviors; persistent people find meaning in their work and invest more energy and stamina to reach a long-term goal.[12] Diana's long-term goal of bringing Amazon teachings to the greater world has meaning for her, and despite the difficulties, she will go to great lengths to see her goal fulfilled.

Integrity may come easily to a woman who is defined by truth. The courageous strength of integrity consists of more than telling the truth, though. Authenticity, congruence, and responsibility for one's own actions and self are factors in integrity.[13] Diana fights to provide an authentic representation of herself and her views through both her teachings and her published essays.[14] People with integrity practice what they preach, embody their moral convictions even when unpopular, and possess sensitivity to the needs of others.[15] Carl Rogers's theory of humanistic psychology is built on the strength of integrity and striving to show integrity.[16] Integrity is correlated with positive mood, life satisfaction, openness to experience, empathy, self-actualization, and conscientiousness.[17] Parents have influence over the development of integrity in their children,[18] such as when Hippolyta encourages the young Diana to be truthful and honest.[19]

Although *vitality* is not typically thought of as a character strength of courage, Peterson and Seligman added it to this virtue late in their classification. They define it as zest, zeal, and love for life.[20] Vitality is the sensation that comes with self-actualization.[21] Enthusiasm radiates from a person with vitality. Diana, who smiles, takes time to help others, and continues her mission despite personal loss, solidifies her position as a woman of courage.[22] Vitality has been shown to be robustly linked to life satisfaction and well-being, along with other strengths, such as love and gratitude.[23] A person with vitality is fully functioning.[24] Diana comes from a society of immortal women, but she still understands the importance of life and enjoying life. She has difficulty fully understanding why a young woman would take her own life yet works to help those coping with loss so that they may live fully once again.[25]

With courage, Wonder Woman can overcome both the mundane and the fantastical trials over the decades. Her courage serves as an example of bravery, persistence, integrity, and vitality.

Comic Book References

All-Star Comics #8 (1941). "Introducing Wonder Woman." Script: W. M. Marston. Art: H. G. Peter.

Wonder Woman #1 (1987). "The Princess and the Power." Script: G. Pérez & G. Potter. Art: G. Pérez & B. Patterson.

Wonder Woman #46 (1990). "Chalk Drawings." Script: G. Pérez & M. Newell. Art: J. Thompson & R. Tanghal.

Wonder Woman #126 (1961). "Wonder Tot and Mister Genie." Script: R. Kanigher. Art: R. Andru & M. Esposito.

Wonder Woman #177 (2002). "Paradise Found." Script: P. Jimenez. Art: P. Jimenez & A. Lanning.

Wonder Woman #195 (2002). "The Mission." Script: G. Rucka. Art: D. Johnson & R. Snyder.

Wonder Woman #209 (2004). "Stoned, Part Four." Script: G. Rucka. Art: D. Johnson & R. Snyder.

Wonder Woman #210 (2005). "Stoned, Conclusion." Script: G. Rucka. Art: D. Johnson & R. Snyder.

Other References

Allan, B. A. (2015). Balance among character strengths and meaning in life. *Journal of Happiness Studies, 16*(5), 1247–1261.

Bolt, M., & Dunn, D. S. (2016). *Pursuing human strengths: A positive psychology guide* (2nd ed.). New York, NY: Worth.

Leontopoulou, S., & Triliva, S. (2012). Explorations of subjective wellbeing and character strengths among a Greek university student sample. *International Journal of Wellbeing, 2*(3), 251–270.

Littman-Ovadia, H., & Lavy, S. (2015). Going the extra mile: Perseverance as a key character strength at work. *Journal of Career Assessment, 21*(4), 1–13.

Park, N., Peterson, C., & Seligman, M. (2004). Strengths of character and well-being. *Journal of Social & Clinical Psychology, 23*(5), 603–619.

Peterson, C., & Seligman, M. (2004). *Character strengths and virtues: A handbook and classification*. Washington, DC: American Psychological Association.

Rogers, C. R. (1961). *On becoming a person: A therapist's view of psychotherapy*. Boston, MA: Houghton Mifflin.

Shepela, A. R., Cook, J., Horlitz, E., Leal, R., Luciano, S., Lutfy, E., Miller, C., Mitchell, G., & Worden, E. (1999). Courageous resistance: A special case of altruism. *Theory & Psychology, 9*(6), 787–805.

Szagun, G., & Schauble, M. (1997). Children's and adults' understanding of the feeling experience of courage. *Cognition & Emotion, 11*(3), 291–306.

Trilling, L. (1972). *Sincerity and authenticity*. Cambridge, MA: Harvard University Press.

Notes

1. Peterson & Seligman (2004).
2. Leontopoulou & Triliva (2012).
3. Peterson & Seligman (2004); Shepela et al. (1999)' Szagun & Schauble (1997).
4. *Wonder Woman* #209 (2004).
5. *Wonder Woman* #210 (2005).
6. Allan (2015); Bolt & Dunn (2016); Peterson & Seligman (2004).
7. *All-Star Comics* #1 (1941); *Wonder Woman* #1 (1987).
8. Peterson & Seligman (2004).
9. Peterson & Seligman (2004).
10. Littman-Ovadia & Lavy (2015).
11. *Wonder Woman* #195 (2003).
12. Littman-Ovadia & Lavy (2015).
13. Peterson & Seligman (2004); Trilling (1972).
14. *Wonder Woman* #195 (2003).
15. Peterson & Seligman (2004).
16. Rogers (1961).
17. Peterson & Seligman (2004).
18. Peterson & Seligman (2004).

19. *Wonder Woman* #126 (1961).
20. Peterson & Seligman (2004).
21. Peterson & Seligman (2004).
22. *Wonder Woman* #177 (2002).
23. Park et al. (2004).
24. Peterson & Seligman (2004).
25. *Wonder Woman* #46 (1990).

THE HUSTLE, BUSTLE, TECHNOLOGY, AND TRAPPINGS OF MODERN LIFE CAN LEAVE A PERSON FEELING ALONE IN A CROWD AND DISCONNECTED FROM CORE PRINCIPLES AND VALUES. WHAT LESSONS CAN A WOMAN FROM AN ANCIENT CULTURE TEACH THE PEOPLE OF TODAY?

PART V

MODERN WORLD

CHAPTER SIXTEEN

Snapping Necks and Wearing Pants: Symbols, Schemas, and Stress Over Change

TRAVIS LANGLEY

"I'm about to make history. By doing something I've never done before."
—Wonder Woman[1]

"Both men and women are resistant to talk about gender, or are quick to dismiss the problems of gender. Because thinking of changing the status quo is always uncomfortable."
—author Chimamanda Ngozi Adichie[2]

Change can be essential to life but can also end it. Whether it arises from things we find pleasant or beneficial (*eustress*) or from things that are unpleasant and detrimental (*distress*), stress taxes our resources and weighs down our mental and emotional loads. Marrying, divorcing, starting jobs, losing jobs, starting school, graduating, dropping out, getting a mortgage, and even taking a vacation will exert pressure, tension, strain—

and that's *stress*.[3] Across lists of *stressors* (whatever factors in life give people stress), the theme is change.[4] Change is stressful.

Is that why readers didn't want Wonder Woman to wear pants?

Why Resist a Hero's Change?

Explanations for why change causes stress include the neurological, endocrinological, philosophical, psychosocial, cognitive, emotional, spiritual, and more.[5] All might be correct. Just as no single explanation can account for all diseases, traffic accidents, or clothing styles, no one theory or hypothesis can cover every aspect or type of stress. A few key concepts, though, may shed some light on why people often resist accepting changes in their heroes: the concepts that relate to why they need and appreciate heroes in the first place.

Incongruence

Carl Rogers, the humanist psychologist who started *client-centered therapy*[6] (now more commonly known as *person-centered therapy*) said that when we are excessively bothered by the difference between how we each see ourselves (*self-image*, the sense of what "I am") and how we think we ought to be (*ideal self*, the sense of what "I should"), the *incongruence* (distressing inconsistency) can damage our sense of self-worth.[7] That ideal self is based on our standards, priorities, and values, the things our heroes tend to represent. Resistance to seeing our heroes change could conceivably grow out of resistance to reconsidering our ideals.

After her creator died, writers repeatedly tried to update Wonder Woman's origin by changing the nature of her relationship with her fellow Amazons, inserting some defining tragedy into her personal biography as if only trauma can make a person heroic, adding male mentors or relatives to her personal history, and occasionally having her wear pants.[8] Repeatedly, those changes have failed to stick. Readers have roared in outrage at many of the changes, disturbed by presentations incongruent with the way they saw their heroine, as if a few writers along the way had failed to get the point.[9]

Symbolism

A *symbol* is something that represents something else, perhaps something with physical substance but perhaps something abstract.[10] Leaders and heroes can symbolize principles, hopes, culture, identity, and ideals.[11] Wonder Woman represents different things to different people: strength, compassion, sensuality, truth, justice, feminism, loving leadership, alien ideology, or gender equality.[12] Because she represents these things, her imagery also represents them. A symbol can deviate only so far before its meaning changes. A red octagon means *STOP*, but morphing it into a yellow triangle should not make the triangle also mean STOP even to those who watched the image morph.

Schemas

From infancy onward, we form connections between ideas and experiences.[13] We find patterns. A mental pattern that developmental psychologist Jean Piaget called a *schema* (a.k.a. *scheme*) comes together as an association of related ideas and details. When the child learns that a penguin is a bird, new information is added to the child's "bird" schema (*assimilation*). When the child realizes that means not all birds fly, the schema itself may change to adapt to the new information (*accommodation*). If learning that Wonder Woman likes a certain breakfast cereal[14] simply adds detail to what a reader knows and thinks about her, then her food preference is merely assimilated into the reader's Wonder Woman schema. The reader who has considered it important that Wonder Woman never kill may have to adapt the schema to accommodate the surprise when the heroine kills the villain Maxwell Lord.[15]

Role Models

We need role models. In fact, we want role models and seek them out. They have the ability to make us become better people as they influence our hopes, aspirations, morals, opinions, and interests, along with the examples we set for others.[16] As we grow older, we learn that our role models are only human. We may accept that, we may judge them harshly for it, or we may resist believing it. "Say it ain't so!"[17] Fear of discovering a respected figure's shortcomings can make an admirer wary of seeing that figure change at all. Even a person who knows logically that clothes do not make the hero can feel discomfort as reasoning and feelings race in from different areas of the brain.

A Discussion with Denny on the "New Wonder Woman"

In turbulent 1968, a manned American space probe orbited the moon for the first time while on Earth wars raged, protesters marched, and leaders were assassinated.[18] Comic book stories changed to adapt to disillusioned times. Writer Denny O'Neil took on the task of revamping the titles *Wonder Woman* and *Justice League of America*. Among the changes, Wonder Woman discards her costume and relinquishes her powers so that she can stay with Steve Trevor as her mother and fellow Amazons all depart to another dimension[19] (right before Steve dies[20]) and moves progressively farther from her roots as O'Neil sought to make her an independent heroine right for the modern age.

We talked to Denny about why he made those changes and the range of reactions they inspired.

> **Langley:** Your take on Wonder Woman moved far away from Marston's.
>
> **O'Neil:** Marston was a really interesting guy, kind of half con man and half genius. My understanding is he micromanaged; he stood over Harry Peter's shoulder. If you look at the first issue of *Wonder Woman*,[21] it's clear he didn't know how to write comics, but I guess he learned. Some of Marston's gamier ideas were finding their way into the comics, at least at first—the bondage imagery, that kind of thing. I may have felt that that didn't have a place in comics. We all draw our own lines.
>
> **Langley:** How did you get involved with Wonder Woman?
>
> **O'Neil:** I don't exactly know. What happened was one of those ill-considered gigs where I was being a freelance editor and a freelance writer. It's something that a lot of the companies have tried. To the best of my knowledge, it's never worked out because the editing half of the equation seems to always get slighted. Editing's a crazy enough job, anyway. No two people do it the same way. My guess is that because Neal Adams and I were sort of the designated character revivers, they offered me that.
>
> **Langley:** Had you grown up reading Wonder Woman?
>
> **O'Neil:** I could just never get involved with that

character even when I was a kid. I would read them because I would read anything that was a comic book when I was six or seven years old. I guess I was entertained by Wonder Woman, but I never had any particular desire to get involved with the character.

Langley: You knew writers wrote her differently after Marston died.

O'Neil: It had evolved quite a lot, but I don't think I would have been at all interested in doing what had become of the character after Marston, either. So I was offered this thing, and they were giving me pretty much a clean slate. Implicit in the offer was "You can change what you don't like."

Langley: What changes did you make?

O'Neil: Well, I thought I was being a feminist. So I took away all of her powers, and I will swear on a stack of Bibles that I had not seen *The Avengers* TV show. I was a Modesty Blaise fan, of both the comic books and Peter O'Donnell's novels. I think the changes I made were kind of in the air. I made her a martial artist. In my head I was serving the cause of feminism because what she did, she did because it was her own human capabilities that allowed her to do those things. I was serving the cause of feminism, and yet Diana got her martial arts chops from an old man. And I added insult to injury by calling that old man *I Ching*, thereby disrespecting one of the five classics of Chinese literature.

Langley: All that ended after *Ms. Magazine* covered how you'd changed her.

O'Neil: When Gloria Steinem came out with her piece—and God bless her for not mentioning my

MADAME PRESIDENT: MS. TO THE RESCUE

JENNA BUSCH

For many girls, Wonder Woman was the first superhero they knew and the first one who looked like them. When the feminist magazine *Ms.* began its run in 1972, Wonder Woman graced the cover. On it, she's saving the world from disaster with her magic lasso near a sign that says, "Peace and Justice in '72."[22] This was in the middle of second wave feminism,[23] and for years, Wonder Woman in the comics had been working with no powers. Sure, she was an expert in the martial arts, but she wasn't the Wonder Woman fans had known for decades. She didn't feel like the hero that Dr. William Moulton Marston created to be "psychological propaganda for the new type of woman who should, I believe, rule the world."[24] She didn't even have the costume.

When founder Gloria Steinem put Wonder Woman on the cover of the magazine, the banner across the top read, "Wonder Woman for President." That cover not only inspired a generation of women but inspired changes in the comics as well. Suddenly, Wonder Woman gets her powers back; wears the red, white, blue, and gold once again; and rejoins the Justice League.[25] Forty years later, in the fall of 2012, she returned to the cover behind women posing with signs saying, "Stop the War on Women."[26]

Cover reprinted with permission of *Ms.* magazine, ©1972.

name—I could certainly see her point of view, and I still can. I think she was more right than I was.

Whole Hero, Whole Truth

Reasons for the reluctance we may feel when heroes change grow out of the fact that change itself disturbs us. We can feel strongly about whatever symbolic value we assign to our role models. Our unease about seeing that value change may arise because altering our existing schemas can be hard, can affect how we feel about the reasons we valued the heroes, and can even rock our perceptions of ourselves. Change stresses us.

Stress is not all bad, though. Stress can be essential. More than a century ago, psychologists Robert Yerkes and John Dillingham Dodson observed that physiological or mental arousal can help us.[27] Their research looked at how we perform better on tasks when arousal goes up, but only to a certain point. Extremely high arousal interferes with functioning. Other researchers since that time have elaborated upon this, showing ways in which we can think, learn, solve problems, enjoy different forms of entertainment, and generally function better in many ways when we are subjected to an optimal level of arousal or stress—not too much but not too little, a Goldilocks zone.[28] We need some change to feel alive. We learn to be wary of change because it can be too much for us. Wonder Woman is not exactly the same character she was in 1941, but she might not be all that different either, with or without the pants.

Comic Book References

Wonder Woman #1 (1942). "The Origin of Wonder Woman." Script: W. M. Marston. Art: H. G. Peter.
Wonder Woman #98 (1959). "The Million-Dollar Penny." Script: R. Kanigher. Art: R. Andru & M. Esposito.

Wonder Woman #178 (1968). "Wonder Woman's Rival." Script: D. O'Neil. Art: M. Sekowsky & D. Giordano.

Wonder Woman #179 (1968). "Wonder Woman's Last Battle." Script: D. O'Neil. Art: M. Sekowsky & D. Giordano.

Wonder Woman #180 (1969). "A Death for Diana!" Script: D. O'Neil. Art: M. Sekowsky & D. Giordano.

Wonder Woman #204 (1973). "The Second Life of the Original Wonder Woman." Script: R. Kanigher. Art: D. Heck & V. Colletta.

Wonder Woman #222 (1976). "Will the Real Wonder Woman Please . . . Drop Dead!" Script: M. Pasko. Art: J. Delbo & T. Blaisdell.

Wonder Woman #219 (2005). "Sacrifice, Part IV." Script: G. Rucka. Art: T. Derenick, G. Jeanty, K. Kerschi, D. Lopez, R. Morales, N. DeCastro, BIT, B. Petrecca, M. Propst, & D. Vines.

Wonder Woman #600 (2010). "Odyssey Prologue: Couture Shock." Script: J. M. Straczynski. Art: D. Kramer & M. Babinski.

Wonder Woman #3 (2012). "Clay." Script: B. Azzarello. Art: C. Chiang.

Other References

Adichie, C. N. (2012). *We should all be feminists*. Speech deliver at TEDxEuston, London, UK.

Anderson, B. (2014, November 18). *Wonder Woman: A new era begins*. Advocate: http://www.advocate.com/arts-entertainment/geek/2014/11/18/wonder-woman-new-era-begins.

Arboleda, L. (2016, January 20). *First footage from "Wonder Woman" film showcases Gal Gadot in all her fighting glory*. Inquisitr: http://www.inquisitr.com/2723160/first-footage-of-wonder-woman/.

Brown, M. E., & Trevino, L. K. (2014). Do role models matter? An investigation of role modeling as an antecedent of perceived ethical leadership. *Journal of Business Ethics, 122*(4), 587–598.

Daniels, L. (2004). *Wonder Woman: The complete history*. San Francisco, CA: Chronicle.

Easterbrook, J. A. (1959). The effect of emotion on cue utilization and the organization of behavior. *Psychological Review, 66*(3), 183–201.

Feldman, D. L. (1985). Ideology and the manipulation of symbols: Leadership perceptions of science, education, and art in the People's Republic of China, 1961–1974. *Political Psychology, 6*(3), 441–460.

Ferguson, J. K., Willemsen, E. W., & Castañeto, M. V. (2010). Centering prayer as a healing response to everyday stress: A psychological and spiritual process. *Pastoral Psychology, 59*(3), 305–329.

Grupe, D. W., Wielgosz, J., Davidson, R. J., & Nitschke, J. B. (2016). Neurobiological correlates of distinct post-traumatic stress disorder symptom profiles during threat anticipation in combat veterans. *Psychological Medicine, 46*(9), 1885–1895.

Gustines, G. G. (2010, June 29). *Makeover for Wonder Woman at 69*. New York Times: http://www.nytimes.com/2010/06/30/books/30wonder.html.

Hansen, A. M., Kaergaard, A., Andersen, J. H., & Netterstrøm, B. (2003). Associations between repetitive work and endocrinological indicators of stress. *Work & Stress, 17*(3), 264–276.

Holmes, T. H., & Rahe, R. H. (1967). The Social Readjustment Rating Scale. *Journal of Psychosomatic Research, 11*(2), 213–218.

Johnson, D. C., & Johnson, L. B. (2010). Reinventing the stress concept. *Ethical Human Psychology & Psychiatry, 12*(3), 218–231.

Johnson, L. (2016, March 8). *Celebrating me and you and Wonder Woman.* Four Elements Coaching: http://4elementscoaching.com/celebrating-me-and-you-and-wonder-woman/.

Jung, C. G., Henderson, J. L., von Franz, M.-L., Jaffé, A., & Jacobi, J. (1964). *Man and his symbols.* New York, NY: Doubleday.

Keitel, A., Ringleb, M., Schwartges, I., Weik, U., Picker, O., Stockhorst, U., & Deinzer, R. (2011). Endocrine and psychological stress responses in a simulated emergency situation. *Psychoneuroendocrinology, 36*(1), 98–108.

Kinsella, E. L., Ritchie, T. D., & Igou, E. R. (2015). Zeroing in on heroes: A prototype analysis of hero features. *Journal of Personality & Social Psychology, 108*(1), 114–127.

Langley, T. (1992). *Cognitive and motivational determinants of appraisal of media violence: Effects of arousal and priming* [doctoral dissertation]. New Orleans, LA: Tulane University.

Linscott, R. B. (1996/2010). *Say it ain't so: Unravelling misquotations.* The Monday Evening Club: http://mondayeveningclub.blogspot.com/2010/04/say-it-aint-so-unravelling.html.

Lupien, S. J., Maheu, F., Tu, M., Fiocco, A., & Schramek, T. E. (2007). The effects of stress and stress hormones on human cognition: Implications for the field of brain and cognition. *Brain & Cognition 65*(3), 209–237.

Matsuuchi, A. (2012). Wonder Woman wears pants: Wonder Woman, feminism, and the 1972 "Women's Lib" issue. *Colloquy, 24,* 118–142.

McLaughlin, K. (2014, July 31). *Eight unforgettable ways 1968 made history.* CNN: http://www.cnn.com/2014/07/31/us/1968-important-events/.

Nussenbaum, K., & Amso, D. (2016). An attentional Goldilocks effect: An optimal mount of social interactivity promotes word learning from video. *Journal of Cognition & Development, 17*(1), 30–40.

Pardo258 (n.d.). *Wonder Woman and what she fights for! Is it needed?* Comics Amino: http://aminoapps.com/page/comics/474773/wonder-woman-and-what-she-fights-for-is-it-needed.

Petrzela, N. M. (2015, May 15). *Do we need Wonder Woman?* Public Books: http://www.publicbooks.org/nonfiction/do-we-need-wonder-woman.

Piaget, J. (1972). Intellectual development from adolescence to adulthood. *Human Development, 15*(1), 1–12.

Piaget, J., & Inhelder, B. (1967). *The psychology of the child.* New York, NY: Basic.

Pitkethley, C. (2009). Recruiting an Amazon: The collision of Old World ideology and New World identity in *Wonder Woman.* In A. Ndalianis (Ed.), *The contemporary comic book superhero* (pp. 164–183). New York, NY: Routledge.

Polo, S. (2011, June 13). *DC inexplicably, quietly changes Wonder Woman's costume . . . again.* The Mary Sue: http://www.themarysue.com/wonder-woman-1-cover-change/.

Rogers, C. (1951). *Client-centered therapy: Its current practice, implications, and theory.* London, UK: Constable.

Rogers, C. (1959). A theory of therapy, personality, and interpersonal relationships as developed in the client-centered framework. In S. Koch (Ed.), *Psychology: A study of the science* (vol. 3). New York, NY: McGraw-Hill.

Rogers, C. R. (1961). *On becoming a person: A psychotherapist's view of psychotherapy.* New York, NY: Houghton Mifflin.

Selye, H. (1976). *The stress of life.* New York, NY: McGraw-Hill.

Sonnentag, T. L., & McDaniel, B. L., (2013). Doing the right thing in the face of social pressure: Moral rebels and their role models have heightened levels of moral trait integration. *Self & Identity, 12*(4), 432–446.

Walker, S. G., & Schafer, M. (2007). Theodore Roosevelt and Woodrow Wilson as cultural icons of U.S. foreign policy. *Political Psychology, 28*(6), 747–776.

Yee, L. (2016). *Wonder Woman at Super Hero High*. New York, NY: Random House.

Yerkes, R. M., & Dodson, J. D. (1908). The relation of strength of stimulus to rapidity of habit-formation. *Journal of Comparative Neurology & Psychology, 18*(5), 459–482.

Young, D. M., Rudman, L. A., Buettner, H. M., & McLean, M. C. (2013). The influence of female role models on women's implicit science cognitions. *Psychology of Women Quarterly, 37*(3), 283–292.

Zandara, M., Garcia-Lluch, M., Pulopulos, M. M., Hidalgo, V., Villada, C., & Salvador, A. (2016). Acute stress and working memory: The role of sex and cognitive appraisal. *Physiology & Behavior, 164*(part A), 336–344.

Notes

1. *Super Friends* episode 4–5, "Universe of Evil" (October 20, 1979).
2. Adichie (2012).
3. Selye (1976).
4. Holmes & Rahe (1967).
5. Ferguson et al. (2010); Grupe et al. (2016); Hansen et al. (2003); Johnson & Johnson (2010); Keitel et al. (2011); Zandara et al. (2016).
6. Rogers (1951).
7. Rogers (1959, 1961).
8. e.g., *Wonder Woman* #98 (1958), #178 (1968), #600 (2010), #3 (2012); see Gustines (2010).
9. e.g., Polo (2011).
10. Jung et al. (1964); Piaget (1972); Piaget & Inhelder (1967).
11. Feldman (1985); Kinsella et al. (2015); Walker & Schager (2007).
12. Anderson (2014); Arboleda (2016); Johnson (2016); Pardo258 (n.d.); Petrzela (2015); Pitkethley (2009).
13. Piaget (1952).
14. Yee (2016).
15. *Wonder Woman* #219 (2005).
16. Brown & Trevino (2014); Sonnentag & McDaniel (2013); Young et al. (2013).
17. A famous *misquote*, as Linscott (1996/2010) explains.
18. McLaughlin (2014).
19. *Wonder Woman* #179 (1968).
20. *Wonder Woman* #180 (1969).
21. *Wonder Woman* #1 (1942).
22. *Ms. Magazine, 1*(1) (1972), cover.
23. Matsuuchi (2012).
24. Quoted in Daniels (2004), p. 22.
25. *Wonder Woman* #204 (1973); *Wonder Woman* #222 (1976).
26. *Ms. Magazine, 40*(1) (2012), cover.
27. Yerkes & Dodson (1908); this is the so-called Yerkes-Dodson law.
28. Anderson et al. (1989); Easterbrook (1959); Langley (1992); Lupien et al. (2007); Nussenbaum & Amso (2016).

CHAPTER SEVENTEEN

First of Her Name: Wonder Woman, the Role Model

MARA WOOD

"I know someone who will always look up to you."
—Artemis, an Amazon[1]

> *"The attainments of others who are similar to oneself are judged to be diagnostic of one's own capabilities."*
> —social psychologist Albert Bandura[2]

The presence of a role model can impact behaviors and attitudes in people who are exposed to that role model.[3] Wonder Woman is a strong role model in both her fictional world and our real one. William Moulton Marston saw the lack of positive female role models in media, stating that "not even girls want to be girls so long as our feminine archetype lacks force, strength, and power."[4] Wonder Woman was also meant to be a model for young boys reading the comic, teaching them the potential women had.[5] While many people look up to Wonder Woman, some more directly emulate her as a role model—for example, the characters Donna Troy and Cassandra Sandsmark, who both aim to model their heroic actions after Diana (by becoming, respectively, the original and then the modern Wonder Girl).[6] Social psychology offers insights into why we learn from models, how we pick models, and the benefits of modeling.

Social Cognitive Theory

Albert Bandura's *social cognitive theory* describes the intricate relationships between people, including the influence of role models. Social cognitive theory encompasses a triumvirate of environmental, behavioral, and personal factors within the concept of *self-efficacy*, a person's belief in his or her ability to perform a task, which is at the crux of learning.[7] People live in an environment full of people and events that respond to their behavior as well as shape their behavior. People's internal workings, their innate personality, also determine their capacity for learning.

Behaviorists like Ivan Pavlov and B. F. Skinner had previously studied learning and proposed that learning was purely a response to explicit environmental stimuli.[8] However, learning is not necessarily the result of explicitly taught reinforcements; it can take place through observation of others. Social psychologist Albert Bandura's Bobo doll experiment demonstrated the effectiveness of *observational learning*. Children observed an adult play with a number of toys. In some situations, the children observed the adult beat up the Bobo doll. When frustration was induced in a play environment, the child imitated the adult's aggressive physical and verbal behavior. The child observed the aggressive behavior and re-created it in a similar environment.[9]

Observational learning provides the foundation for our understanding of role models. A person can learn a behavior vicariously, that is, by observing a behavior and the subsequent consequences of that behavior.[10] The observer is aware of the outcomes of the model's behavior. Superheroes can serve as models; the observer can see an outcome of the heroic action as desirable in some way, whether by receiving an external reward, reaching the fulfillment of personal goals, or becoming the ideal person the observer wants to become.[11] The cognitive aspect of Bandura's social cognitive theory explains that observers undergo a series of subprocesses to determine what modeled behavior they learn.[12]

Attention
People are constantly surrounded by a number of environmental stimuli. What we attend to in our environment sets the stage for what we consider models. We typically attend to models that are interesting. A model that is set apart from the environmental stimuli around it is more likely to be attended to by an observer. Another relevant factor in attending to models is the association between the model and the observer. Those who are near us most often are attended to the most.[13] For children, parents are the models who are most often in their field of attention. As children grow, other caregivers and peers enter their lives and can therefore become models of behavior. Observers pay attention to models who embody characteristics they are interested in possessing themselves. Seeing a model with the elements we desire to see in ourselves draws our attention.[14] The model's affective value, functional value, complexity, and prevalence also impact the degree of attention from the observer.[15]

Wonder Woman comes directly into Cassandra Sandsmark's attentional field when she takes a job with Cassie's mother,

Helena Sandsmark.[16] Cassie witnesses Wonder Woman in action shortly after their introduction. With that kind of exposure, Wonder Woman's actions are interesting and important to Cassie because they differ from her previous, everyday experience. Donna Troy, on the other hand, grew up in an environment similar to Diana's, by some accounts the only other child on Paradise Island.[17] Donna's attention would naturally gravitate toward Diana, her only peer.

Retention

Another cognitive factor involved in emulating a role model is the degree of retention the observer has of the model's behavior. Retention relies on the memory of the observer. To retain the modeled behavior, the observer must be able to encode the behavior using imaginal and verbal methods. The combination of the two processes allows observers to "see" themselves perform the action as well as talk themselves through the steps. By organizing the behavior symbolically, observers are engaging in the highest level of observational learning.[18] The behavior is stored in the observers' memory in the way they can best remember it. This process requires effort on the part of observers, indicating that modeled behaviors that undergo the retention stage are relevant to the observer and carry some meaning. In Wonder Woman's case, her very outfit is iconic and memorable, fostering retention of her words and actions in those who see her.[19]

Reproduction

The retained behavior is then reproduced by observers. Observers must have some spatial awareness and relevant cognitive ability in order to reproduce the behavior. An untrained observer may have difficulty re-creating a complicated gymnastics routine, for instance, no matter how much attention is paid to the model or how much of the routine is retained in the observer's memory. If the observer is able to perform some of the modeled behavior, the discrepancy between the modeled behavior and the observer's behavior can provide the observer with corrective feedback. The observer can then continue to concentrate on and perfect the modeled behavior.[20] The two Wonder Girls reproduce Diana's modeled heroic behaviors through the use of similar tools, such as bracelets and lassos.

Motivation

Observational learning also informs the observer of the possible outcomes of the behavior. Positive outcomes can determine what modeled behaviors are attended to, and they can also motivate the observer to perform the behavior itself. The presence and practice of a behavior rely on the motivation to perform the behavior, including direct reward, vicarious reward, or some sort of self-produced outcome.[21] Vicarious rewards provided to the model induce similar feelings of success in the observer. They stimulate a neural response similar to receiving the reward yourself. This feeling of reward is even stronger in the observer if the model is similar to the observer or likable.[22]

Donna and Cassie have seen Diana's performance as Wonder Woman time and time again. Because Diana is both a public figure and a personal friend, it is easy for them to witness the consequences of her actions and determine the behaviors that led to the end result. Both young women must have found something motivating in the role as a hero, particularly one attached to a name as prominent as Wonder Woman, to follow in Diana's footsteps.

Looking Up to Wonder Woman

These four cognitive subprocesses help to guide the observer in selecting behavior to model. Other factors are at work, though. Models are often chosen based on their proficiencies.[23] The selection of a model indicates the predictive expectations of the person. Both Donna and Cassie carried the title Wonder Girl, evoking the Wonder Woman brand.[24]

Close to the Real Thing
Social comparison theory is the self-appraisal of ability when compared to worse- or better-off people.[25] It is natural to compare yourself to others. Children in school are interested in knowing how peers did on a test. Athletes want to know the times and scores of other athletes in their field. Employees are curious about their co-workers' job performance. In the fictional world of comics, heroes are peers and evoke comparisons between abilities (resulting in years of heated discussion by fans). Social comparison can also increase self-efficacy. Seeing others who are similar to yourself successfully perform a task can increase your belief in your ability to complete that same task. When seeking out a role model, we tend to look for someone similar to us, with a degree of competency greater than our own.[26]

Observers may choose their role models based on superficial reasons, like hair color or physical appearance, but models chosen based on potential ability are most effective.[27] Personal characteristics shared by the observer and the model indicate some degree of predictive capability of the observer.[28] It is as if observers believe they have the innate ability to perform the same task. Donna and Diana have much in common on the surface, but their similarity is greater than that. Like Wonder Woman, Donna has grown up on Themyscira, raised by the

Amazons in the same manner.[29] In some cases, she is referred to as a mirrored "snapshot" of Diana when she was twelve years old, possessing all the traits of the princess at that time.[30] Cassie, on the other hand, seeks out that similarity by asking Zeus to grant her powers like Wonder Woman.[31] In the early days of her time as Wonder Girl, Cassie even wears the wig Diana wore while Artemis served as Wonder Woman.[32] Cassie, by artificially changing her short blond hair to sleek black, sends a message to those she rescues that she is similar to Wonder Woman.

Seeing a model similar to us successfully perform a task evokes a sense of accomplishment in the observer. Like a vicarious reward, the observer feels benefit from the success of the model.[33] That same principle works against models who are unsuccessful in the behavior they model. When the observer sees a model fail, that evokes a degree of despair in the observer. Diana steps down from her title as Wonder Woman, and Donna Troy steps into the new role. However, Donna worries about her performance as Wonder Woman, thinking, "If she couldn't do it, what chance do I have?"[34] Since role models are often chosen based on their perceived expertise and knowledge, an "even they cannot do it" thought rests in the mind of the observer. Luckily for Donna, she did not have to carry the burden of fully emulating her role model for very long.[35]

As a role model, Wonder Woman has an added power over the two Wonder Girls, especially Cassie. The effectiveness of a role model can be enhanced when that role model has the ability to provide rewards to the observer.[36] Parents model appropriate behavior, but they can also provide their children with rewards when they perform the modeled behavior. Wonder Woman rewards Cassie's behavior as Wonder Girl directly. When Cassie performs the correct behavior in line with the Wonder Woman model, she is rewarded with the opportunity to fight by Wonder Woman's side.[37]

A Role Model for the People

Through symbolic modeling, Wonder Woman sets herself up as a role model for a wider audience. Symbolic modeling describes the mass distribution, usually through media, of behaviors that can be replicated.[38] Diana is initially hesitant to engage in any public speaking. Her attitude about that changes after meeting Myndi Mayer, who genuinely believes that Diana has a message worth spreading around the world.[39] Wonder Woman's widespread publicity also elevates her status and power. Models with power and status—in addition to competence—are more effective than models who are lower in status.[40] It can certainly be inferred that Wonder Woman has a high, prominent status in the DC Universe. The first woman to join Earth-2's Justice Society of America,[41] Despite joining as the JSA's secretary, Wonder Woman is soon treated as an equal among the superheroes. Her status grows as she associates with Earth-1's Justice League of America as a member,[42] Superman as a friend,[43] and Themyscira as a representative and diplomat.[44] Throughout her published stories, a number of reporters interview Wonder Woman and write interest pieces on her because of her prominence in society.[45] Wonder Woman's distinction from other potential models indicates her success as a heroine.

A Capable Woman

Female role models are especially important to women, even more than male role models are to men.[46] In a study regarding role model selection, men did not differ in their selection of male or female role models. Women, on the other hand, were significantly stronger in their same-sex role model preference.[47] A female role model acts as a proxy for the female observer, especially if there is similarity between the model and the observer. Women are also acutely aware of the barriers to success their gender faces, which may increase the preference

Diana's time as Wonder Woman has inspired more than just the formation of the Wonder Girls. There are times when Diana is unable to perform her role as Wonder Woman. In those cases, other women have stepped into the role and tried to embody what it means to be called Wonder Woman:

- Artemis of Bana-Mighdall is the victor of a contest held by Hippolyta in an effort to strip the title of Wonder Woman from Diana. Artemis grows up in a much different environment than Diana, and her approach to the title differs greatly.[48]
- Queen Hippolyta fills the role of Wonder Woman after Diana's death. Her physical appearance is similar to Diana's, and she joins the Justice Society of America during the Second World War.[49]
- Donna Troy assumes the identity of Wonder Woman shortly after Diana steps down. Her reign is short, and she relinquishes it to Diana prior to rejoining the Titans.[50]
- Circe, the Sorceress takes the powers from Diana, Donna, and Cassie to create her own version of Wonder Woman. Though her methods are more violent, she uses her time as Wonder Woman to rescue women from hopeless situations.[51]
- Cassie Sandsmark becomes Wonder Woman in an alternate future after the death of Diana.[52]

Each woman brings a different aspect of the role to the foreground during her tenure as Wonder Woman, but it is clear that the position created by Diana is important to each one.

for a successful female role model over a successful male role model.[53]

Wonder Woman is not positioned as a role model solely because of her unique abilities. Prior to creating Wonder Woman, William Moulton Marston realized that people need female role models. While it is possible for readers both male and female to look up to one of the many already established male heroes, a female role model offers distinctive benefits to her observers. One real-world area in which the gender of role models can be explored is math ability in women. It is a commonly held stereotype that women are weaker in math than men.[54] This gender stereotype informs women's math performance. The presence of a female role model who demonstrates competency in math can counter women's poorer math performance.[55] Wonder Woman's success as a hero is important to the other heroines she meets. Her powers are stereotypically masculine in nature: super strength, flight, and military training. She blends these powers with more feminine characteristics, such as restraint, defense, and preaching peace. Her approach defies stereotypes of women in general, which in turn makes her a draw as a role model for other women.[56]

A Role Model for Everyone

Role models are only as effective as the observer will allow them to be. For role models to be effective, their success must be viewed as attainable, they must be somewhat similar to the observer, and the observer needs to care about the behavior being modeled.[57] Bandura's social cognitive theory helps us understand how we learn from viewing and what impacts our model selection. In the end, it is subjective to each viewer what they want to see in a model. For Donna and Cassie, Diana is a heroine who models the life they want to live. For readers, Wonder Woman is a character worth looking up to.

Comic Book References

All-Star Comics #12 (1942). "The Black Dragon." Script: G. Fox. Art: J. Burnley.
Brave and the Bold #28 (1960). "The Justice League of America." Script: G. Fox. Art: M. Sekowsky.
Brave and the Bold #60 (1965). "The Astounding Separated Man." Script: B. Haney. Art: B. Premiani.
Teen Titans #17 (2005). "Titans Tomorrow, Part 1: Big Brothers and Big Sisters." Script: G. Johns. Art: M. McKone & M. Alquiza.
Teen Titans #22 (1969). "Halfway to Holocaust." Script: M. Wolfman. Art: G. Kane & N. Cardy.
Wonder Woman #53 (1952). "The Crime Master of Time." Script: R. Kanigher. Art: H. G. Peter.
Wonder Woman #158 (1965). "The End—or the Beginning!" Script: R. Kanigher. Art: R. Andru & M. Esposito.
Wonder Woman #8 (1987). "Time Passages." Script: G. Pérez & L. Wein. Art: G. Pérez & B. D. Patterson.
Wonder Woman #37 (1989). "Strangers in Paradise." Script: G. Pérez & M. Newell. Art: C. Marrinan & S. Montano.
Wonder Woman #50 (1991). "Embrace the Coming Dawn." Script: G. Pérez. Art: J. Thompson & R. Tanghal.
Wonder Woman #105 (1996). "Lifelines, Part 1." Script/Art: J. Byrne.
Wonder Woman #111 (1996). "Level 3." Script/Art: J. Byrne.
Wonder Woman #113 (1996). "Are You Out of Your Minds?!" Script/Art: J. Byrne.
Wonder Woman #122 (1997). "Judgment of the gods." Script/Art: J. Byrne.
Wonder Woman #128 (1997). "Shell Game." Script/Art: J. Byrne.
Wonder Woman #134 (1998). "Who Is Donna Troy?" Script/Art: J. Byrne.
Wonder Woman #140 (1999). "Trinity 98." Script: E. Luke. Art: Y. Paquette & B. McLeod.
Wonder Woman #170 (2001). "She's a Wonder!" Script: P. Jimenez. Art: P. Jimenez & A. Lanning.
Wonder Woman #1 (2006). "Who Is Wonder Woman? Part 1." Script: A. Heinberg. Art: T. Dodson & R. Dodson.
Wonder Woman #4 (2006). "Who Is Wonder Woman? Part 4." Script: A. Heinberg. Art: T. Dodson & R. Dodson.
Wonder Woman Annual #1 (2007). "Who Is Wonder Woman? Part 5." Script: A. Heinberg. Art: T. Dodson & R. Dodson.

Other References

Bandura, A. (1977). *Social learning theory.* Englewood Cliffs, NJ: Prentice-Hall.
Bandura, A. (1986). *Social foundations of thoughts and actions: A social cognitive theory.* Englewood Cliffs, NJ: Prentice-Hall.
Bandura, A. (1997). *Self-efficacy: The exercise of control.* New York, NY: Freeman.
Bandura, A., Ross, D., & Ross, S. A. (1961). Transmission of aggression through imitation of aggressive models. *Journal of Abnormal & Social Psychology, 63*(3), 575–582.

Cronin, B. (2009). *Was Superman a spy? And other comic book legends revealed.* New York, NY: Plume.

Daniels, L. (2000). *Wonder Woman: The complete history.* San Francisco, CA: Chronicle.

Jett, B. (2015, October 9). *Who is WW? The mistaken little sister.* World of Superheroes: http://www.worldofsuperheroes.com/2015/10/who-is-ww-the-mistaken-little -sister/.

Lockwood, P. (2006). "Someone like me can be successful": Do college students need same-gender role models? *Psychology of Women Quarterly, 30*(1), 36–46.

Lockwood, P., & Kunda, Z. (1997). Superstars and me: Predicting the impact of role models on the self. *Journal of Personality & Social Psychology, 73*(1), 91–103.

Marston, W. M. (1943). Why 100,000,000 Americans read comics. *American Scholar, 13*(1), 35–44.

Marx, D. M., & Roman, J. S. (2002). Female role models: Protecting women's math test performance. *Personality & Social Psychology Bulletin, 28*(9), 1183–1193.

Skinner, B. F. (1963). *Operant behavior. American Psychologist, 18*(8), 503–515.

Wolpe, J., & Plaud, J. J. (1997). Pavlov's contributions to behavior therapy: The obvious and the not so obvious. *American Psychologist, 52*(9), 966–972.

Notes

1. *Wonder Woman* #140 (1999).
2. Bandura (1997), p. 87.
3. Bandura (1977).
4. Marston (1943).
5. Daniels (2000).
6. Technically, the original Wonder Girl was supposed to be Wonder Woman herself as a girl until a writer unaware of this depicted Wonder Girl as a separate character (*Brave and the Bold* #60, 1965). See Cronin (2009) or Jett (2015). *Wonder Woman* #158 (1965) addressed the retroactive change to Wonder Woman's history.
7. Bandura (1997).
8. Skinner (1963); Wolpe & Plaud (1997).
9. Bandura et al. (1961).
10. Bandura (1977).
11. Bandura (1977).
12. Bandura (1997).
13. Bandura (1977).
14. Bandura (1977).
15. Bandura (1997).
16. *Wonder Woman* #105 (1996).
17. *Wonder Woman* #134 (1998).
18. Bandura (1977).
19. *Wonder Woman* #140 (1999).
20. Bandura (1977).
21. Bandura (1997).
22. Lockwood & Kunda (1997).
23. Bandura (1997).
24. Beginning in *Brave and the Bold* #60 (1965) for Donna and *Wonder Woman* #111 (1996) for Cassie.
25. Bandura (1997).
26. Bandura (1997).

27. Bandura (1997).
28. Bandura (1997).
29. *Teen Titans* #22 (1969).
30. *Wonder Woman* #134 (1998).
31. *Wonder Woman* #122 (1997).
32. *Wonder Woman* #111 (1996).
33. Bandura (1997).
34. *Wonder Woman* #1 (2006).
35. *Wonder Woman Annual* #1 (2007).
36. Bandura (1986).
37. *Wonder Woman* #113 (1996).
38. Bandura (1986).
39. *Wonder Woman* #8 (1987).
40. Bandura (1986).
41. *All-Star Comics* #12 (1942).
42. *Brave and the Bold* #28 (1960).
43. *Wonder Woman* #37 (1989).
44. *Wonder Woman* #50 (1991).
45. *Wonder Woman* #53 (1952); *Wonder Woman* #170 (2001).
46. Lockwood (2006).
47. Lockwood (2006).
48. *Wonder Woman* #93 (1995).
49. *Wonder Woman* #128 (1997).
50. *Wonder Woman* #1 (2006).
51. *Wonder Woman* #4 (2006).
52. *Teen Titans* #17 (2005).
53. Lockwood (2006).
54. Marx & Roman (2002).
55. Marx & Roman (2002).
56. Marx & Roman (2002).
57. Marx & Roman (2002).

CHAPTER EIGHTEEN

Balancing the Warrior and the Peace Ambassador: Self-Concepts and Moral Complexity

Eric D. Wesselman, Emilio J. C. Lobato, and J. Scott Jordan

"Perfection . . . sometimes it's our worst enemy. I tried to be perfect once. Decided to just try to be better. Found a good way to start that is by accepting who you are."
—Wonder Woman[1]

"Superheroes are magnificent inventions . . . we are given the opportunity to stretch our own moral imaginations by wondering along with these heroes about the most appropriate and correct course of action."
—psychologist Lawrence C. Rubin[2]

Defining heroism can be difficult even without the added complication of determining what a superhero is.[3] Definitions of both commonly involve abiding by a culturally valued

moral code, enforcing justice, and protecting people altruis-
tically (sometimes with special powers, at other times not).[4]
Heroes and superheroes can struggle with the moral dilemma
of using violence to enforce justice and protect the innocent
but still remain true to the moral codes that are rooted in their
self-concepts.[5] Psychologists who study moral decision-making
often examine how aspects of individuals' self-concept relevant
to conceptions of morality—sometimes called a *moral identity*—
influence their adherence to moral values and ultimately the
way they respond when someone (including themselves) acts in
contrary ways.[6] Wonder Woman's struggle arises in part because
her self-concept encompasses disparate identities that sometimes
conflict with one another: ambassador of peace versus Amazon
warrior who has trained all her life in the arts of war.[7] A major
theme in Wonder Woman's stories is how she balances her
desire to teach others to live peacefully with knowing that using
force is sometimes necessary.[8] She is challenged constantly to
ensure peace and justice and use violence only when she deems
it morally appropriate. A key moment in Women Woman's
character development—her killing of Maxwell Lord[9]—and
the reactions of her superhero peers Batman and Superman
(the so-called DC Trinity)[10] can help illustrate how individuals'
self-concepts drive their moral decision-making.

Self-Complexity and Balancing Identities

*"I am a warrior as much as I am a woman of peace. I can
never place one half of my soul above the other. . . ."*
—Wonder Woman[11]

> *"By maintaining distinctions among various aspects of
> the self, one is more likely to maintain positive feelings*

about some aspects, which act as a buffer against negative
happenings or negative thoughts about other specific aspects."
—psychologist Patricia W. Linville[12]

An individual's *self-concept* is the way a person describes or perceives herself or himself,[13] and it involves various aspects of that person's social life (e.g., personal characteristics, interpersonal relationships, culture).[14] Wonder Woman is an immortal Amazon, a warrior from the idyllic island of Themyscira who serves both as a peace ambassador to the United Nations and as a heroic member of the Justice League to protect the people of Earth. She recognizes that her mission will be difficult because although she lives among humans, she is not a human herself. Unfortunately, individuals often do not trust others who are different from them (i.e., not perceived as part of their *in-group*).[15] Research on intergroup conflict demonstrates that trust is imperative for cooperation and positive interactions between groups; distrust often leads to prejudice, aggression, and social avoidance.[16] Wonder Woman realizes that both the people she is trying to help and her fellow heroes may distrust her, not understand fully her actions and motives, and even refuse her help.[17]

Individuals strive for consistency across the various aspects of their self-concept,[18] but as they negotiate the complexities of daily life, conflicts inevitably emerge.[19] Some individuals are more effective than others at managing these complexities, and this management can affect the way they evaluate themselves and others.[20] These differences can be seen among the DC Trinity: Batman and Superman often have difficulty reconciling their identities as civilians and superheroes.[21] Superman, like Wonder Woman, also has to negotiate his emotional identification with humans even though he is technically not one of them.[22] Wonder Woman appears to be the best of the three in terms of balancing the different aspects of her self-concept, proclaiming confidently

INCLUSION OF OTHER IN SELF

The *Inclusion of Other in Self* measure assesses how much individuals integrate relationship partners into their self-concept, with each partner represented by a circle.[23] Researchers have adapted this measure to examine individuals' commitment to social groups.[24] Individuals who indicate complete overlap between themselves and their social group (*identity fusion*) can exhibit high levels of devotion and engage in extreme actions, such as being willing to die or kill to benefit their group.[25] Wonder Woman is not a human. She was created by the gods and is an Amazon—beings who are immortal as long as they do not leave Themyscira and are not killed in combat.[26] However, Wonder Woman strives to live among humans and work within their laws and customs; she believes her mission to teach humans how to live peacefully would be most effective that way.[27] Thus, Wonder Woman willingly brings humanity into her self-concept even though some individuals explicitly tell her she is still not one of *them*.[28] Wonder Woman likely sees a high degree of overlap between her self-concept and humanity (perhaps letter F or G in the diagram). This overlap can explain her willingness to risk serious harm or death without hesitation to save others' lives.[29]

that she will fulfill whichever role (warrior, ambassador, or princess) the world needs her to play whenever the need arises.[30]

Morality Convictions and Lethal Methods

"I walk with death. I do not follow death. Nor do I lead.
Rather, death is at my side, the uneasy, constant companion
of any warrior."
—Wonder Woman[31]

"Moral convictions demonstrably provide people with the
moral courage and fortitude to 'go it alone' if necessary and
to defend their point of view, even when it is very lonely to
stand up for what they are convinced is right."
—psychologist Linda J. Skitka[32]

Individuals' moral beliefs influence how they define (and evaluate) their self-concepts.[33] Moral beliefs also influence how individuals evaluate the appropriateness of specific actions (their own and others') and their general attitudes toward sociopolitical issues (e.g., death penalty, military action).[34] One belief individuals often use to determine the morality of an action is whether that action harms someone.[35] Certain that Maxwell Lord will use his mind control powers to force Superman to kill others,[36] Wonder Woman takes Lord's life.[37] When individuals witness someone engaging in an action that violates the perceivers' moral values, those individuals will judge that person negatively, especially if the behavior is something they find distasteful.[38] By choosing to kill Lord, Wonder Woman incurs moral condemnation from Batman and Superman because both believe that it is wrong to kill a human, even a villain who is trying to harm or kill others.[39]

Individuals often experience the moral beliefs central to

their self-concept as *convictions*—beliefs that are self-evident, are indisputable, and often lead to reflexive reactions in judging others.[40] Both Batman and Superman immediately respond adversely to Wonder Woman's decision to kill Lord,[41] probably due to the oaths they have sworn to never purposefully take another's life.[42] Wonder Woman believes that all human life is precious and abhors *murder*,[43] yet she has sometimes been depicted as not having the same compunction against *killing* if it is necessary to protect lives.[44] Wonder Woman is clear that her killing of Lord was not "murder," and whenever she describes the event, she says she "slew," "killed," or had to "take his life."[45] Whereas Batman argues that killing is never an option for superheroes, Wonder Woman argues that moral decisions are not always as clear-cut as he and Superman seem to view them.[46] Indeed, most Amazons acknowledge that moral ambiguity often exists, such as the necessity of violence and killing;[47] their tolerance for ambiguity is likely due to the increased self-complexity inherent in being raised in a culture that yearns for peace yet trains for war.[48]

Individuals generally have difficulty with moral ambiguity when harm is involved because when they consider the morality of an action, they often define the other individuals involved as being either *agents* (i.e., the source of the behavior—either a hero or a villain) or *patients* (i.e., the target of the behavior—either a beneficiary or a victim).[49] It is hard for someone to be seen as both.[50] Thus, it may be difficult for Wonder Woman's peers and especially for the general public that did not have access to the full context of the incident[51] to see Lord as both a villain and a victim. Indeed, many individuals within the DC Universe have difficulty reconciling Wonder Woman and the Amazons' peace–war dichotomy and view them suspiciously because of this perceived contradiction;[52] perhaps some readers may even have difficulty reconciling this dichotomy.[53] Research suggests that there is a thin line between being perceived as a hero and being seen as a villain; individuals afford heroes little leniency when they exhibit flaws or in engage in something perceived as immoral and have little trouble blaming them for it.[54] Wonder Woman receives blame and distrust from the general public after they learn she has killed Lord; she is given little leeway even though she has a record of heroic acts and selfless altruism.[55]

Psychologists who study moral convictions find that these convictions inspire individuals to adhere to their moral codes even in the face of extreme adversity and at personal cost.[56] Wonder Woman's moral conviction focuses on protecting innocent lives regardless of the physical[57] or social costs (such as threatening her friendships with Batman and Superman or potentially incurring legal punishment).[58] Wonder Woman does not regret making these difficult choices.[59] She even encourages the Amazons to flee the mortal realm permanently to protect them from destruction even though she knows it means being isolated from them indefinitely.[60] Individuals who are chronically excluded or isolated from others often experience severe physical (e.g., cardiovascular and immunity problems) and psychological outcomes (e.g., depression)[61]—Wonder Woman's moral convictions empower her to take on these harmful outcomes willingly.

Her Mission Continues . . .

"Heroine, demigoddess, solider, peacemaker—I am all of these things in part, yet none of them completely. In truth, I am most like the people of Man's World—a being of contrasts and contradictions."
—Wonder Woman[62]

Individuals have self-concepts that involve multiple aspects, and certain aspects can become more or less salient depending on the situation. Even though individuals strive for consistency among these myriad aspects, some individuals can tolerate greater complexity than others can. Moral beliefs often form a core aspect of one's self-concept—what psychologists call an individual's *moral identity*—and the moral conflicts that emerge in one's life (whether a comic book superhero or a real-life person) can cause intense distress if a person cannot tolerate complexities in his or her moral self-concept. Superheroes often struggle with whether to use violence (especially lethal methods) when protecting the lives of others. We argue that Wonder Woman embodies a high level of psychological self-complexity and thus can tolerate more ambiguity in her moral self-concept than can someone who has less self-complexity (e.g., Batman and Superman). She exhibits the most self-complexity of the three because her behavior reflects the ability to act in ways that acknowledge the seemingly contradictory[63] nature of the two most salient aspects of her self-concept (her role as a peace ambassador and her training as an Amazon warrior). Wonder Woman's ability to manage high self-complexity allows her to deal with any threats to her self-concept better than do individuals who harbor less-complex self-concepts.[64] Further, Wonder Woman's *moral conviction* to protect innocent life at all costs affords her the strength to sacrifice her own well-being for that of the people she wishes to protect. When Wonder Woman and Superman are comforting each other after a friend's death, she navigates this complexity when she says that they are "never everything we wish to be . . . and rarely are we everything we appear to be." Superman simply responds, "You are."[65]

Comic Book References

Batman #509 (1994). "KnightsEnd, Part 1: Spirit of the Bat." Script: D. Moench. Art: M. Manley & D. Giordano.

Batman/Superman/Wonder Woman: Trinity #1 (2003). Script: M. Wagner. Art: M. Wagner.

Batman: War on Crime (1999). Story: A. Ross & P. Dini. Script: P. Dini. Art: A. Ross.

Blackest Night: Wonder Woman #1 (2010). "The Living." Script: G. Rucka. Art: N. Scott, P. Rollins, J. Glapion, W. Wong, & D. Geraci.

Flash #219 (2005). "Truth or Dare Part 1" Script: G. Johns. Art: Justiniano, J. Livesay, & W. Wong.

Identity Crisis #4 (2004). "Chapter Four: Who Benefits." Script: B. Meltzer. Art: R. Morales & M. Bair.

Infinite Crisis #1 (2005). "Infinite Crisis." Script: G. Johns. Art: P. Jiminez & A. Lanning.

Legends of the Dark Knight #62 (1994). "KnightsEnd Part 4: Devils." Script: C. Dixon. Art: R. Wagner & R. McCain.

Shadow of the Bat #29 (1994). "Manimal: Proving Ground." Script: A Grant. Art: B. Blevins & B. Smith.

Superman #219 (2005). "Sacrifice (Part I of IV): Touch." Script: M. Verheiden. Art: E. Benes, M. Benes, R. Lea, & A. Lei.

Superman: Peace on Earth (1999). Story: A. Ross & P. Dini. Script: P. Dini. Art: A. Ross.

The Untold Legend of the Batman #1 (1980). "In the Beginning." Script: L. Wein. Art: J. Byrne & J. Aparo.

Wonder Woman #210 (2005). "Stoned, Conclusion." Script: G. Rucka. Art: D. Johnson & R. Snyder.

Wonder Woman #217 (2005). "The Bronze Doors Conclusion." Script: G. Rucka. Art: R. Morales & M. Propst.

Wonder Woman #219 (2005). "Sacrifice (Part IV of IV)." Script: G. Rucka. Art: T. Derenick, G. Jeanty, K. Kerschl, D. Lopez, R. Morales, N. DeCastro, BIT, B. Petrecca, M. Propst, & D. Vines.

Wonder Woman #220 (2005). "Affirmative Defense." Script: G. Rucka. Art: D. Lopez & BIT.

Wonder Woman #221 (2005). "Pride of the Amazons." Script: G. Rucka. Art: R. Morales, C. Richards, M. Bair, M. Propst, & R. Snyder.

Wonder Woman #222 (2005). "Blood Debt." Script: G. Rucka. Art: C. Richards & R. Snyder.

Wonder Woman #223 (2005). "Marathon Part 1." Script: G. Rucka. Art: C. Richards, R. Morales, M. Bair, & R. Snyder.

Wonder Woman #224 (2005). "Marathon Part 2." Script: G. Rucka. Art: C. Richards & R. Snyder.

Wonder Woman #225 (2005). "Nothing Finished, Only Abandoned." Script: G. Rucka. Art: C. Richards & R. Snyder.

Wonder Woman #226 (2005). "Cover Date." Script: G. Rucka. Art: C. Richards & R. Snyder.

Wonder Woman #7 (2007). "Love and Murder Part 2." Script: J. Picoult. Art: D. Johnson, R. Snyder, & R. Ramos.

Wonder Woman #9 (2007). "Love and Murder Part 4." Script: J. Picoult. Art: T. Dodson & R. Dodson.

Wonder Woman #25 (2008). "Personal Effects." Script: G. Simone. Art: B. Chang.

Wonder Woman #22 (2013). "The Calm." Writer: B. Azzarello. Art: C. Chiang.

Wonder Woman: Spirit of Truth (2001). Story: A. Ross & P. Dini. Script: P. Dini. Art: A. Ross.

Other References

Agnew, C. R., Van Lange, P. A. M., Rusbult, C. E., & Langston, C. A. (1998). Cognitive interdependence: Commitment and the mental representation of close relationships. *Journal of Personality & Social Psychology, 74*(4), 939–954.

Aquino, K., & Reed, A. (2002). The self-importance of moral identity. *Journal of Personality & Social Psychology, 83*(6), 1423–1440.

Aron, A., Aron, E. N., & Smollan, D. (1992). Inclusion of other in the self scale and the structure of interpersonal closeness. *Journal of Personality & Social Psychology, 63*(4), 596–612.

Brewer, M. B., & Gardner, W. (1996). Who is this "We"? Levels of collective identity and self representations. *Journal of Personality & Social Psychology, 71*(1), 83–93.

Coogan, P. (2013). The hero defines the genre, the genre defines the hero. In R. S. Rosenberg & P. Coogan (Eds.), *What is a superhero?* (pp. 3–10). New York, NY: Oxford University Press.

Daniel, L. (2004). *Wonder Woman: The complete history.* San Francisco, CA: Chronicle.

DeScioli, P., & Kurzban, R. (2008). Cracking the superhero's moral code. In R. S. Rosenberg (Ed.), *The psychology of superheroes: An unauthorized exploration* (pp. 245–259). Dallas, TX: BenBella.

Fiske, S. T. (2000). Stereotyping, prejudice, and discrimination at the seam between the centuries: Evolution, culture, mind, and brain. *European Journal of Social Psychology, 30*(3), 299–322.

Forgas, J. P., & Williams, K. D. (2002). The social self: Introduction and overview. In J. P. Forgas & K. D. Williams (Eds.), *The social self: Cognitive, interpersonal, and intergroup perspectives* (pp. 1–18). New York, NY: Psychology Press.

Gaertner, L., & Schopler, J. (1998). Perceived ingroup entitativity and intergroup bias: An interconnection of self and others. *European Journal of Social Psychology, 28*(6), 963–980.

Gómez, Á., Morales, J. F., Hart, S., Vázquez, A., & Swann, W. B. (2011). Rejected and excluded forevermore, but even more devoted irrevocable ostracism intensifies loyalty to the group among identity-fused persons. *Personality & Social Psychology Bulletin, 37*(12), 1574–1586.

Graham, J., Haidt, J., & Nosek, B. A. (2009). Liberals and conservatives rely on different sets of moral foundations. *Journal of Personality & Social Psychology, 96*(5), 1029–1046.

Gray, K., & Wegner, D. M. (2011). To escape blame, don't be a hero—be a victim. *Journal of Experimental Social Psychology, 47*(2), 516–519.

Gray, K., & Wegner, D. M. (2012). Morality takes two: Dyadic morality and mind perception. In M. Mikulincer & P. R. Shaver (Eds.), *The social psychology of morality: Exploring the causes of good and evil* (pp. 109–127). Washington, DC: American Psychological Association.

Haidt, J. (2008). Morality. *Perspectives on Psychological Science, 3*(1), 65–72.

Hawkley, L. C., & Cacioppo, J. T. (2003). Loneliness and pathways to disease. *Brain, Behavior, & Immunity, 17*(1), 98–105.

Higgins, E. T. (1987). Self-discrepancy: A theory relating self and affect. *Psychological Review, 94*(3), 319–340.

Koleva, S. P., Graham, J., Iyer, R., Ditto, P. H., & Haidt, J. (2012). Tracing the threads: How five moral concerns (especially purity) help explain culture war attitudes. *Journal of Research in Personality, 46*(2), 184–194.

Linville, P. W. (1985). Self-complexity and affective extremity: Don't put all of your eggs in one basket. *Social Cognition, 3*(1), 94–120.

Linville, P. W., & Carlston, D. E. (1994). Social cognition of the self. In P. G. Devine, D. L. Hamilton, & T. M. Ostrom (Eds.), *Social cognition: Impact on social psychology* (pp. 143–193). San Diego, CA: Academic Press.

Markus, H., & Wurf, E. (1987). The dynamic self-concept: A social psychological perspective. *Annual Review of Psychology, 38*(1), 299–337.

Miller, R., & Cushman, F. (2013). Aversive for me, wrong for you: First-person behavioral aversions underlie the moral condemnation of harm. *Social & Personality Psychology Compass, 7*(10), 707–718.

Miller, R. M., Hannikainen, I. A., & Cushman, F. A. (2014). Bad actions or bad outcomes? Differentiating affective contributions to the moral condemnation of harm. *Emotion, 14*(3), 573–587.

Monin, B., & Jordan, A. H. (2009). The dynamic moral self: A social psychological perspective. In D. Narvaez & D. K. Lapsley (Eds.), *Personality, identity, and character: Explorations in moral psychology* (pp. 341–354). New York, NY: Cambridge University Press.

Pagnoni Berns, F. G. (2014). War, foreign policy, and the media: The Rucker years. In J. J. Darowski (Ed.), *The ages of Wonder Woman: Essays on the Amazon princess in changing times* (pp. 194–203). Jefferson, NC: McFarland.

Reeder, G. D., Pryor, J. B., Wohl, M. J., & Griswell, M. L. (2005). On attributing negative motives to others who disagree with our opinions. *Personality & Social Psychology Bulletin, 31*(11), 1498–1510.

Rosenberg, R. S. (2008). Introduction. In R. S. Rosenberg (Ed.), *The psychology of superheroes: An unauthorized exploration* (pp. 1–4). Dallas, TX: BenBella.

Rosenberg, R. S., & Coogan, P. (Eds.) (2013). *What is a superhero?* New York, NY: Oxford University Press.

Rubin, L. C. (2013). Are superhero stories good for us? Reflections from clinical practice. In R. S. Rosenberg (Ed.), *Our superheroes, ourselves* (pp. 37–52). New York, NY: Oxford University Press.

Sachdeva, S., Iliev, R., & Medin, D. L. (2009). Sinning saints and saintly sinners: The paradox of moral self-regulation. *Psychological Science, 20*(4), 523–528.

Skitka, L. J. (2012). Moral convictions and moral courage: Common denominators of good and evil. In M. Mikulincer & P. R. Shaver (Eds.), *The social psychology of morality: Exploring the causes of good and evil* (pp. 349–365). Washington, DC: American Psychological Association.

Steele, C. M., & Liu, T. J. (1983). Dissonance processes as self-affirmation. *Journal of Personality & Social Psychology, 45*(1), 5–19.

Steinem, G. (1972). Introduction. In P. Chesler (Author), *Wonder Woman* (pp. 1–6). New York, NY: Holt, Rinehart & Winston.

Swann Jr., W. B., Gómez, A., Seyle, D. C., Morales, J., & Huici, C. (2009). Identity fusion: The interplay of personal and social identities in extreme group behavior. *Journal of Personality & Social Psychology, 96*(5), 995–1011.

Swann, W. B., Gómez, Á., Dovidio, J. F., Hart, S., & Jetten, J. (2010). Dying and killing for one's group: Identity fusion moderates responses to intergroup versions of the trolley problem. *Psychological Science, 21*(8), 1176–1183.

Swann, W. B., Jr., Rentfrow, P. J., & Guinn, J. (2003). Self-verification: The search for coherence. In M. Leary & J. Tangney (Eds.), *Handbook of self and identity* (pp. 367–383). New York, NY: Guilford.

Tam, T., Hewstone, M., Kenworthy, J., & Cairns, E. (2009). Intergroup trust in Northern Ireland. *Personality & Social Psychology Bulletin, 35*(1), 45–59.

Vezzali, L., Capozza, D., Stathi, S., & Giovannini, D. (2012). Increasing outgroup trust, reducing infrahumanization, and enhancing future contact intentions via imagined intergroup contact. *Journal of Experimental Social Psychology, 48*(1), 437–440.

Wesselmann, E. D., VanderDrift, L. E., & Agnew, C. R. (2016). Religious commitment: An interdependence approach. *Psychology of Religion & Spirituality, 8*(1), 35–45.

Yuki, M., Maddux, W. W., Brewer, M. B., & Takemura, K. (2005). Cross-cultural differences in relationship- and group-based trust. *Personality and Social Psychology Bulletin, 31*(1), 48–62.

Notes

1. *Wonder Woman* #22 (2013).
2. Rubin (2013), pp. 48–49.
3. Rosenberg & Coogan (2013).
4. Coogan (2013); DeScioli & Kurzban (2008); Rosenberg (2008).
5. DeScioli & Kurzban (2008); Rosenberg (2008).
6. Aquino & Reed (2002); Haidt (2008).
7. *Wonder Woman: Spirit of Truth* (2001).
8. Steinem (1972).
9. *Wonder Woman* #219 (2005).
10. *Batman/Superman/Wonder Woman: Trinity* #1 (2003).
11. *Wonder Woman: Spirit of Truth* (2001).
12. Linville (1985), pp. 94–95.
13. Linville & Carlston (1994); Markus & Wurf (1987).
14. Brewer & Gardner (1996); Forgas & Williams (2002).
15. Fiske (2000).
16. Fiske (2000); Tam et al. (2009); Vezzali et al. (2012); Yuki et al. (2005).
17. *Flash* #219 (2005); *Infinite Crisis* #1 (2005); *Wonder Woman: Spirit of Truth* (2001).
18. Higgins (1987); Steele & Liu (1983); Swann et al. (2003).
19. Brewer & Gardner (1996).
20. Linville (1985).
21. *Batman: War on Crime* (1999); *Legends of the Dark Knight* #62 (1994); *Shadow of the Bat* #29 (1994); *Superman: Peace on Earth* (1999); *The Untold Legend of the Batman* #1 (1980); *The Untold Legend of the Batman* #3 (1980): *Wonder Woman* #226 (2005).
22. *Infinite Crisis* #1 (2005); *Superman: Peace on Earth* (1999); *Wonder Woman: Spirit of Truth* (2001).
23. Agnew et al. (1998); Aron et al. (1992).
24. Gaertner & Schopler (1998); Swann et al. (2009); Wesselmann et al. (2016).
25. Gómez et al. (2011); Swann et al. (2010).
26. *Wonder Woman* #221 (2005); *Wonder Woman* #226 (2005); *Wonder Woman: Spirit of Truth* (2001).
27. *Wonder Woman* #221 (2005); *Wonder Woman* #222 (2005); *Wonder Woman* #223 (2005); *Wonder Woman* #225 (2005); *Wonder Woman: Spirit of Truth* (2001).
28. *Infinite Crisis* #1 (2005); *Wonder Woman* #220 (2005); *Wonder Woman* #7 (2007); *Wonder Woman* #9 (2007); *Wonder Woman: Spirit of Truth* (2001).
29. *Wonder Woman* #210 (2005); *Wonder Woman* #217 (2005); *Wonder Woman* #220 (2005).
30. *Infinite Crisis* #1 (2005); *Wonder Woman: Spirit of Truth* (2001).
31. *Blackest Night: Wonder Woman* #1 (2010).
32. Skitka (2012), p. 360.
33. Monin & Jordan (2009); Sachdeva et al. (2009).

34. Graham et al. (2009); Koleva et al. (2012); Reeder et al. (2005).
35. Graham et al. (2009); Gray & Wegner (2012).
36. *Wonder Woman* #219 (2005).
37. *Wonder Woman* #219 (2005).
38. Miller & Cushman (2013); Miller et al. (2014).
39. *Wonder Woman* #220 (2005).
40. Haidt (2008); Skitka (2012).
41. *Wonder Woman* #220 (2005).
42. *Batman* #509 (1994); *Superman* #219 (2005).
43. *Blackest Night: Wonder Woman* #1 (2010); *Wonder Woman* #210 (2005); *Wonder Woman: Spirit of Truth* (2001).
44. *Blackest Night: Wonder Woman* #1 (2010); *Wonder Woman* #210 (2005); *Wonder Woman* #25 (2008).
45. *Blackest Night: Wonder Woman* #1 (2010); *Wonder Woman* #220 (2005); *Wonder Woman* #221 (2005); *Wonder Woman* #223 (2005).
46. *Infinite Crisis* #1 (2005).
47. *Wonder Woman* #224 (2005).
48. *Wonder Woman: Spirit of Truth* (2001).
49. Gray & Wegner (2012).
50. Gray & Wegner (2012).
51. *Wonder Woman* #220 (2005); *Wonder Woman* #221 (2005); *Wonder Woman* #223 (2005).
52. *Flash* #219 (2005); *Wonder Woman* #220 (2005); *Wonder Woman* #221 (2005); *Wonder Woman* #222 (2005).
53. Daniels (2004); Pagnoni Berns (2014).
54. Gray & Wegner (2011); Gray & Wegner (2012).
55. *Wonder Woman* #221 (2005); *Wonder Woman* #222 (2005).
56. Skitka (2012).
57. *Wonder Woman* #210 (2005); *Wonder Woman* #220 (2005).
58. *Infinite Crisis* #1 (2005); *Wonder Woman* #220 (2005); *Wonder Woman* #223 (2005).
59. *Wonder Woman* #220 (2005); *Wonder Woman* #221 (2005).
60. *Wonder Woman* #224 (2005).
61. Hawkley & Cacioppo (2003); Wesselmann et al. (2016).
62. *Wonder Woman: Spirit of Truth* (2001).
63. Daniel (2004); *Flash* #219 (2005); Pagnoni Berns (2014); *Wonder Woman* #220 (2005); *Wonder Woman* #221 (2005); *Wonder Woman* #222 (2005).
64. Linville (1985).
65. *Wonder Woman* #226 (2005).

CHAPTER NINETEEN

Coffee with Your Hero: The Benefits of Parasocial Relationships

JANINA SCARLET AND ALAN KISTLER

"Please take my hand. I give it to you as a gesture of friendship and love, and of faith freely given. I give you my hand and welcome you into my dream."
—Wonder Woman[1]

> *"Because true belonging only happens when we present our authentic, imperfect selves to the world, our sense of belonging can never be greater than our sense of self-acceptance."*
> —social worker and researcher Brené Brown[2]

Belonging is an innate human desire to be a part of something that is greater than oneself.[3] From birth, humans and other mammals yearn for attachment and physical comfort. If actual human contact is not available, mammals often search for a surrogate source of comfort, such as a stuffed animal.[4] Sometimes such attachments include fictional characters. Forming an attachment to a fictional character or another individual from media (e.g., a celebrity who is not fictional but also is not a direct participant in the individual's life) in such a way that one feels connected is called a *parasocial relationship* (PSR) or *social surrogacy*.[5] Are there benefits to forming a PSR with a fictional character such as Princess Diana of Themyscira, the hero called Wonder Woman?

Parasocial Relationships

PSRs and Child Development

Both children[6] and adults[7] can benefit from positive PSRs. By forming a connection with a character such as Wonder Woman, children might be able to learn moral values and behaviors[8] as well as improve their decision-making skills,[9] improve their language acquisition[10] and executive functioning,[11] better their communication skills,[12] and improve their ability to cooperate with others.[13] For instance, when confronting her frequent opponent Cheetah, Diana has often reached out while acknowledging that there are bad feelings and history between them. Rather than dismissing this enemy's feelings of anger, betrayal, and self-loathing, Diana responds to her by speaking not to a cheetah-creature but instead to Dr. Barbara Ann Minerva, the human being who long ago was transformed into the Cheetah: "Love can exist with hatred, each preying on the other. . . . You are no beast. You are a woman."[14] Thus, seeing a beloved character behave in a certain way or handle a conflict in a specific fashion can allow educators and parents to use that character as a model for discussion and behavior emulation.[15]

PSRs and Health

Superhero PSRs can also serve as positive role models for healthy eating and exercise. In fact, when children are asked to consider what their favorite superhero might like to eat, they are significantly more likely to make healthier food choices themselves.[16] There are several stories in which Diana makes sure to engage in exercise, increasing her already considerable strength and optimizing her health. She engages in regular sparring matches with other heroes, such as Batman,[17] and advocates that superhumans have their own version of the Olympics so that they can celebrate and hone their abilities in a positive manner rather than primarily using them to fight criminals, terrorists, and conquerors.[18]

As difficult as it is to make healthy decisions in the first place, it is even more difficult to maintain them. Self-control, which is necessary to make continuous healthy decisions, is finite. Specifically, when someone uses self-control (to resist an unhealthy snack, for instance), he or she is less likely to be able to use it later.[19] However, this effect is reversed when an individual is able to be compassionate toward him- or herself by resting, using kind phrases,[20] or watching a favorite television show.[21] In fact, watching a favorite TV program, such as *Wonder Woman,*[22] can restore self-control and improve one's mood.[23]

Processing Trauma and Grief

Grief, a painful breakup, and abuse can have devastating consequences on both children and adults. However, PSRs may serve as a tool to help individuals better understand and process loss.[24] In particular, PSRs both help the individual to feel less alone in his or her experience and provide an indirect connection through which that person may process painful loss.[25] After her younger sister and apprentice Donna Troy dies in battle, Diana puts on a brave face for most of her friends and colleagues at the funeral. But when she's alone with Batman, she finally releases her grief, sobbing as she laments, "I should have been there to protect her. I should've sensed that she needed me."[26]

In addition to processing grief, superheroes such as Wonder Woman can help children understand how to process and stop physical or sexual abuse.[27] In fact, children who read comics about a superhero who experienced abuse[28] were more likely to disclose their own abuse history.[29] In addition, when sexual assault survivors are able to process their trauma through the use of beloved heroes, they tend to have an easier time communicating their emotions about the assault, which is an important element in healing. In addition, many are able to find courage and strength through PSRs.[30] In the live-action Wonder Woman series starring Lynda Carter, the episode "Formula 407" involves Diana dealing with repeated sexual harassment and shaming from a man. Many who find it uncomfortable to discuss the sexual harassment they have suffered may find the subject easier to talk about after seeing Wonder Woman deal with it.

Becoming a Hero through Acceptance

Acceptance of Others

PSRs can help people learn compassion and empathy toward other people. Empathy learned through PSRs can extend toward people from typically stigmatized groups, such as immigrants, members of the LGBTQ community, and the homeless population.[31] In particular, when people read about the suffering of another character, they are more likely to be empathic toward others.[32] This finding was especially true when the observed character was from a diverse population,[33] suggesting that diverse representation can be beneficial for comic book readers and TV show viewers.[34] In addition, neuroscience studies find that when people read about a fictional character's struggle, the compassion centers of their brain become activated,[35] thus treating the PSR as real.[36] In one of her earliest comic book

PSI VERSUS PSR

Parasocial interaction (PSI) and parasocial relationship (PSR) are sometimes used interchangeably, but there is some difference. PSI tends to refer to a perceived communication with a movie, book, television, or video game character or a character from the mass media.[37] For example, if a person read one of the several comics in which Diana advocates acceptance and tolerance of same-sex marriage, including one in which she officiates at such a wedding,[38] the reader might feel that the character is speaking directly to him or her about the issue.

In contrast, PSRs tend to develop over time and refer to a type of relationship, by which the media character serves as a surrogate for social support. PSRs tend to last longer than PSIs, and often PSIs develop into PSRs over time.[39] Both PSIs and PSRs appear to be universal. However, different cultures value different aspects of PSRs. Whereas people from collectivistic countries such as Mexico appear to value the similarity of the character to their own values, people from individualistic countries such as Germany are more likely to value the achievement of these characters.[40]

adventures, Diana is captured by an enemy and bound with chains. Unable to break free, she feels that she is a failure to herself and to others relying on her help.[41] Many readers can relate to such feelings of helplessness and failure from some experience in their lives and can then feel connected to Diana's hope when she arrives at a solution to her problem.

The increase in compassion and empathy through PSRs is especially important as it can allow people to be more kind toward others and reconnect with their sense of purpose. In fact, when medical students viewed and reflected on fictional characters that seemed compassionate toward their patients, they reported an intention to be more compassionate toward their own patients.[42] Throughout her many adventures, Diana is someone who often strives to understand the views of others—whether friend, enemy, or stranger—and argues that such understanding is achievable by all people, not just superheroes. While speaking at a university in France, she invites an exchange of viewpoints and ideas, even if she disagrees with them, from people in the audience rather than asking them simply to listen quietly to her lecture. She is a teacher who also hopes to learn.[43]

Acceptance of the Self

In addition to playing a role in increasing acceptance of others, PSRs can help individuals become more accepting of themselves. Self-esteem, the evaluation of self-worth, can be negatively affected by social rejection and bullying.[44] This is not surprising in light of the universal need for connection and belonging.[45] The Justice League has experienced many membership lineups and incarnations. During a time of reformation for the team, Diana remarks that such a group is important not only to unify heroes to form an effective defense for the Earth but to provide a community for those heroes to intermingle with others who understand their unusual lives and stresses.[46]

Interestingly, PSRs can help people recover from the damaging effects of rejection and loneliness. In fact, when people experience the painful effects of social rejection, they are more likely to watch their favorite TV show rather than a random television program.[47] Thus, the PSRs in this case appear to function as a form of self-soothing rather than "escapism." Moreover, when people are upset about a fight with a loved one, talking or writing about a favorite TV show significantly reduces the negative effects of social rejection.[48]

Through deep emotional connections with fictional characters, many of which are treated as a real friendship,[49] individuals are able to create a sense of belonging. Throughout her career, Wonder Woman gathers many friends and allies, as well as apprentices such as Donna Troy and Cassie Sandsmark, both of whom use the code name Wonder Girl at different times. Diana also starts the Wonder Woman Foundation, an international nonprofit charity that works to encourage and promote equality for women and the LGBTQIA community as well as providing aid to various people and other charities.[50] When a PSR develops, individuals are likely to identify themselves as similar to their favorite characters (e.g., a member of the Justice League).[51]

The biggest obstacle people tend to face when it comes to self-acceptance is the acceptance of specific attributes or characteristics of oneself of which one may be ashamed.[52] These individuals are often driven toward societal norms of what is considered acceptable or desirable. Examples of personal features that many people might feel ashamed of include appearance and body image, finances, success, social status, relationship status, ability or disability, and sexual performance, among many others.[53] Interestingly, PSRs appear to eliminate the negative effects of shame,[54] increasing self-acceptance[55] and self-esteem.[56] At times, Diana struggles with what her role as Wonder Woman truly means: whether she is to be a warrior or a diplomat or a teacher. Whenever this happens, she inevitably is reminded by friends, allies, or even her own magic lasso of truth that a person is capable of being many things at once, including contradictions.[57]

Cultivating Belongingness through PSRs

Most mammals want to experience a sense of connection and belonging. PSRs with fictional characters such as superheroes can help with that. Among superheroes, Wonder Woman in particular does not see herself as above or separate from humanity and deals with emotions and losses just as we do, which makes her an excellent character with whom to establish a PSR. In fact, establishing PSRs with someone like Diana allows people to better cope with grief[58] and trauma,[59] improve body image[60] and self-esteem,[61] and reduce the negative effects of loneliness and rejection.[62] Thus, by observing her, viewers can learn how to get support when they need it. Diana draws strength from community, from her family both literal and found, and makes herself available to those who need her special help or simply need a friend who will listen. When people worry that they are not strong enough for a challenge, Wonder Woman lovingly reassures them that they are.

Comic Book References

DC One Million #1 (1998). "Riders on the Storm." Script: G. Morrison. Art: V. Semeiks & P. Rollins.

Infinite Crisis #5 (2006). "Faith." Script: G. Johns. Art: P. Jimenez, J. Ordway, I. Reis, A. Lanning, J. Ordway, & A. Thibert.

JLA Secret Files & Origins #3 (2000). "Blame." Script: D. C. Johnson. Art: P. Raimondi, C. St. Aubin, & D. Meikis.

Justice League America #0 (1994). "Home Again." Art: G. Jones & C. Wojtkiewicz.

Sensation Comics Featuring Wonder Woman #48 (2014). "A Day in Our Lives." Script: J. Badower. Art: J. Badower.

Spider-Man and Power Pack #1 (1984). "Secrets." Script: N. Allen & J. Salicrup. Art: J. Mooney & M. Esposito.

Teen Titans/Outsiders Secret Files & Origins #1 (2003). "A Day After." Script: J. Winick & G. Johns. Pencils: I. Reis, C. Barberi, M. Campos, & N. Rapmund.

Wonder Woman #2 (1943). "The God of War." Script: W. M. Marston. Art: H. G. Peter.

Wonder Woman #8 (1987). "Time Passages." Script: L. Wein & G. Pérez. Art: G. Perez & B. D. Patterson.

Wonder Woman #167 (2001). "Gods of Gotham Part 4." Art: P. Jimenez & A. Lanning.

Wonder Woman #170 (2001). "She's a Wonder." Script: P. Jimenez & J. Kelly. Art: P. Jimenez & A. Lanning.

Wonder Woman #3 (2016). "Lies, Part Two." Script: G. Rucka. Art: L. Sharp.

Wonder Woman: Earth One (2016). Script: G. Morrison. Art: Y. Paquette.

Other References

Adams, C. E., & Leary, M. R. (2007). Promoting self-compassionate attitudes toward eating among restrictive and guilty eaters. *Journal of Social & Clinical Psychology, 26*(10), 1120–1144.

Bauer, K., & Dettore, E. (1997) Superhero play: What's a teacher to do? *Early Childhood Education Journal, 25*(1), 17–21.

Brown, B. (2012). *Daring greatly: How the courage to be vulnerable transforms the way we live, love, parent, and lead.* New York, NY: Penguin.

Cohen, J. (2004). Parasocial break-up from favorite television characters: The role of attachment styles and relationship intensity. *Journal of Social & Personal Relationships, 21*(2), 187–202.

Cummins, R. G., & Cui, B. (2014). Reconceptualizing address in television programming: The effect of address and affective empathy on viewer experience of parasocial interaction. *Journal of Communication, 64*(4), 723–742.

Derrick, J. (2013). Energized by television: Familiar fictional worlds restore self-control. *Social Psychological & Personality Science, 4*(3) 299–307.

Derrick, J. E., Gabriel, S., & Hugenberg, K. (2009). Social surrogacy: How favored television programs provide the experience of belonging. *Journal of Experimental Social Psychology 45*(2), 352–362.

Dyson, A. H. (1997) *Writing superheroes: Contemporary childhood, popular culture, and classroom literacy.* New York, NY: Teachers College Press.

Eyal, K., & Cohen, J. (2006). When good friends say goodbye: A parasocial breakup study. *Journal of Broadcasting & Electronic Media, 50*(3), 502–523.

Farsides, T., Pettman, D., & Tourle, L. (2013). Inspiring altruism: Reflecting on the personal relevance of emotionally evocative prosocial media characters. *Journal of Applied Social Psychology, 43*(11), 2251–2258.

Fitzsimons, G. M., & Finkel, E. J. (2011). Outsourcing self-regulation. *Psychological Science, 22*(3), 369–375.

Gabriel, S., & Young, A. F. (2011). Becoming a vampire without being bitten: The narrative collective-assimilation hypothesis. *Psychological Science, 22*(8), 990–994.

Garbarino, J. (1987). Children's response to a sexual abuse prevention program: A study of the Spiderman comic. *Child Abuse & Neglect, 11*(1), 143–148.

Gardner, W. L., & Knowles, M. L. (2008). Love makes you real: Favorite television characters are perceived as "real" in a social facilitation paradigm. *Social Cognition, 26*(2), 156.

Harlow, H. (1958). The nature of love. *American Psychologist, 13*(12), 673–685.

Hsu, C. T., Conrad, M., & Jacobs, A. M. (2014). Fiction feelings in Harry Potter: Haemodynamic response in the mid-cingulate cortex correlates with immersive reading experience. *Neuroreport, 25*(17), 1356–1361.

Huang, J. Y., Ackerman, J. M., & Bargh, J. A. (2013). Superman to the rescue: Simulating physical invulnerability attenuates exclusion-related interpersonal biases. *Journal of Experimental Social Psychology, 49*(3), 349–354.

Kostelnik, M. J., Whiren, A. P., & Stein, L. C. (1986). Living with He-Man: Managing superhero fantasy play. *Young Children, 41*(4), 3–9.

Lather, J., & Moyer-Gusé, E. (2011). How do we react when our favorite characters are taken away? An examination of a temporary parasocial breakup. *Mass Communication & Society, 14*(2), 196–215.

Luke, M. A., Sedikides, C., & Carnelley, K. (2012). Your love lifts me higher! The energizing quality of secure relationships. *Personality & Social Psychology Bulletin, 38*(6), 721–733.

Markell, K. A., & Markell, M. A. (2013). *The children who lived: Using Harry Potter and other fictional characters to help grieving children and adolescents.* New York, NY: Routledge.

Martin, J. F. (2007). Children's attitudes toward superheroes as a potential indicator of their moral understanding. *Journal of Moral Education, 36*(2), 239–250.

Nylund, D. (2007). Reading Harry Potter: Popular culture, queer theory and the fashioning of youth identity. *Journal of Systemic Therapies, 26*(2), 13–24.

Orellana, M. F. (1994). Appropriating the voice of the superheroes: Three preschoolers' bilingual language uses in play. *Early Childhood Research Quarterly, 9*(2), 171–193.

Pardales, M. J. (2002) So, how did you arrive at that decision? Connecting moral imagination and moral judgment. *Journal of Moral Education, 31*(4), 429–436.

Rubin, L., & Livesay, H. (2006). Look, up in the sky! Using superheroes in play therapy. *International Journal of Play Therapy, 15*(1), 117–133.

Schlozman, S. C. (2000). Vampires and those who slay them. *Academic Psychiatry, 24*(1), 49–54.

Schmid, H., & Klimmt, C. (2011). A magically nice guy: Parasocial relationships with Harry Potter across different cultures. *International Communication Gazette, 73*(3), 252–269.

Vezzali, L., Stathi, S., Giovannini, D., Capozza, D., & Trifiletti, E. (2015). The greatest magic of Harry Potter: Reducing prejudice. *Journal of Applied Social Psychology, 45*(2), 105–121.

Walker, J. S. (2004). The impact of superheroes on self-esteem, with emphasis on individuals of color. *Dissertation Abstracts International Section A, 64,* 3084.

Wansink, B., Shimizu, M., & Camps, G. (2012). What would Batman eat? Priming children to make healthier fast food choices. *Pediatric Obesity, 7*(2), 121–123.

White, R. E., & Carlson, S. M. (2015). What would Batman do? Self-distancing improves executive function in young children. *Developmental Science, 19*(3), 419–426.

Young, A. F., Gabriel, S., & Hollar, J. L. (2013). Batman to the rescue! The protective effects of parasocial relationships with muscular superheroes on men's body image. *Journal of Experimental Social Psychology, 49*(1), 173–177.

Young, T. J. (1993). Women as comic book super-heroes: The "weaker sex" in the Marvel Universe. *Psychology: A Journal of Human Behavior, 30*(2), 49–50.

Notes

1. *Wonder Woman* #167 (2001).
2. Brown (2012), p. 145.
3. Brown (2012).
4. Harlow (1958).
5. Derrick (2013).
6. Martin (2007).
7. Gardner & Knowles (2008).
8. Martin (2007).
9. Pardales (2002).
10. Orellana (1994).
11. White & Carlson (2015).
12. Bauer & Dettore (1997).
13. Kostelnik et al. (1986).
14. *Wonder Woman* #3 (2016).
15. Bauer & Dettore (1997); Martin (2007).

16. Wansink et al. (2012).
17. *JLA Secret Files & Origins* #3 (2000).
18. *DC One Million* #1 (1998).
19. Derrick (2013).
20. Adams & Leary (2007).
21. Derrick (2013).
22. *Wonder Woman: Earth One* (2016).
23. Derrick (2013); Fitzsimmons & Finkel (2011); Luke et al. (2012).
24. Markell & Markell (2013); Schlozman (2000).
25. Cohen (2004); Eyal & Cohen (2006); Lather & Moyer-Gusé (2011); Schlozman (2000).
26. *Teen Titans/Outsiders Secret Files & Origins* #1 (2003).
27. Garbarino (1987); Rubin & Livesay (2006).
28. *Spider-Man and Power Pack* #1 (1984).
29. Garbarino (1987).
30. Rubin & Livesay (2006).
31. Huang et al. (2013).
32. Vezzali et al. (2015).
33. Vezzali et al. (2015).
34. Dyson (1997); Young (1993).
35. Hsu et al. (2014).
36. Gardner & Knowles (2008).
37. Cummins & Cui (2014).
38. *Sensation Comics Featuring Wonder Woman* #48 (2014).
39. Cummins & Cui (2014).
40. Schmid & Klimmt (2011).
41. *Wonder Woman* #2 (1943).
42. Farsides et al. (2013).
43. *Wonder Woman* #170 (2001).
44. Brown (2012); Derrick et al. (2009).
45. Brown (2012).
46. *Justice League America* #0 (1994).
47. Derrick et al. (2009).
48. Derrick (2009).
49. Gardner & Knowles (2008).
50. *Wonder Woman* #8 (1987).
51. Gabriel & Young (2011).
52. Brown (2012).
53. Brown (2012).
54. Young et al. (2013).
55. Nylund (2007).
56. Derrick et al. (2009); Walker (2004).
57. *Infinite Crisis* #5 (2006).
58. Markell & Markell (2013); Schlozman (2000).
59. Garbarino (1987); Rubin & Livesay (2006).
60. Young et al. (2013).
61. Derrick et al. (2009); Walker (2004).
62. Derrick et al. (2009).

CHAPTER TWENTY

Truth in Treatment: Who Wields the Magic?

TRAVIS LANGLEY AND MARA WOOD

"Does the truth hurt, Steve?"
—Diana[1]

"The human intellect has not shown itself elsewhere to be endowed with a very good scent for truth. . . ."
—psychoanalyst Sigmund Freud[2]

Like her creator with his lie detector test,[3] Wonder Woman with her magic lasso seeks truth,[4] both for practical purposes such as determining guilt and for therapeutic benefit to the individual forced to face reality.[5] Not everybody, though, agrees that "the truth will set you free."[6] Many forms of therapy help clients pursue their personal truth, but many others do not. Some professionals argue that shoring up defenses against unpleasant thoughts and memories can sometimes do more good than confronting them[7] and that some self-deception may help clients "overcome conflicts and grow in their emotional, creative, and relationship lives."[8] Even aside from the fact that treatments such as *behavior modification* (applying behaviorist principles to change behavior[9]) focus on altering how we act without delving into underlying truths about past experiences, unconscious conflicts, or unrealistic self-concepts, some therapies use fantasy as therapeutic devices,[10] while others, such as guided imagery[11] and hypnotherapy,[12] are accused of fostering false memories.

What is truth? Should a therapist who believes clients must face facts concentrate on helping them look at the past or the present? Internal or external experience? Subjective or objective reality? When Wonder Woman lassos half a dozen of Batman's enemies to make them "face their deepest fears, the engine that drives their madness,"[13] what kind of therapist is she?

Where the Truth Lies

Out of the many therapists who believe people need to seek truth, to try to understand themselves and their world better, come many different means of pursuing it. Carl Rogers, Sigmund Freud, and Albert Ellis—the three most influential psychotherapists, according to one survey of North American psychologists[14]—varied in where each thought the truth must lie. Although the psychologist who created Wonder Woman died before Ellis entered the scene,[15] Rogers had begun to make a name for himself[16] and Freud preceded them all, dying two years before William Moulton Marston's Wonder Woman would debut.[17]

Living in the Past: Psychoanalysis

Despite popular misconception, Sigmund Freud did not found psychology or psychiatry.[18] He founded an approach to treatment, *psychoanalysis*, based on investigating an individual's past conflicts and unconscious desires. Also despite popular misconception, Freud rarely mentioned the "subconscious"[19] and, in fact, criticized the term as vague.[20] It was Pierre Janet who coined the French term *subconscient* (translated into English as *subconscious*)[21] and connected past experience to individuals' present distress shortly before Freud did.[22] Freud promoted the more comprehensive term *unconscious*[23] for a vast reservoir of ideas and memories not easily accessed by the conscious mind, along with deeper drives and purposes that can never be fully knowable at the conscious level. Wonder Woman's creator used the terms *subconscious* and *unconscious* interchangeably,[24] perhaps because the unconscious mind Freud proposed had become popularly known as the subconscious.[25]

Marston believed that the subconscious influences us and that his lie detector test could "disclose subconscious secrets of which the subject is utterly unaware."[26] He also considered his belief that people enjoy submission when it's administered with love, not cruelty, to be "a universal truth, a fundamental subconscious feeling of normal humans," so he represented that in his stories. Referring to his belief that women enjoy submission and being bound, he said, "This I bring out in the Paradise Island sequences where the girls beg for chains and enjoy wearing them."[27] Regarding males, too, Marston said, "If they go crazy over Wonder Woman, it means they're longing for a beautiful, exciting girl who's stronger than they are" and that Wonder Woman reached "the subconscious, elaborately disguised desire of males to be mastered by a woman who loves them."[28] Viewing these or any other mental influences as subconscious or unconscious, though, can be problematic because that creates the risk of interpreting human experience from a point of view that can be narrow, dogmatic, and even a bit arrogant: "Oh, you can't think of evidence to indicate that my assertion about you is true? Then it's unconscious and now I have to help you see your mind the way I see it." A common criticism of the psychoanalytic approach is that many of its key concepts lack *falsifiability*, meaning they cannot be empirically confirmed or disconfirmed due to their untestable nature.[29]

Although Marston looked at the influence of a person's past experience, he did not emphasize it the way Freud did.[30] "Wonder Woman and her sister Amazons have to wear heavy bracelets to remind them of what happens to a girl when she lets a man conquer her," Marston said,[31] talking about one deliberate, conscious reminder of the past as a cautionary lesson to remember in the present and the future. When he wrote about the subconscious in his stories, he tended to write in terms of immediate influence on behavior, not normally preoccupation with the past. During a story in which Wonder Woman suffers amnesia, her unconscious mind retains the knowledge and skills her conscious mind has forgotten. When criminals fire guns at her, she reflexively deflects the bullets in the heat of the moment because, the narrative says, "something in her subconscious urges Wonder Woman to repel the bullets with her bracelets!"[32]

Even though Marston believed the subconscious or unconscious mind exerts a powerful influence on us and incorporated that into his Wonder Woman stories, he expressed some skepticism regarding the power of psychoanalytic methods to discern truth. With some dismay, he recounted how he once remarked that he had enjoyed a stage play about facing the afterlife only to have a prominent psychoanalyst interpret his choice of words as a declaration of Marston's Oedipal conflict.[33]

Freud's view of human nature was, at times, pessimistic. He

believed that we are inherently selfish creatures, driven by *id* (the part of personality each person is born with) and its *pleasure principle* (seeking instant gratification; that is, immediate fulfillment of needs and desires). The id has no self-control and resists restrictions.[34] According to Freud, we have to learn the *reality principle*, the idea that reality can provide us with greater satisfaction if we learn self-control, in order to develop the *ego* (the part of personality we think of as ourselves) and later the *superego* (essentially, our conscience). Marston also believed that self-control is learned and added the importance of letting others exert control: "The only hope for peace is to teach people who are full of pep and unbound force to enjoy being bound."[35] When an enemy removes Wonder Woman's bracelets in one Marston story, Diana loses her self-control and goes on a rampage, boasting, "I'm completely uncontrolled! I'm free to destroy like a man!"[36] Later, she welcomes her bracelets' return: "It's wonderful to feel my strength bound again—power without self-control tears a girl to pieces!" So her bracelets serve not only as a reminder of the past but also as a cue for self-control during the present, but only in Marston's stories. Despite this partial alignment with basic Freudian principles, Marston and Wonder Woman take a more optimistic view of human nature,[37] making them less like Freud and perhaps more like Rogers.

Living in the Person: Client-Centered Therapy

Carl Rogers believed that people are inherently good and naturally want their *actual selves* (who they really are) to progress toward becoming more like their *ideal selves* (who they feel they should be).[38] Rogers did not feel the therapist should tell the client how to get there, though. Unlike Sigmund Freud, who might tell someone what his or her unconscious truth must be, Carl Rogers believed that each person should find his or her own truth without being pushed into it. A Rogerian therapist is supposed to help people in a *nondirective* way, refraining from controlling the direction therapy takes or explaining clients' experiences for them.[39] For Rogers, the client should direct the course of therapy—which he called *client-centered therapy*, more widely known as person-centered therapy today.[40] In this, Marston likely fell more on the Freudian side because he believed people should direct others for their own good.[41] He depicted this through his stories of a heroine whose magic lasso compelled obedience and whose fellow Amazons forced rehabilitation upon enemies at their Reform Island.[42]

Otherwise, though, the character Marston created to represent the ideal woman[43] also fits the qualities Rogers believed the ideal client-centered therapist should exhibit: genuineness, unconditional positive regard, and empathy.

Genuineness. The client-centered therapist must be genuine with each client and must convey this authenticity for the sake of the therapeutic relationship. The Rogerian therapist conveys this *genuineness* by eliminating the "false face" of professionalism and reacting with true feelings.[44] When Lois Lane expresses skepticism regarding her ability to trust Wonder Woman with Superman, she confronts Diana and asks how she handles "contradictions" in her character. Instead of getting defensive, Wonder Woman raises her lasso and says that carrying it on her at all times leaves her no choice but to accept the truth and own all of her contradictions and flaws.[45] Much as the Rogerian client supposedly reacts to the client-centered therapist more receptively upon seeing that the therapist is genuine, Lois becomes better able to trust Wonder Woman when she recognizes the superhero's genuineness.

Unconditional positive regard. No matter what the client has said or done, the therapist will continue to value him or her as a worthwhile human being without *conditions of worth* (requirements for the client to be valued).[46] *Unconditional positive regard* means prizing the client as a worthwhile human being regardless of his or her actions or words. Wonder Woman provides such acceptance when one of her earliest nemeses, a spy named Baroness Paula von Gunther,[47] not only reforms but also becomes the Amazons' ally and one of Wonder Woman's best friends. Instead of judging Paula for becoming a spy to protect her daughter, Diana provides her with resources to improve herself.[48]

Empathy. Having and demonstrating *empathy*, the ability to recognize and understand emotions, is crucial. Clients who receive empathy from their therapist enjoy the freedom to explore and express their own emotions.[49] Rogers felt that the key to empathy is really listening to what the client is communicating.[50] Wonder Woman often couples her empathy with action. When the supervillain Silver Swan screams that she wants to be left alone and that she is "so tired, so tired," Wonder Woman does not dismiss her ravings. She calmly replies, I know you are. I know." In the midst of battle, she shows her awareness of Silver Swan's feelings and responds to them with empathy.

> *"The curious paradox is that when I accept*
> *myself just as I am, then I change.*
> —psychologist Carl R. Rogers[51]

Living in the Present: REBT

Renowned psychologist Albert Ellis came to see psychoanalytic focus on the past and the unconscious as pointless: "I thought foolishly that Freudian psychoanalysis was deeper and more intensive than other, more directive forms of therapy, so I was trained in it and practiced it. Then I found that it intensively went into every irrelevancy under the sun—and that it didn't work. People got insights into what was bothering them, but they hardly did a damn thing to change."[52] Ellis created *rational emotive behavior therapy (REBT)* to help clients improve how they feel and act by viewing life more rationally. By seeing themselves more accurately and logically, recognizing that they are not Superman or Wonder Woman as he put it,[53] he felt people could make better, more constructive choices, instead of destructive choices, and therefore lead more satisfying lives. In Wonder Woman's first live theatrical appearance, she is seen as "the most rational and stable character,"[54] free from the kind of irrational, self-defeating beliefs that Ellis believed cause dysfunction.

Like Ellis, Wonder Woman believes in facing reality and, unlike Rogers, often pushes others to face it as well. Also like Ellis, she looks at present circumstances while acknowledging the rest of life: "Kal looks to the future, Batman looks to the past. And I reside in the present, securely bridging the two."[55]

Truth and Lies

Psychoanalyst Robert J. Langs categorized any therapeutic approach that tried to help clients and therapists find truth as a *truth therapy* and any approach that didn't as a *lie therapy*.[56] While he received criticism for dichotomizing the methods, ignoring those that neither pursue truth nor promote mistrust, valuing investigation over healing, neglecting approaches other than psychoanalytic, and perhaps dogmatically asserting that truth can be determined,[57] he was right that some methods seek truth while others do not. Wonder Woman's lasso, with its power to compel obedience, becomes commonly known as the lasso of truth because the hero who wields it continually seeks truth, even subjecting herself to a daily ritual in which Diana places the lasso on her shoulders in order to see through any lies she might be telling herself.[58] The mere idea that she might unknowingly lie to herself is consistent with the psychoanalytic view taken by Langs, the Freuds, and others,[59] while this exercise fits Ellis's position that becoming and staying healthy requires ongoing effort to root out whatever misconceptions and delusions the person might hold.[60]

The heroine created to represent her creator's views on psychology shares some qualities of all three of those great thinkers in psychology, and she differs from them each as well. Like Freud, she looks deep for truths that may lurk outside the individual's conscious awareness. Like Rogers, she treats others with genuineness, empathy, and unconditional positive regard. Like Ellis, she cuts to the point faster than Freud and is more directive than Rogers. Because her approach to seeking truth is a bit *eclectic*, a mix of professional approaches, Wonder Woman as therapist remains true to the psychologist who created her, eschewing a one-size-fits-all way of treating people.

> *"Once again—you're human.*
> *Not Superman or Wonder Woman.*
> *Not a god or goddess. Always fallible."*
>
> —psychologist Albert Ellis[61]

Comic Book References

JLA: A League of One (2000). Script/Art: C. Moeller.

Sensation Comics #4 (1942). "School for Spies." Script: W. M. Marston. Art: H. G. Peter.

Sensation Comics #6 (1942). "Summons to Paradise Island." Script: W. M. Marston. Art: H. G. Peter.

Sensation Comics #19 (1943). "The Unbound Amazon." Script: W. M. Marston. Art: H. G. Peter.

Sensation Comics #26 (1944). "The Masquerader." Script: W. M. Marston. Art: H. G. Peter.

Sensation Comics Featuring Wonder Woman #1 (2014). "Gothamazon." Script: G. Simone. Art: E. Van Sciver & M. Di Chiara.

Wonder Woman #3 (1943). "The Secret of Baroness von Gunther." Script: W. M. Marston. Art: H. G. Peter.

Wonder Woman #4 (1943). "Man-Hating Madness!" Script: W. M. Marston. Art: H. G. Peter.

Wonder Woman #141 (1999). "Trinity 98, Part II." Script: E. Luke. Art: Y. Paquette & B. McLeod.

Wonder Woman #170 (2001). "She's a Wonder!" Script: P. Jimenez & J. Kelly. Art: P. Jimenez & A. Lanning.

Other References

APA Monitor (2002). Eminent psychologists in the 20th century. *APA Monitor, 33*(7), 29.

Berry, W. (2012, May 6). *The truth will not set you free.* Psychology Today: https://www. psychologytoday.com/blog/the-second-noble-truth/201205/the-truth-will-not-set-you-free.

Boscarino, J. A., & Figley, C. R. (2009). The impact of repression, hostility, and post-traumatic stress disorder on all-cause mortality: A prospective 16-year study. *Journal of Nervous & Mental Disease, 197*(6), 461–466.

Breuer, J., & Freud, S. (1895/1936). *Studies in hysteria.* Washington, DC: Nervous & Mental Disease.

Carveth, D. L. (1998). Is there a future in disillusion? Constructionist and deconstuctionist approaches in psychoanalysis. *Journal of the American Academy of Psychoanalysis & Dynamic Psychiatry, 27*(2), 325–358.

Cherry, K. (2016, June 21). *10 most influential psychologists: A look at eminent thinkers in psychology.* Very Well: https://www.verywell.com/most-influential-psychologists-2795264.

Cook, J. M., Biyanova, T., & Coyne, J. C. (2009). Influential psychotherapy figures, authors, and books: An internet survey of over 2,000 psychotherapists. *Psychotherapy, 46*(1), 42–51.

Daniels, L. (2000). *Wonder Woman: The complete history.* San Francisco, CA: Chronicle.

Ellenberger, H. F. (1970). *The discovery of the unconscious: The history and evolution of dynamic psychology.* New York, NY: Basic.

Ellis, A. (1951). *The folklore of sex.* Oxford, UK: Boni.

Ellis, A. (1999/2007). *How to make yourself happy and remarkably less disturbable.* Atascadero, CA: Impact.

Epstein, R. (2001, January 1). *The prince of reason: An interview with Albert Ellis, developer of rational emotive therapy.* Psychology Today: https://www.psychologytoday.com/articles/200101/the-prince-reason.

Eysenck, H. J. (1985). *Decline and fall of the Freudian empire.* New York, NY: Viking.

Freud, A. (1936). *The ego and defense mechanisms.* London, UK: Imago.

Freud, S. (1912/1958). A note on the unconscious in psychoanalysis. *The standard edition of the complete psychological works of Sigmund Freud* (vol. XII, pp. 255–266). London, UK: Hogarth.

Freud, S. (1920). *Beyond the pleasure principle.* London, UK: Norton.

Freud, S. (1923/1927). *The ego and the id.* London, UK: Norton.

Freud, S. (1926/1927). The question of lay analysis. In J. Strachey (Ed. & Trans.), *The standard edition of the complete psychological works of Sigmund Freud* (vol. XX, pp. 177–258). London, UK: Hogarth.

Freud, S. (1939). *Moses and monotheism.* New York, NY: Knopf.

Green, J. P., Lyn, S. J., & Malinoski, P. (1998). Hypnotic pseudomemories, prehypnotic warnings, and malleability of suggested memories. *Applied Cognitive Psychology, 12*(5), 413–444.

Guthrie, A. (2008). *The problem of therapeutic action in child psychoanalysis: What to do, how to be, why it works* [doctoral dissertation]. Toronto, Ontario, Canada: University of Toronto.

Hanley, T. (2014). *Wonder Woman unbound: The curious history of the world's most famous heroine.* Chicago, IL: Chicago Review Press.

Herndon, P., Myers, B., Mitchell, K., Kehn, A., & Henry, S. (2014). False memories for highly aversive early childhood events: Effects of guided imagery and group influence. *Psychology of Consciousness: Theory, Research, & Practice, 1*(1), 20–31.

Janet, P. (1886). Deuxième note sur le sommeil provoqué à distance et la suggestion mental pendant l'état somnambulique. *Bulletin de la Société de Psychologie Physiologique, 2,* 70–80.

Janet, P. (1910). Chapter four. In H. Münsterberg, T. Ribot, P. Janet, J. Jastrow, B. Hart, & M. Prince (Authors), *Subconscioius phenomena* (pp. 53–70). Boston, MA: Gorham.

LaBier, D. (2013, February 18). *Why self-deception can be healthy for you: Deceiving yourself can help you achieve your goals.* Psychology Today: https://www.psychologytoday.com/blog/the-new-resilience/201302/why-self-deception-can-be-healthy-you.

Langs, R. J. (1981). Truth therapy/lie therapy. In R. Langs (Ed.), *Classics in psychoanalytic technique* (pp. 499–515). New York, NY: Aronson.

Look (1938, December 6). Would YOU dare take these tests? *Look, 2*(24), pp. 16–17, 27.

Lynn, S. J., Rhue, J. W., Myers, B. P., & Weekes, J. R. (1994). Pseudomemory in hypnotized and simulating subjects. *International Journal of Clinical & Experimental Hypnosis, 42*(2), 118–129.

Marston, W. M. (1917). Systolic blood pressure symptoms of deception. *Journal of Experimental Psychology 2*(2), 117–163.

Marston, W. M. (1928). *Emotions of normal people.* London, UK: Kegan Paul, Trench, Trubner.

Marston, W. M. (1947). Lie detection's bodily basis and test procedures. In P. L. Harriman (Ed.), *Encyclopedia of psychology* (pp. 354–363). New York, NY: Philosophical Library.

Martin, G., & Pear, J. (2007). *Behavior modification: What it is and how to do it* (8th ed.). Upper Saddle River, NJ: Pearson Prentice Hall.

McNally, R. J. (2005). Debunking myths about trauma and memory. *Canadian Journal of Psychiatry, 50*(13), 817–822.

Mota, C., & Blumer, M. L. C. (2013). Incorporating fiction and fantasy into family therapy. *Journal of Psychotherapy, 24*(2), 139–154.

Panda, I. (2015, July 11). *Analysis of Batman v Superman trailer—Wonder Woman, Jason Todd, motivations, & more.* The Insightful Panda: https://theinsightful-panda.com/2015/07/11/analysis-of-batman-v-superman-trailer-wonder-woman-jason-todd-motivations-more/.

Popper, K. R. (1963). *Conjectures and refutations: The growth of scientific knowledge.* London, UK: Routledge & Kegan Paul.

Porter, S., Yuille, J. C., & Lehman, D. R. (1999). The nature of real, implanted, and fabricated memories for emotional childhood events: Implications for the recovered memory debate. *Law & Human Behavior, 23*(5), 517–537.

Rees, C. L. (1998). *An examination of patients' responses to framework breaks in psychotherapy in an institutional context* [doctoral dissertation]. Grahamstown, East Cape, South Africa: Rhodes University.

Richard, O. (1944, August 14). Our women are our future. *Family Circle,* pp. 14–17, 19.

Rogers, C. R. (1939). *Clinical treatment of the problem child.* Boston, MA: Houghton Mifflin.

Rogers, C. R. (1942). *Counseling and psychotherapy: Newer concepts in practice.* Boston, MA: Houghton Mifflin.

Rogers, C. R. (1951). *Client-centered therapy: Its current practice, implications, and theory.* London, UK: Constable.

Rogers, C. R. (1961). *On becoming a person: A therapist's view of psychotherapy.* Boston, MA: Little, Brown.

Rogers, C. R. (1980). *A way of being.* Boston, MA: Houghton Mifflin.

Rogers, C. R. (1985). The necessary and sufficient conditions of therapeutic personality change. *Journal of Consulting Psychology, 21*(2), 95–103.

Roudinesco, E. (2016). *Freud: In his time and ours.* Cambridge, MA: Harvard University Press.

Scheidler, T. (1972). Use of fantasy as a therapeutic agent in latency-age groups. *Psychotherapy: Theory, Research, & Practice, 9*(4), 299–302.

Schelling, F. W. J. (1800/1978). *System of transcendental idealism.* Charlottesville, VA: University Press of Virginia.

Sheehan, P. W., Green, V., & Truesdale, P. (1992). Influence of rapport on hypnotically induced pseudomemory. *Journal of Abnormal Psychology, 101*(4), 690–700.

Smith, D. (1982). Trends in counseling and psychotherapy. *American Psychologist, 37*(7), 802–809.

Tudor, K., & Worrall, M. (2006). *Person-centered therapy: A clinical philosophy.* New York, NY: Routledge.

Webster, R. (1995). *Why Freud was wrong: Sin, science, and psychoanalysis.* Halesworth, Suffolk, UK: Orwell.

Wertheimer, M. (1987). *A brief history of psychology* (3rd ed.). New York, NY: Holt, Rinehart & Winston.

Wolpe, J. (1968). Psychotherapy by reciprocal inhibition. *Conditional Reflex, 3*(4), 234–240.

Woodworth, R. S. (1917). Some criticisms of the Freudian psychology. *Journal of Abnormal Psychology, 12*(3), 174–194.

Notes

1. *Wonder Woman* (2009 animated motion picture).
2. Freud (1939), pp. 203–204.
3. Marston (1917, 1947).
4. Beginning in *Sensation Comics* #6 (1942).
5. e.g., *Sensation Comics Featuring Wonder Woman* #1 (2014).
6. John 8:32. Berry (2012) disagrees.
7. e.g., Boscarino & Figley (2009).
8. LaBier (2013).
9. Martin & Pear (2007); Wolpe (1968).
10. e.g., Mota & Blumer (2013); Scheidler (1972).
11. e.g., Herndon et al. (2014); Porter et al. (1999).
12. e.g., Green et al. (1998); Lynn et al. (1994); Sheehan et al. (1992).
13. *Sensation Comics Featuring Wonder Woman* #1 (2014).
14. In that order, as reported by Smith (1982). Others, though, would rank them differently—e.g., APA Monitor (2002); Cherry (2016); Cook et al. (2009).
15. His books started with Ellis (1951).
16. Rogers (1939, 1942).
17. Roudinesco (2016).

18. Wertheimer (1987).
19. Breuer & Freud (1895/1936).
20. Freud (1926/1927).
21. Janet (1886, 1910).
22. Ellenberger (1970).
23. A term coined by the philosopher Friedrich Wilhelm Joseph Schelling in 1800.
24. Example: "I have three times succeeded in eliminating altogether the unpleasant-ness of severe toothache by changing my 'subconscious' or 'unconscious' motor set from one of resistance to one of complete acceptance of the stimuli imposed."—Marston (1928), p. 60.
25. Ellenberger (1970).
26. Look (1938), p. 16.
27. Quoted by Daniels (2000).
28. Hanley (2014), pp. 48–49.
29. Eysenck (1985); McNally (2005); Popper (1963); Webster (1995); Woodworth (1917).
30. Marston (1928).
31. Quoted by Byrne writing as Richard (1944), p. 19.
32. *Sensation Comics* #26 (1944).
33. Marston (1928).
34. Freud (1920).
35. Marston (1943, February 20), letter to Max Gaines. Quoted by Daniels (2000), p. 63.
36. *Sensation Comics* #19 (1943).
37. Marston (1928).
38. Rogers (1961).
39. Rogers (1951, 1985).
40. Tudor & Worrall (2006).
41. Marston (1928).
42. *Wonder Woman* #4 (1943).
43. Daniels (2000).
44. Rogers (1980).
45. *Wonder Woman* #170 (2001).
46. Rogers (1980).
47. *Sensation Comics* #4 (1942).
48. *Wonder Woman* #3 (1943).
49. Rogers (1961).
50. Rogers (1980).
51. Rogers (1961), p. 17.
52. Epstein (2001).
53. Ellis (1999/2007), p. 35.
54. Panda (2015).
55. *Wonder Woman* #141 (1999).
56. Langs (1981).
57. Carveth (1998); Guthrie (2008); Rees (1998).
58. *JLA: A League of One* (2000).
59. Langs (1981); A. Freud (1936); S. Freud (1912/1958)
60. Ellis (1999/2007).
61. Ellis (1999/2007), p. 35.

Diana transcends the mortal world and becomes the Goddess of Truth.
Wonder Woman #127 (1997). Art: J. Byrne. ®DC Comics.

Transcendence

T R A V I S   L A N G L E Y

In the last group of positive traits covered in the *Character Strengths and Virtues* (CSV) handbook, the virtue *transcendence* goes beyond mundane existence "to embrace part or all of the larger universe."[1] A sense of connection to things greater than ourselves can help provide meaning in our lives, which may make some feel distant and removed but makes others feel more fully human and alive.[2] Few superheroes—not even Superman, who comes from another planet[3] elsewhere in the universe—seem as transcendent as Wonder Woman.

The key transcendent strength is *spirituality*, a sense of connection and commitment to nonmaterial nature or universal, sacred, or divine nature. Spirituality involves religiosity, faith, and purpose. According to the CSV handbook, "It is the most human of the character strengths as well as the more sublime."[4] Growing up with powers gifted to her by the gods and among Amazons straight out of Greek mythology[5] makes

Diana conscious of her divine nature, as does communicating with goddesses such as Aphrodite as part of her everyday life.[6] A person can grow up without retaining community or parental values,[7] of course. Diana remains so dedicated to her gods that they reward her devotion by granting her divinity and making her the Goddess of Truth for a while.[8] Repeatedly in her stories, though, she gives up immortality because she can do the greatest good for humankind as one of them.[9]

Other transcendent strengths (hope, gratitude, humor, appreciation of beauty and excellence) can help the person find meaning and value in life, but they can also help the person escape, overcome, or persevere. Even though each can serve immediate purposes unrelated to transcending everyday life, these strengths provide the potential and they often seem to go together.[10] Optimism[11] ties these strengths together. Each is a form of appreciation—of that which is or that which might be. These qualities can foster resilience and mental health.[12] Wonder Woman does not merely hope for the best; she works to bring out the best in people, to encourage them to have faith, and to make the world a wonderful place.[13] Her sense of humor may have been easier to see during the Golden Age, when a core tenet of her personality was that she wanted fun challenges,[14] but she persists in showing her hope and appreciation.

By showing these transcendent strengths, the role model inspires them in others.[15] We can experience hope and gratitude vicariously through someone else.[16] We can learn to hope.[17] We can learn to marvel at the universe within ourselves and all around. While the psychologists who developed the *Character Strengths and Virtues* handbooks considered spirituality to be the prototype for all the transcendent strengths, those strengths are all about appreciation of one kind or another—appreciation for people, the future, the world around us, and the invisible world we sense beyond it all. The transcendent strengths at their greatest are about being in awe of things outside ourselves, about *wonder*. Unlike so many other superhero names, *Wonder Woman* does not simply describe the hero's own traits or abilities. The name describes what she feels and what she inspires: a sense of wonder.

Comic Book References

Action Comics #1 (1938). "Superman, Champion of the Oppressed." Script: J. Siegel. Art: J. Shuster.

All-Star Comics #8 (1941). "Introducing Wonder Woman." Script: W. M. Marston. Art: H. G. Peter.

Wonder Woman #1 (1942). "The Origin of Wonder Woman." Script: W. M. Marston. Art: H. Peter.

Wonder Woman #2 (1942). "Ares, the God of War." Script: W. M. Marston. Art: H. Peter.

Wonder Woman #102 (1958). "Secret Origin of Wonder Woman!" Script: R. Kanigher. Art: R. Andru & M. Esposito.

Wonder Woman #127 (1997). "Transfiguration." Script & Art: J. Byrne.

Wonder Woman #164 (2001). "Discordia." Script: P. Jimenez & J. M. DeMatteis. Art: P. Jiminez & A. Lanning.

Other References

Abadsidis, S. (2013, August 8). *She's a wonder: Three men chat about one Wonder Woman.* The Good Men Project: https://goodmenproject.com/arts/gmp-shes-a-wonder-three-men-chat-about-one-wonder-woman/.

Alarcon, G. M., Bowling, N. A., & Khazon, S. (2013). Great expectations: A meta-analytic examination of optimism and hope. *Personality & Individual Differences, 54*(7), 821–827.

Benner, D. G. (2011). *Soulful spirituality: Becoming fully alive and deeply human.* Ada, MI: Brazos.

Brinkman, B. G., & Jedinak, A. (2014). Exploration of a feminist icon: Wonder Woman's influence on U.S. media. *Sex Roles, 70*(9–10), 434–435.

Ecklund, E. H., & Lee, K. S (2011). Atheists and agnostics negotiate religion and family. *Journal for the Scientific Study of Religion, 50*(4), 728–743.

Howell, A. J., Bailie, T., & Buro, K. (2015). Evidence for vicarious hope and gratitude. *Journal of Happiness Studies, 16*(3), 687–704.

McEntee, M., L., Dy-Liacco, G. S., & Haskins, D. G. (2013). Human flourishing: A natural home for spirituality. *Journal of Spirituality in Mental Health, 15*(3), 141–159.

Ong, A. D., Edwards, L. M., & Bergeman, C. S. (2006). Hope as a resource of resilience in later adulthood. *Personality & Individual Differences, 41*(7), 1263–1273.

Peterson, C., & Seligman, M. E. P. (2004). *Character strengths and virtues: A handbook and classification.* Washington, DC: American Psychological Association.

Smigelsky, M. (2013). Becoming fully human: The promotion of meaning and spirituality in professional relationships and contexts. *Journal of Constructivist Psychology, 26*(4), 316–318.

Stegman, R. L., & McReynolds, W. T. (1978). "Learned helplessness," "learned hope-fulness," and "learned obsessiveness": Effects of varying contingencies on escape responding. *Psychological Reports, 43*(3), 795–801.

Sun, H., Tan, Q., Fan, G., & Tsui, Q. (2014). Different effects of rumination on depression: Key role of hope. *International Journal of Mental Health Systems, 8,* article 53.

Tiger, L. (1979). *Optimism: The biology of hope.* New York, NY: Simon & Schuster.

Wu, H. (2011). The protective effects of resilience and hope on quality of life of the families coping with the criminal traumatisation of one of its members. *Journal of Clinical Nursing, 20*(13–14), 1906–1915.

Notes

1. Peterson & Seligman (2004), p. 519.
2. Benner (2011); McEntee et al. (2013); Smigelsky (2013).
3. *Action Comics* #1 (1938).
4. Peterson & Selgiman (2004), p. 533.
5. *Wonder Woman* #1 (1942); #102 (1958).
6. e.g., *Wonder Woman* #2 (1942).
7. Ecklund & Lee (2011).
8. *Wonder Woman* #127 (1997).
9. e.g., *All-Star Comics* #8 (1941); *The New Original Wonder Woman* (1975 television movie).
10. e.g., hope and spirituality linked by Tiger (1979) and others.
11. Alarcon et al. (2013).
12. Ong et al. (2006); Sun et al. (2014); Wu (2011).
13. *Wonder Woman* #164 (2001).
14. Abadsidis (2013).
15. Brinkman & Jedinak (2014).
16. Howell et al. (2015).
17. Steman & McReynolds (1978).

Final Word: Humanity

MARA WOOD

Wonder Woman's lasting impact is a testament to her foundation in psychology. William Moulton Marston's heroine displays the virtues of wisdom, courage, justice, temperance, and transcendence, but the strengths that make up *humanity* are the ones that have endeared her to her decades of readers. Through love, kindness, and social intelligence (the strengths that positive psychologists associate with humanity)[1], Wonder Woman becomes something more than just a superhero.

Love is the sharing of aid, comfort, and acceptance. Love is not limited to romance; it is the foundation of deep relationships. Relationships between people make us human. Marston chose Aphrodite, the Greek goddess of love, to be the patron of the Amazons. He aligned the cause of women with Aphrodite and promoted the concept of women as the gender with a higher capacity for love. Wonder Woman's relationships are founded in love, whether it is her relationship with her mother, Hippolyta; her friend Etta; her lover and friend, Steve; or even her enemies. Love has been linked to life satisfaction, indicating that the relationships we form with others are essential to our well-being.[2]

Kindness is best conceptualized as being nice, but it is more complex than that. It is a concern for the well-being of others and compassion. Altruism, or selfless acts, is also a hallmark of kindness. Trina Robbins and Colleen Doran's *The Once & Future Story* displays Wonder Woman's capacity for kindness. She acts as part of a team of women to provide the needed support to help a woman leave a domestic abuse situation.

Diana's *social intelligence* stems from her ability to interpret the feelings, motives, and various psychological states relevant to

317

the well-being of others. She is not oblivious to the pain and suffering others experience; rather, she strives to understand it. She sees the signs of domestic abuse in another woman without being forewarned about the situation.

Diana's lasso has the ability to seek out truth, but it also allows the user to read the emotion of the bound individual. Social intelligence (reasoning about social information and ability to apply it) gives Diana the skills she needs as ambassador for Themyscira: assessing motives, fostering cooperation, assessing her own performance, understanding the connection between emotion and relationships, and identifying emotional content in others. With this arsenal of skills, Diana develops relationships and advocates for the Amazons and women everywhere.

Diana's humanity is what makes her Wonder Woman. At the encouragement of his wife Elizabeth and with inspiration from Olive Byrne,[3] psychologist William Moulton Marston created her to teach others, and she does that through the use of love, kindness, and social intelligence. At times, she wonders if she is truly human or just a clay golem to carry out the gods' will.[4] The masterful display of the strengths of humanity proves Wonder Woman to be connected to and in touch with the people who surround her. She is truly a woman to whom we can all look up, filled with wonder.

Comic Book References

Wonder Woman #147 (1999). "Godwar Revolution." Script: E. Luke. Art: Y. Paquette & B. McLeod.

Other References

New York Times (1993, April 3). Elizabeth H. Marston, inspiration for Wonder Woman, 100 (obituary). *New York Times* (late edition), section 1, p. 11.

Park, N., Peterson, C., & Seligman, M. (2004). Strengths of character and well-being. *Journal of Social and Clinical Psychology*, 23(5), 603–619.

Peterson, C., & Seligman, M. E. P. (2004). *Character strengths and virtues*. Washington, D.C.: American Psychological Association.

Notes

1. Park et al. (2004); Peterson & Seligman (2004).
2. Park et al. (2004); Peterson & Seligman (2004).
3. *New York Times* (1993); personal communication from P. Marston to T. Langley (2016).
4. *Wonder Woman* #147 (1999).

About the Editors

Travis Langley, PhD, professor of psychology at Henderson State University, is the Popular Culture Psychology series editor. He is volume editor and lead writer for *The Walking Dead: Psych of the Living Dead; Star Wars Psychology: Dark Side of the Mind; Game of Thrones Psychology: The Mind is Dark and Full of Terrors; Doctor Who Psychology: A Madman with a Box; Star Trek Psychology: The Mental Frontier; Supernatural Psychology: Roads Less Traveled;* and *Captain America vs. Iron Man: Freedom, Security, Psychology.* He authored the acclaimed book *Batman and Psychology: A Dark and Stormy Knight.* Documentaries such *Legends of the Knight* and *Necessary Evil: Super-Villains of DC Comics* feature him as an expert and educator. *Psychology Today* carries his blog, "Beyond Heroes and Villains." As **@Superherologist**, he is one of the ten most popular psychologists on Twitter.

He happily points out that Wonder Woman's creator was a fellow psychologist and that troublemaker Fredric Wertham was not, and in front of any number of witnesses he will correct anybody who gets those mixed up.

Mara Whiteside Wood, PhD, is a school psychology special-ist in the Rogers Public School district in Arkansas. Her focus of practice is consultation, assessment of children for special education services, academic and behavioral interventions, and therapy using comics. She contributed chapters to *The Walking Dead Psychology: Psych of the Living Dead, Star Wars Psychology: Dark Side of the Mind,* and *Captain America vs. Iron Man: Free-dom, Security, Psychology,* and has served as editorial assistant on several volumes in Sterling's Popular Culture Psychology series. She hosts the "Talking Comics" podcast, co-hosts the "Legendary Runs" podcast, and is a contributor to the Talking Comics website. She tweets as **@MegaMaraMon,** where she shares her favorite comic moments.

About the Contributors

 **Jenna Busch** is a writer, host, and founder of Legion of Leia, a website to promote and support women in fandom. She co-hosted "Cocktails With Stan" with comic book legend Stan Lee, and has appeared in the film *She Makes Comics*, as a guest on *Attack of the Show*, NPR, Al Jazeera America, and ABC's *Nightline*. She is a comic book author, podcast co-host, and weekly feminist columnist for Metro. Busch has co-authored a chapter of *Star Wars Psychology*, *Game of Thrones Psychology*, *Star Trek Psychology*, *Doctor Who Psychology*, and *Captain America vs. Iron Man Psychology*. Her work has appeared all over the web. She can be reached on Twitter @JennaBusch.

 **Erin Currie**, PhD, is driven to use her psychology superpowers for good. By day she is a Consultant/Founder of MyPsychgeek, LLC, helping individuals and small businesses find their own superpowers through personalized professional development and team development. By night she gives her inner geek free reign to ponder and write about the psychological causes of the behaviors of her favorite characters. She also wrote for *Game of Thrones Psychology* and *Doctor Who Psychology*. Find her on Twitter: @mypsychgeek.

 Annamaria Formichella-Elsden is a professor of English and the Dean of the School of Communication and Arts at Buena Vista University in Storm Lake, Iowa. She earned her bachelor's degree in English at the University of New Hampshire, then earned her MFA in creative writing at Emerson College and PhD in American literature from Tufts University.

Dr. Formichella-Elsden has won the George Wythe Award for Excellence in Teaching, and she has published numerous articles dealing with American writers, travel, and gender.

Wind Goodfriend is a professor of psychology, director of the trauma advocacy program, and assistant dean of graduate programs at Buena Vista University in Storm Lake, Iowa. She earned her bachelor's degree at Buena Vista University, then earned her Master's and PhD in social psychology from Purdue University. Dr. Goodfriend has won the "Faculty of the Year" award at BVU several times and has won the Wythe Award for Excellence in Teaching. She is also the Principal Investigator for the Institute for the Prevention of Relationship Violence.

Tim Hanley is a comic book historian and the author of *Wonder Woman Unbound: The Curious History of the World's Most Famous Heroine*, *Investigating Lois Lane: The Turbulent History of the Daily Planet's Ace Reporter*, and *The Many Lives of Catwoman: The Felonious History of a Feline Fatale*. His work has appeared in the *Los Angeles Review of Books* and *The Comics Journal*, and he writes the monthly "Gendercrunching" column for *Bleeding Cool*. You can find him on Twitter @timhanley01.

Lara Taylor Kester, M.A., holds a degree in Counseling Psychology as well as a certificate in Traumatology and Treatment from Holy Names University. A registered Marriage and Family Therapy Intern who works with at-risk and foster youth in the San Francisco Bay Area, she co-hosts Therapy Podcast and serves as a contributing editor at GeekTherapy.com. She has authored chapters in *The Walking Dead Psychology*, *Game*

of Thrones Psychology, and *Captain America vs. Iron Man: Freedom, Security, Psychology*. Find her on Twitter @geektherapist.

Nina Taylor Kester holds a BFA in Cartooning and Illustration from the School of Visual Arts. As the Program Coordinator for the Cartoon Art Museum in San Francisco, California, she incorporates diversity and cultural awareness into educational and public programing. She launched the Peanuts brand social media presence at Charles M. Schulz Creative Associates/Peanuts World Wide and ran public relations at Archie Comics. Her most mindful work was as a colorist for *Peanuts* monthly issues and original graphic novels for BOOM! Studios.

Alan Kistler is the author of the *New York Times* best seller *Doctor Who: A History*. He is an actor and writer living in Los Angeles, and the creator/host of the podcast *Crazy Sexy Geeks*. He is a storytelling consultant and pop culture historian focusing on science fiction and American superheroes. He has contributed to the books *Walking Dead Psychology, Doctor Who Psychology, Star Trek Psychology*, and *Captain America vs. Iron Man: Freedom, Security and Psychology*. Twitter: @SizzlerKistler

Rebecca M. Langley, MS, LPC, is a therapist who has worked with chronically mentally ill populations, at-risk youth, and adolescents in long-term foster care. She has been licensed as a professional counselor since 2007. Her therapeutic method has been eclectic because, like Wonder Woman's creator, she does not believe in one-size-fits-all treatment. Now a full-time psychology instructor at Henderson State

University, she teaches courses such as abnormal psychology, developmental psychology, and infancy and childhood.

Martin Lloyd, PhD, LP, received his doctorate in Clinical Psychology from the University of Minnesota. He has worked in various prisons and high-security hospitals, including the U.S. Medical Center for Federal Prisoners. He currently practices as a forensic psychologist in Minnesota and occasionally teaches Forensic Psychology at Gustavus Adolphus College. As a Post-Doctoral Fellow at Patton State Hospital, he installed a Wonder Woman light switch plate in his office, to honor William Moulton Marston's contributions to forensic psychology. He hopes it is still there.

Mike Madrid is the author of *The Supergirls: Fashion, feminism, fantasy, and the history of comic book heroines*, which *Entertainment Weekly* called "sharp and lively" and NPR named as one of the "Best 5 Books of 2009 to Share With Your Friends." His other books are the Golden Age comic collections *Divas, Dames & Daredevils* and *Vixens, Vamps & Vipers*. He has written for *The Huffington Post* and is featured in the award-winning documentary film *Wonder Women! The Untold Story of American Superheroines*. He can be found at www.heaven4heroes.com.

Jeff Pisciotta is a biomechanist and martial artist. He has studied wing chun gung fu under a few different masters. A fateful encounter with Bruce Lee gave him a "crash course" in Jeet Kune Do (JKD) and a "lecture" on the science of biomechanics that forever changed his approach to his study of the martial arts and also led Pisciotta to pursue graduate studies in biomechanics and to his eventual career. He founded Applied

Innovation Research, a biomechanics consulting company, and is also acting CEO at JKD Biomechanics LLC, where he seeks to perpetuate the science of JKD.

Janina Scarlet, PhD, is a Licensed Clinical Psychologist, a scientist, and a full-time geek. She uses Superhero Therapy to help patients with anxiety, depression, chronic pain, and PTSD at the Center for Stress and Anxiety Management and Sharp Memorial Hospital and is also a professor at Alliant International University, San Diego. Dr. Scarlet is the author of *Superhero Therapy* with Little Brown Book Group and has also authored chapters in the Sterling Publishing works *The Walking Dead Psychology, Star Wars Psychology, Star Trek Psychology, Game of Thrones Psychology, Doctor Who Psychology,* and *Captain America vs. Iron Man Psychology.* She can be reached via her website at www.superhero-therapy.com or on Twitter: @shadowquill.

Laura Vecchiolla, PsyD, is a clinical psychologist using the empowering themes of myth and the Hero's Journey in therapy to help others on their journey toward growth and healing. When she is not slaying her own dragons, she is pursuing her academic interests, which include the mythopoetic nature of the psyche and the curative powers of stories. She contributed to *Star Wars Psychology: Dark Side of the Mind* and *Game of Thrones Psychology: The Mind is Dark and Full of Terrors.*

Caitlin Yogerst, MSE, LPC-IT, is a mental health and substance abuse therapist in Milwaukee, Wisconsin. Caitlin built her expertise in various locations ranging from the Winnebago Mental Health Institute to drop in centers for the severe and persistent mentally ill and at-risk youth. Caitlin has also worked with Wisconsin's inmate population at the Wisconsin Resource Center. As a mental health clinician Caitlin found solace in popular culture as part of her self-care regimen.

 Chris Yogerst, PhD, is assistant professor of communication for the University of Wisconsin Colleges where he teaches the popular course "Superheroes and Society." His love for comics began when he was given *The Dark Knight Returns* as a kid. Also a film historian, Chris is author of the book *From the Headlines to Hollywood: The Birth and Boom of Warner Bros.* (Rowman & Littlefield) and authored a chapter in *The Laughing Dead: The Horror-Comedy Film from Bride of Frankenstein to Zombieland*. Chris can be reached at his website (chrisyogerst.com) and on Twitter (@chrisyogerst).

 **E. Paul Zehr**, PhD, is professor, author, and martial artist at the University of Victoria, where he teaches in the neuroscience, kinesiology, and Island Medical programs. His pop-sci books include *Becoming Batman* (2008), *Inventing Iron Man* (2011), *Project Superhero* (2014), and the forthcoming *Creating Captain America* (2018). *Maxim*, CNN, NPR, and others have interviewed him for his diverse expertise. Paul writes for *Psychology Today*, *Scientific American*, and *ComiConverse.com*.

Special Contributors

Elizabeth Holloway Marston was born to American parents in 1893 in Douglas, Isle of Man. The family moved to Massachusetts and she grew up in the Boston area. Majoring in psychology at Mount Holyoke, she was awarded an AB degree in 1915 and entered Boston University School of Law. ("Those dumb bunnies at Harvard wouldn't take women, so I went to Boston University.") She was awarded an LLB degree in 1918. She married psychologist William Moulton Marston and continued her education, conducting research at the Harvard University psychology department on the physiological signs of deception. Her studies on testimony became the subject of her thesis, which led to an MA degree awarded by Radcliffe in 1921. The Marstons collaborated on the development of what is commonly (if imprecisely) known as the lie detector. Elizabeth's career included indexing the documents of the first fourteen Congresses; lecturing on domestic relations, commercial law, and ethics; and serving on the editorial staffs of a number of publications included the *Encyclopedia Brittanica*. She died in Bethel Connecticut on March 27, 1993, at age 100. (Information comes from her obituary, courtesy of the Wonder Woman Network Family Museum.)

Retired underground cartoonist and current comics historian **Trina Robbins** has been writing graphic novels, comics, and books for almost half a century. Her subjects have ranged from Wonder Woman and the Powerpuff Girls to her own teenage superheroine, *Go Girl!*, and from women cartoonists and superheroines to women who kill. She's won an Inkpot Award and was inducted in the Will Eisner Hall of

Fame at the San Diego Comic-Con. She lives in a moldering, 100+-year-old house in San Francisco with her cats, shoes, and dust bunnies. She illustrated and co-authored the comic book series *The Legend of Wonder Woman*.

Index